the new

Golden Retriever

Am. Can. Ch. Comstock Sunfire O'Hillcrest UDT, MH, WCX, VCX; Can. CDX, WCI; GRCA Outstanding Dam. "Ritz" is a daughter of Can. Ch. Comstock's Carmel Nut UDTX, SH, WCX, VCX, Can. UD, WCX. She has several times been Highest Scoring Dog in Trial, completed her championships very quickly, and has a ***daughter (qualified for All-Age in Field Trials) and a group-placing champion son. Owner Kathy McCue says: "She has always done everything and anything I asked of her."

the new

Golden Retriever

by marcia r. schlehr

All drawings by the author

HOWELL
BOOK
HOUSE

Howell Book House

Macmillan General Reference
A Simon & Schuster/Macmillan Company
1633 Broadway
New York, NY 10019

Library of Congress Cataloging-in-Publication Data
Schlehr, Marcia R.
    The new golden retriever / Marcia R. Schlehr.
    p. cm.
ISBN 0-87605-187-5
1. Golden Retrievers. I. Title.
SF429.G63S345—1996
636.7'52—dc20   95-48299
    CIP

Design by George J. McKeon

Manufactured in the United States of America
10 9 8 7 6 5 4 3 2 1

Photo: *Anne Bissette*

Dedicated to all those who enter our lives so trustingly.
May we strive not to betray them.

Blueprint
of the Golden Retriever

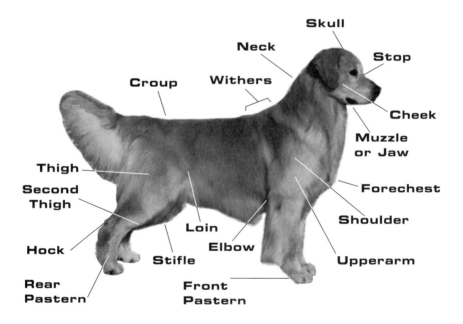

Contents

Acknowledgments

Every book is in some respect affected by many individuals other than the named author. If it were not for the efforts of thousands of devotees of the Golden Retriever over the last century and a quarter, there would be no subject for this book. To them, we all owe much, and they should serve to remind us that we did not "invent" the Golden Retriever:

The deepest appreciation must be extended to Rachel Page Elliott—all Golden folk are fortunate beyond words to have this scholar of the canine as a special friend of the Golden. As a historian of the breed, she has no peer, and her suggestion that I write this book was an extraordinary compliment.

Helen W. (Betty) Gay, lifelong friend and mentor in Goldens, who shares not only an interest in canine conformation and function but who also loaned her impressive file of early pedigrees, and whose pertinent comments so often give me direction when needed—Betty has always been an invaluable sounding board and information resource.

Friends Walt and June Faubion; Walt for being my "computer guru" while I'm learning to handle this electronic beast, and June for all the wonderful meals at their gracious, Golden-filled home on Thistle Ridge. Ed and Marallyn Wight as well, dear friends who started out with two puppies in 1972 and have done so much, and taught me so much over the years; I should have paid *them* to take the puppies.

The many individual Golden owners who supplied photographs must be acknowledged and thanked for entrusting their precious photos for this project. Special thank-yous to Peggy Hilton and Emily Smith Cain, who gave me much unpublished historical material, and to John K. Wallace Jr., for so generously passing on many dog photos and memorabilia from his father, which will now become part of the GRCA's Archives.

The Archives of the Golden Retriever Club of America, a collection originally established by Pagey Elliott and now in the care of Archivist Carole Johnson.

Valerie Foss of England, for the pedigree research made available in her two editions of the *Golden Retriever Book of Champions*.

And very special thanks to all the Goldens who have been subject and inspiration; especially Tuck, for he was my first, my friend, my teacher. Their willingness, joy in life, acceptance and forebearance are humbling indeed.

All the Good Dogs

What purpose did they serve, all the good dogs that once ran through the world and wait now in the shadowy quiet of the past.

They lightened our burdens and drove away our enemies and stayed when others left us. They gave aid and comfort, protection and security. They held a mirror wherein we might see ourselves as we long to be. They gave us a glimpse of the world beyond the narrow confines of our own species.

Although we make dull students, slowly they help us learn how to command and to protect with wisdom and justice and imagination.

They taught and still teach us the joy of giving generosity and kindness and love—without thought of gainful return.

And now—all the fleet hounds, the staunch mastiffs, the loyal shepherds, the dancing toys, the fumbling puppies, pets on silk pillows, workers plodding at their tasks, the special ones you loved best, those of ours we still miss—all the good dogs, goodbye, until on some brighter day, in some fairer place you run out again to greet us.

Dogs and People, 1954
by George and Helen Papashvily

Drawn from the painting by John Charlton in the GRCA archives, depicting a dog which accords closely with descriptions of the Tweed Water Spaniel. The coat is close to the body and curled, the legs and face smooth; some slight feathering.

Foreword

Here, in one volume, is a sweeping overview of the background, development and the many ways in which the Golden Retriever gives joy and service to humans. It is a book in which the author has skillfully coordinated countless references stretching into two hundred or more years of retriever history, much of which has not been told before.

The text flows from one phase of history to another, as random and experimental crosses of bloodlines laid the foundation for a variety of retriever types designed to meet the needs of sportsmen who, with the advancing knowledge about firearms, wanted dogs that could not only seek but fetch game from both land and water. As the story unfolds, readers become acquainted with generations of sporting families who shared this challenge and who, in spite of the devastation of wars that threatened many a breeding program, managed to preserve the strong lines that contribute to the breed's versatility and to which all present-day registered Golden Retrievers can be traced.

Early pedigrees are discussed in detail, with comments about overall type, color, head shape and general conformation. The variables of structure, correct and incorrect, are cleverly illustrated with the author's line drawings, and throughout the text are warnings regarding the pitfalls of genetic faults that plague Goldens. I particularly like the powerful chapter entitled "Thinking About Breeding?" Read this section carefully, word for word.

In perusing these pages, one often has the feeling that the writer is talking directly to the readers, answering any questions they might ask. The text is interesting and informative, lightened here and there by subtle, humorous and thought-provoking comments. What is more, whereas the book is written for Golden Retriever people in particular, much of the content is beneficial for dog owners in general.

It is an honor to be asked to write the Foreword for Marcia Schlehr's book. I am confident that it will take its place as the most complete reference yet published on the breed.

Rachel Page Elliott

Introduction

When I met my first Golden Retriever in 1946, our neighbors' "Treva" was one of what was almost a rare breed. In that year, 994 Goldens were registered with the AKC, and that was nearly double the number of the previous year. From 1932, when the breed was recognized as such, through 1945, a total of some 2,000 Goldens had been registered.

The end of World War II was the beginning of a great increase not just in Goldens but in all purebred dogs. Purebred dogs became not just the avocation of wealthy fanciers with large kennels and hired help, but more and more a part of everyday life as companions and, increasingly, a hobby for the individual—the hunter needing a retriever to fill the day's bag and conserve game, participants in training for the newly developed Obedience Trials or retriever Field Trials, and those involved in conformation competition.

And Goldens grew in popularity. By 1955, when I acquired the Golden who "sold" me on the breed so absolutely and completely, about 2,000 Goldens a year were registered by the AKC—as many as in all the first thirteen years of recognition. In the early 1970s, registrations began to increase precipitously, and by 1992, it took about *eleven days* to gain those 2,000 Goldens, the total for the year being more than 68,000.

The Golden is presently in the top five breeds in number of registrations. Such numbers can't all come from dedicated, responsible, conscientious breeders, the sort who originated the breed and brought the Golden to the highest level of development. It has been said that fewer than 10 percent are produced by conscientious breeders; the balance comes from commercial sources ("puppy mills") and casual breedings. The last accounts for the vast majority; the people who breed "Sandy" to "Prince" down the street, for no other reason than to get puppies of the same breed. "Sandy" and "Prince" no doubt have some notable names in the far reaches of their pedigrees, if one cares to go back that far; but that is scarcely a guarantee of quality.

The history and development of the Golden Retriever breed is an area of special interest to me. As dog breeds go, the Golden is a fairly young breed, and its development in the late 19th and the 20th century means it is reasonably well documented with both written and photographic records. Still, there is much area for conjecture.

What I offer here is based on the findings of such acknowledged historians of the breed as Elma Stonex and Rachel Page Elliott; on other findings in old stud records; various books, old paintings and other artwork; and personal correspondence. No one will ever know *everything* about the history of the Golden Retriever, but from what is known we can try to develop a coherent picture of the breed's development.

Why is this important? Who cares how the breed was created? Whether owner, exhibitor or judge, if anyone wishes to understand any breed as fully as possible, this is a part of that understanding. If you're a trainer, an understanding of temperament and intrinsic capabilities is essential. The potential breeder needs to understand that varying conformation features may have a genetic basis from the origins of the breed. If one desires to keep the breed in balance (which is necessary to retain characteristic features of the breed), it certainly helps to understand the forces which shift that balance.

The growth of the breed and its activities has been so phenomenal in the last twenty-five years, that it is impossible to treat this in detail. General trends and shifts have been described, and a few outstanding individuals noted, but a comprehensive listing of all notable kennels, dogs and people would require a virtual encyclopedia. If one wants to delve into detail, the primary source is the Golden Retriever Club of America's *Yearbook,* a biannual compilation of records, titles, pedigrees and photographs covering every phase of Golden activity in this country.

There are so many excellent books available on the topics of training, health and breeding that no attempt has been made to cover these in detail. These topics are covered rather generally, but areas of particular importance to Goldens are included.

Throughout the book I've tried to emphasize the Golden as a versatile breed, a "generalist" rather than a "specialist." While particular interests will determine the areas in which any individual is active with Goldens, one of the breed's greatest features is its suitability for a wide range of activities and performance. In an era of increasing specialization, the Golden's inherent versatility is of great value. Of course it is quite possible to produce subtypes that excel in narrow areas of endeavor, but this is nearly always at the expense of some other area, and one loses the wonderful balance and wide capabilities that are so much a part of the true Golden Retriever.

It is the hope that this book will make more people aware of the full range of potential within the Golden Retriever, perhaps to start them on the way to appreciating and utilizing those breed characteristics, and to help keep our Goldens the splendid canines they should be.

Marcia R. Schlehr
1995

chapter 1

The Many Facets of the Golden Retriever

While the Golden Retriever was originally intended to be a personal gundog and retriever of feathered game, the qualities which make the breed ideal for that purpose also enable it to achieve in many other areas. The willingness to work for and with people, and the intelligence and trainability that have been bred for, make most Goldens willing pupils, whatever the kind of training.

Strong retrieving instincts, a keen nose and a soft mouth not only enable the Golden to bring home game that is fit for the table but provide the breed with a foundation for work as unusual as detecting hidden contraband or explosives. The Golden's size and strength, sound build and easy-to-care-for qualities make the breed suitable for tracking as well as for work as guide dogs and service dogs. And their wise, amiable personality and rapport with people make Goldens standout candidates for therapy work and companionship.

Ch-AFC Lorelei's Golden Rockbottom UD, born 1948. Rocky was a fast and impressive field worker. He completed his show title at barely a year of age and is the only Field Champion Golden to win an all-breed Best in Show. Owned, trained and handled by breeder Reinhard Bischoff, sired by Ch. Lorelei's Golden Rip** out of Lorelei's Golden Tanya.

1

Ch. Malagold Beckwith Om K Ivan CD (Ch. Beckwith's Copper Ingot x Ch. Beckwith's Frolic of Yeo CDX) was an exceptional hunting dog on both waterfowl and upland game, right to the end of his life at age 12½. Ivan is pictured in the 1960s with owner Marilyn Hartman, Landican Goldens. Ivan was also a GRCA Outstanding Sire.

Complete coverage of all areas in which Goldens have excelled would far exceed the bounds of one book. The reader is advised to consult some of the many excellent texts available on the various topics and areas of training. Some are listed in the Appendix, and the shelves at any good-sized bookstore will doubtless carry many more.

This chapter will serve as an overview of those areas in which the achievements of Goldens are notable, and their aptitude is limitless. All Golden Retriever owners are encouraged to try any or all of these activities for fun or competition. Your Golden will love them, too. Enjoy!

THE HUNTING DOG

The first purpose of the Golden Retriever was to be a helper in the hunting field. Bred from generations of dogs selected for retrieving fallen feathered game, Goldens were originally used for this purpose, and still are.

In the 19th century, retrievers were used as "nonslip" retrievers—that is, the dogs remained in a designated position until given the command to retrieve game which had been shot. Later, in North America, Goldens (and other retrievers) were also used as were spaniels—to find and flush upland game, then to retrieve it. For the hunter who kept only one dog, this procedure was logical. Many Golden owners who run in Trials and Hunting Tests also use their dogs when actually hunting. A dog with the training and experience required for Derby Trials, or Senior Hunting Tests, should readily be useful for actual hunting, either upland or waterfowl. Even if the practical hunter has no expectations of entering any organized events, the basic training will certainly enhance the dog's usefulness in the field.

Ron Bischke of Alberta, Canada, with the only two Goldens to carry the unique combination of Field Trial Champion and Obedience Trial Champion (Canadian UD). Left, Can. FTCh-OTCh Windbreaker Bulrush Buddy (male, by Am. AFC Yankee's Smok'n Red Devil x Am. FC Windbreakers Razzmatazz). Right, Can. FTCh-OTCh Kipp's Cotton Jenny (female, by Am. FC-NAFTC Topbrass Cotton x Can. FTCh Windbreakers Khaki Kipp); Jenny qualified for the Canadian National Retriever Trial several times.

The Golden's structure and coat type are well suited to cold-weather waterfowling, which may entail patient waiting in a hidden blind next to a farm pond or by a spread of decoys on a wind-whipped lake. A dog who remains waiting quietly, is steady to wing and shot, marks the falls and then retrieves quickly and efficiently, is of great value.

In many areas the retriever works ahead of the gun to quarter and search out game in the same manner as a spaniel does. Most retrievers work closely enough to flush the birds within range; a few will hesitate or actually flash-point before going in for the flush. While they may not bump the birds out with the zest of a busy springer, the exquisite nose of a good Golden will probably find just as many birds, and retrieve them wherever they may fall. The Golden has served as a topnotch pheasant dog for more than a half-century in North Dakota, Minnesota and other areas of the Midwest.

In the same fields, or from the icy waters of the Great Lakes and the St. Lawrence, the Golden will retrieve the largest of American game birds, the Canada goose, from the blinds where hunter and dog await the feeding flocks. A tough old goose needs a strong retriever to bring it to hand, and the good Golden with heart, sense and soundness can do it.

The Golden is less well suited to the southlands, where a heavy coat is an impediment in warm weather and could cause overheating. Goldens in the warmer climates acclimate to some extent and carry much lighter coats than in the colder areas, but high humidity along with parasites and skin diseases often cause problems.

The Golden has been used to walk at Heel behind Pointers and Setters until the bird is pointed, flushed and shot. This is not as true in Great Britain, where hunting is more often an organized event for many. In this country, most hunters work singly or in pairs, and one dog is sufficient. The Golden's true versatility, willingness and biddability make the breed a good choice for many hunters who want a useful dog who is also a pleasant companion outside of hunting season.

FIELD TRIALS

The first Field Trials for retrievers were held in England at the turn of the century. One of the first winners was a liver-colored Flat-Coat, Don of Gerwn, sired by the second Lord Tweedmouth's Golden dog, Lucifer. Mrs. Charlesworth's Noranby Sandy and Noranby Tweedledum were the first registered Goldens to gain recognition, about 1912, when they won Certificates of Merit at Field Trials.

In the USA, some Trials were held in the early 1930s in the east. By the end of the 1930s, there were Trials in the upper Midwest and in the St. Louis area where Goldens were placing, and growth has been steady throughout the country. At retriever Trials, aside from the very few Specialty Field Trials, all retriever breeds compete on equal footing, and since Field Trial champions continue to compete in the All-Age stakes where championship points are won, competition is extremely tough. Unlike dogs in dog shows, the Field Trial dog is competing directly against experienced champions for the points.

Originally Field Trials were set up so as to simulate a day's hunting. Tests in the 1930s and 1940s were (by today's standards) fairly simple, but much emphasis was placed on the dog's *natural abilities* (nose, marking) and working out problems such as following a crippled bird. All dogs did not necessarily get the same test, and there were variations such as walk-ups and working out of a blind that are seldom used today. As the dogs got better by selection and breeding, and amateur and professional training skills advanced, the competition became more intense as well. Annual awards for achievements and the National Championship Trials gave impetus to development of competition dogs. Today, serious competition in retriever Field Trials requires a tremendous commitment of time, energy and financial resources for training and competition. Goldens are far outnumbered by Labradors but account for a good percentage of placements and two or three Field Championships yearly.

The successful Field Trial retriever these days is a dog with an admirable capacity for accepting training. They need the natural talents of marking ability, memory and concentration, plus the intensity, style and speed that will make the judges remember them and add a bit to their scores. If two dogs complete the same test with equal efficiency, the one with the style and speed will always score higher.

Field Trials have several levels of competition. **Derby** stakes are for dogs from six months to two years of age. Tests are singles and double marks, sometimes a triple, on land and water. Dogs must be steady and deliver to hand. Natural abilities and style are given a bit more emphasis than degree of training for complex tests (although that certainly can be an asset). "Derby

Ch. Signature's Natural Wonder, owned by Judy and Kurt McCauley. Judy handled Woody quite successfully to his title and as a champion. Early in 1994 he went to California for a few months, and under professional handling earned 4 Best in Show awards and became the top-winning male Golden of the year. Erik Strickland handles him here to a Best in Show.

points" are credited toward annual awards given by *Retriever Field Trial News,* but there is no AKC-recognized title.

Qualifying stakes are a step up from Derby, for dogs of any age who have not won championship points or placed in All-Age stakes. Placing first or second in a Qualifying stake earns the dog status as a "Qualified All-Age" dog—that is, the dog can be counted as one of the twelve "qualified" dogs necessary in an All-Age stake competition in order for championship points to be awarded. Dogs in the Qualifying stake must be capable of triple marks (watching and remembering three birds downed), blind retrieves (taking direction to an unseen fall) and honoring (remaining in place while another dog works).

All-Age stakes are where the work is most demanding, and where championship points are earned. **Amateur All-Age** is for dogs who are handled by bona fide amateurs. No professional handlers are allowed; although a dog may have had professional training, the person *handling* him must be an amateur. Some of the "amateurs" these days are every bit as capable and experienced as the "pros," both as trainers and as handlers, so the competition is on a very high level. Points earned in AAA stakes credit toward the title of Amateur Field Champion (AFC).

Open All-Age stakes are, as implied, open to all. Amateur, professional, champion or aspirant, all compete equally. Here you can see the ultimate in dog training on exhibit, and tests limited by little except the judges' imagination. An Open dog is expected to mark and remember as many as four falls on land and water, to "take a line" exactly as indicated and then to take the handler's directions smartly at distances of 200 yards or more, often in the face of extreme distractions. The dog must face any cover or obstacle fearlessly and perform with style and intensity in any circumstances.

Limited and Special All-Age stakes include those limited to dogs meeting special restrictions on entry, such as the National Retriever Championship and the National Amateur Retriever Championship competitions. Each dog must have won placements at a certain level in order to enter the National

Ch. Landican's Ocoee Opportunity CD. "Sunshine" had an amazing show career, completing her championship from the puppy class within 26 days from first point to last, including 3 Best of Breed wins. By sixteen months of age, she qualified for the GRCA Show Dog Hall of Fame, the youngest ever to do so. Owned by Ellen Reiss and Kathy Lorentzen, Sunshine was a registered Therapy Dog, a treasured companion, and a most intelligent, intuitive dog. By Ch. Libra Malagold Coriander x Ch. Landican's Lady Diana CD WC.

Championships, and the winner is entitled to the official designation of National Field Champion (NFC) or National Amateur Field Champion (NAFC). Four Goldens have won the NFC; one, the NAFC.

Field Championships are earned through a point system. In All-Age stakes, there must be twelve qualified dogs competing in order to award points. First place earns five points; second, three points; third, one point and fourth, half a point. Judges' Award of Merit (JAM) is awarded at the discretion of the judges to any dog who completes all tests satisfactorily but does not place. Ten points in Open are required for an FC. An AFC requires fifteen points, but these may be won in either Open or Amateur if amateur-handled. Both titles require a first-place win in all-breed retriever competition.

Field Trials consist of a series of land and water tests designed by the judges, making best use of the available terrain. Each series will have approximately equal and similar tests for all dogs running. Dogs who commit major errors or fail a test are dropped; the others are called back for the next series. Judges use notes and an informal scoring system to determine which dogs are to be dropped or kept, and the relative standings of each dog. A small

Pride of achievement. To breed, train and handle a talented dog to honors is the goal of many dedicated Golden people. "Solo" (Can. Ch. Heritage Winter Solstice, Am. Can. CDX, JH, WC, Can. CDX, WC) started her Obedience career with a Highest Scoring Dog in Trial win from Novice B class, trained and handled by Cynthia Olson. By Am. Can. Ch. Kyrie Legendarian, Am. CDX TD WC, Can. CDX WC, out of Can. Ch. JoNoRe's Courthill Tradition, Am. Can. UD WC.

stake may have three or four series and be completed in the course of a day. A large stake may take two days; and the National Championships running ten series, with eighty or more dogs entered, may take four or five days to complete.

The GRCA (Golden Retriever Club of America) uses the "star system" to designate dogs who have placed in a licensed (or member) trial: ** indicates a dog with a placement or a JAM in Derby, or a third or fourth place or JAM in Qualifying. First or second in Qualifying, or any placement or JAM in All-Age stakes (qualified dog), is ***.

CONFORMATION SHOWS

Goldens were shown in England first about 1908, in classes for Flat-coated (or Wavy-coated) retrievers "of any color." In Canada and the U.S., the first record of Goldens in show competition was in the early 1920s; at that time, all retrievers were lumped together, and a class might have Labradors, Goldens and Flat-coats together. Goldens were officially recognized for separate competition in Great Britain about 1911 and in the U.S. in 1932.

In conformation or "bench show" competition, the dogs are judged solely on the dog's adherence to a specific breed Standard—that is, physical attributes, structure and shape, gait and way of going, size, color and coat. All these characteristics are described by the Standard, a document that attempts to put into words the "ideal" for that breed. No written description is equal to seeing and getting your hands on a few really outstanding specimens; only then can one form an accurate mental image of that elusive ideal.

In the early years of the Golden's history, Goldens were a varied lot. There were not many shown, and judges had little experience with the breed. For most Golden fanciers, the main interest was in comparing dogs within breed level competition, and completing a championship. It was not a usual thing for Goldens to place in the Sporting Group against the glamor and show-manship of the elegant setters and the beautifully turned-out spaniels. The sturdy, workmanlike retrievers just did not catch the eye of many judges.

However, there were a few top winning show dogs. In the 1950s, **Ch. Golden Knolls Shur Shot CD** and his son **Ch. Golden Knolls King Alphonzo** set an unprecedented record of wins. King was a large, dark, upstanding dog. Today, he would be considered too large and "settery" in outline, but he was sound, and caught the judges' eye for twenty-four Bests in Show.

By 1970 "show" type had changed considerably. The revised breed Standard had moderated height, although many dogs were impressively heavy-boned (often too much so). A lighter, brighter shade of gold became popular, and Goldens developed more glamor—profuse coats, increased showmanship and much more extensive grooming to create that "showdog" look. Dogs such as **Ch. Cummings Goldrush Charlie** and his half-brother **Ch. Misty Morn's Sunset CD TD WC** were campaigned professionally and to an unprecedented extent in all-breed competition. Their showmanship and obvious personality brought them as many wins as did their physical attributes. "Sammy's" wide use and prepotency as a sire made him the all-time top sire with more than 135 Champion or UD offspring. Charlie's

At work in the Obedience ring, doing the Utility Scent Discrimination exercise. Richland Kyrie Liberty Belle, Am. Can. UD, Am.WCX, Can. WC, was Neida Huesinkvelt's devoted companion and running partner for more than 14 years. In her only two litters, Libbe produced five UDs (three of them OTCHs), Hunting Test titlists and show winners, earning the designation GRCA Outstanding Dam.

There's nothing quite like passing your first Tracking Test! Successful Tracking requires great confidence in and understanding of your individual dog. In center is Jan Thompson, clutching that precious glove, and Galyarde Second Chance (later Am. TDX, Can TD, Am. Can. CD), flanked by the two judges.

record of forty-two Best in Show wins stood for many years. Goldens were now commonly placing in the fiercely competitive Group and BIS rings.

In the 1980s the major show lines were based on descendants of Sam and Charlie. Probably many breeders who never looked farther back than a three- or four-generation pedigree never realized how pervasive the influence of these two sons of **Ch. Sunset's Happy Duke** really was. One linebred Sammy descendant was the Best in Show winning bitch, **Ch. Amberac's Asterling Aruba,** bred by Ellen Manke and owned by Mary (Weustenberg) Burke. Aruba proved not only a successful winner in the ring but through her offspring, of which an unprecedented number completed championships (thirty-two) and won in Group competition, became the progenitor of a new fashion of show dogs.

By the late 1980s there were so many dog shows that a dog could attend more than 100 of the 1,100 or so shows held in a year. Showmanship, coat and glamor became essential to winning. Group and Best in Show wins far overshadowed wins or placements in the breed, and top dogs were usually campaigned by a professional, often spending weeks and months on the road. As much money might be spent on a top dog's advertising campaign as on all other expenses. This trend is even more pronounced in the mid-1990s.

"Alamo"—Am. Can. Ch. Farm Fresh Apple Pie Ala Mode, CDX, MH, WCX Can. CD, bred and owned by Leslie Dickerson. The Hunting Test program has proven very popular with owners wanting to prove their dogs' abilities in field work outside of the fiercely competitive area of formal Field Trials. Quite a few "show bred" Goldens have demonstrated that working aptitude has not necessarily been lost because of show ring success.

In conformation, dogs compete first within each breed at the class level, then for the Winners' Dog or Winners' Bitch award, which gives points toward the championship title. The point winners at each show, along with the champion dogs and bitches, then compete for Best of Breed and Best of Opposite Sex to Best of Breed awards. All Best of Breed winners are entitled to compete in their particular Group for placements, and the seven Group winners go on to competition for Best in Show.

Goldens compete in the Sporting Group, which includes all the gundogs such as the various setters, pointers, spaniels and retrievers. The AKC's booklet *Rules and Regulations Applying to Registration and Dog Shows* sets forth the exact requirements for all such matters, and must be read by anyone intending to show.

The usual classes within each breed and sex are the following. *Puppy*, for entries between six and twelve months of age; often, two puppy classes are offered, six to nine months and nine to twelve months. *Twelve to Eighteen Months* class is for entries within those age limits. *Novice* class is for dogs who have not won a first place in any class other than Puppy or Novice (may win three firsts in Novice), nor any championship points. *Bred by Exhibitor* class is for entries who are bred and handled by their owners. *American-bred* class is for any dog (except champions) who was whelped in the U.S. from a mating that took place in the U.S. *Open* class is open to all dogs eligible to be shown; usually exhibitors don't plan on entering Open until the dog is reasonably mature and ready for serious competition. In *Winners'* class all the first-place class winners at a given show compete for the championship points: A Winners' Dog is chosen from all male class winners; Winners' Bitch, from the females. In each sex, a Reserve Winners'

Dog/Bitch is also chosen—a "first runner-up," so to speak—but this win does not carry any points.

Dogs and bitches who have completed the requirements championships may enter Best of Breed competition (or as it was known some years ago, "For Specials Only," which meant for special awards, such as Best of Breed—not that the *dogs* were "special," although that became the connotation). From this group, which also includes the WD and WB and the winners of any single-entry nonregular classes such as Veterans, a Best of Breed and a Best of Opposite Sex to Best of Breed (BOS) are chosen, and a Best of Winners (either the WD or WB).

Points are awarded on the basis of how many dogs the WD or WB defeats. The number of entries required for points is established yearly by the AKC by means of a formula which tries to ensure that only a certain percentage of shows will be three-points or higher ("major") shows in each breed. Depending on the number of class entries competing within each breed and sex, a show may have from zero to five points available. No more than five points may be won at any one show. Fifteen points won under at least three different judges are required for a championship; at least two "majors" (three points or higher) under different judges are required.

In Canada the system is similar but simpler. Ten points are needed under three different judges, but at present, no majors are required. The classes are similar, although there is no Novice class. Puppy classes are always divided into Junior Puppy (six to nine) and Senior Puppy (nine to twelve), and (of course) it is Canadian-bred class rather than American-bred. All puppies compete for Best Puppy in Breed, Group and Show parallel to the All-Age competition, but no championship points are given for Puppy awards.

In this country Goldens have become a very popular show dog, and Goldens are often among the two or three breeds with the largest entries. Only one Golden dog and one bitch at any show will earn points, so in a total entry of perhaps 20 to 150 or more—even 300 to 500 at large Specialty shows—competition is far from easy.

OBEDIENCE TRIALS

Goldens have been a presence at formal Obedience Trials since the beginning. The first Golden CD (Companion Dog) was in 1942; there were for years very few Obedience Trials overall, but by the early 1950s there was a marked increase in the number of Obedience training classes. Many of the instructors for these classes had learned their craft during World War II, working with sentry, guard and messenger dogs. The basics of training that were learned for war work applied as well to making civilians' dogs into more mannerly canines, and the move into formal Obedience Trials was a natural one.

Early Obedience exercises were, indeed, based on what was taught to the military canine. Heel, Sit, Down, Stay, Recall, Retrieve a wooden dumbbell, Retrieve over an obstacle, even Tracking—all derive from military and police work. In the 1940s and 1950s, the top winners at Obedience Trials were often the "working" breeds such as German Shepherd Dogs and Dobermans. The standout Golden in Obedience in the 1940s was **Goldwood Michael UD** (first CDX Golden), trained and handled by Capt. Schendel for owner Morgan Brainard; Michael had no less than twelve perfect 200 scores to his credit.

By the early 1950s, Golden Retrievers were consistently winning. By the 1960s and 1970s, Goldens were dominating Obedience Trials, and some breeders were devoting themselves to developing lines of Goldens specifically for Obedience competition. A short-coupled dog, active and athletic, not burdened with excess "bone" and substance, who learned quickly, could forgive handler's errors and not fold up under intense training was a good candidate for competition training. Especially in the Midwest, trainer/exhibitors wanted a fast, stylish, "hard-driving" dog for the intensely competitive trial competition, and many times found it by breeding to dogs from field trial lines or purchasing young dogs from field stock. After all, they had been bred for many years for the same qualities.

Some astonishing records have been set by Goldens in Obedience. The proliferation of Trials in the last three decades, and advances in teaching and training, have set the stage for performers such as **Bernie Brown's OTCh Tanbark's Bristol Creme**, whose lifetime total of 5,619 OTCh points (enough for *fifty-six* Obedience Trial Championships) was the highest for all breeds until surpassed in 1994. Goldens in recent years have accounted for as much as one-quarter of all High in Trial awards. Records like these require not only an exceptional dog but a highly dedicated and skillful owner/trainer.

But one of the nicer things about Obedience is that one can set one's own goals. Relatively few dogs and handlers attain the heights of Highest Scoring Dog in Trial or Obedience Trial Champion (a title introduced in 1977), but nearly any owner/trainer with a Golden can aspire to earning the CD, CDX or UD titles. Goldens account for more titles in Obedience than nearly any other breed, and almost all the dogs are owner-trained.

CD, or Companion Dog, is a dog who has demonstrated the basics of training that any dog should know, whether he is "just a pet" or learning the basics for further work in any area, including advanced titles. CD work is much the same as the basic training or "yard work" given to retrievers as a basis for field training. The CD is earned in the Novice class at Obedience Trials; the exercises include Heeling both on-lead and off, Stand for Examination, Recall, Long Sit (one minute) and Long Down (three minutes) with the dogs lined up in a group, their handlers in sight across the ring. There is no retrieving or jumping. While the exercises are simple, high scores require good teamwork and precision. Novice A is for owners who have never put an Obedience title on a dog, Novice B is for those owners who have.

"Devin" is a graduate of the Guide Dog Foundation, one of several organizations that train Goldens and other breeds as guides for the blind. Goldens are valued for their adaptability, easygoing temperament and trainability.

CDX title (Companion Dog Excellent). In the Open Class, all work is done off-lead. There is Heeling; a Recall, which includes a Drop (dog lies down on command) while the dog is coming toward the handler; Retrieve a dumbbell both on the flat and over a High Jump (at $1^1/_4$ times the dog's shoulder height) and a Broad Jump of low hurdles set to cover twice the distance of the High Jump. The three-minute Sit and five-minute Down are done with the dogs lined up in a group and the handlers leaving the ring, to remain out of sight for the designated time. Open A is for dogs who have not yet earned the CDX title; Open B is where the CDX and UD dogs may continue to compete for honors. Hot competition in the Open B class often means that scores are very high; even a 198 might not get you in the ribbons at many Trials.

The **UD** title (Utility Dog) requires qualifying in the Utility Class. The Signal Exercise incorporates a Heeling pattern, Stand and Stay, Down from a distance, then Sit in place, Recall and Finish—all solely on hand signals. Scent Discrimination entails the dog retrieving metal and leather articles scented by the handler from a group of ten other identical articles. The "Moving Stand" has the dog Heeling, then left on a Stand-Stay as the handler continues; the dog is briefly examined by the judge, then is recalled directly to Heel position by the handler. Directed Jumping requires the dog to leave the handler on command, go to the far side of the ring, stop and Sit on command; the dog is then directed by the handler to jump either of the hurdles designated by the judge (High Jump and Bar Jump) at right and left, and return to the handler. The exercises are much more complex than in Novice or Open,

Many Goldens serve admirably as Assistance Dogs, readily learning whatever may be required; as the needs of each person using the dog differ, so the training will vary. The dogs are not only helpers but also valued companions. "Sherlock" earned a CD and WC before changing careers to become Cal's Assistance Dog; that training gave him a sound basis for the specialized work.

requiring an intricate sequence of actions by the dog. There are so many opportunities for the dog to fail an exercise that this class is sometimes wryly referred to as "Futility" class.

Each of the aforementioned titles requires that the dog qualify three times, under three different judges. Dogs are scored by points taken off for various errors, from perhaps a half-point for a very minor deviation in position to zero points for a complete exercise that is failed. All dogs enter the ring with a perfect 200 points (and it's downhill from there, to quote one handler!) and in order to qualify, they must have a total score of at least 170 points, earning at least 50 percent of the points in every exercise. All qualifiers are called back into the ring when the awards are given out, and receive a green ribbon. Those who place first through fourth receive appropriate ribbons or rosettes, and perhaps trophies as well.

The Obedience Trial Championship (OTCh) was established in 1977. It was designed to be a title that was won by placing over competition, in somewhat the same fashion that show championships are won by dogs placing over numbers of other dogs. The OTCh title requires that the dog first earn the UD title, then earn 100 points in Open B and Utility classes, with at least three first-place wins, one in each class and another in either class. Points are given for first and for second, based on the number of dogs competing in the class, and range from one for second place in a small class, to as much as forty for first in a Utility B class of forty-one or more. Dogs in an area where entries are small may have to win at a great many Trials; or a "hot" dog in big classes could finish up quickly.

The UDX (1994) was designed to recognize the consistent performer regardless of scores; any dog who qualifies at the same trial in both the Open

Wisperwind Willoughby, CD, U-CD, is a career Therapy Dog, a member of the Therapet program in Ann Arbor, Michigan. Willie draws smiles from those in pain, encourages mobility in the disabled, comforts the sad and has even drawn responses from the comatose. His constant slow wag and friendly face make him a friend to all; Willie gives of himself without reservation. Owned by Susan F. Fischer.

B and the Utility class ten times earns the UDX title. One reason for the establishment of this title was the frustration felt by exhibitors being shut out of chances for earning points toward the OTCh title; OTCh points are given only for first and second place, and with entries as large as they often are and competition as stiff as it is now, many creditable performers just didn't get into the first two places.

TRACKING TESTS

For a short time in the mid-1940s, a qualification in Tracking was required for the UD title, but this presented obvious difficulties, and Tracking was made an independent title. AKC Tracking is based on man-tracking as used by the police and military, although it is simple by the standards of dogs used for tracking in "real life." For the TD (Tracking Dog) title, the dog must follow the scent of a stranger over a trail 440 to 500 yards in length and locate an article such as a glove at the end. The start of the track is indicated by two "flags," one at the beginning, the other thirty yards along the track. There must be at least two ninety-degree turns, usually three or four, and the dog will start not less than thirty minutes or more than one hour after the track has been laid. The regulations specify in detail how the track is to be planned by the two judges and laid by the tracklayer.

Before entering a test, a dog must be certified as capable of performing by a Tracking judge. This is done by having the dog actually run a track under the observation of the approved Tracking judge, although it may be done anytime agreed upon by the judge and handler. In essence, then, when a dog successfully passes a licensed Tracking Test, its work has been deemed "qualifying" by three judges—the one who certified the dog and the two judging the test. Only one "pass" is required for the title.

Many dogs are used to detect substances such as illegal drugs, but few of them are as highly titled as "Mindy," who now works as a drug detection dog for the U.S. Forest Service in Florida. Formally, she is Ch. Richochet's Morning Star, UD, MH, WCX, VCX, and is owned by Glenda and Tracy Manucy.

Tracking Tests are always held outdoors, in whatever kind of weather may occur. The type of fields or terrain used varies considerably depending on the area of the country and what land is available. This could range from the lush alfalfa fields of Midwest farmland to the rocky deserts of Arizona or the brown pasturelands of California. The dog wears a harness allowing the head to go down for easy scenting and free use of body and legs, and must work at the end of a twenty- to forty-foot line. Without this, the handler would very quickly be outdistanced by the dog. The start of the track is indicated by two markers, but the rest of it is unmarked and unknown to the handler.

Advanced Tracking, where the dog can earn a **TDX** title, makes TD testing look like a "walk in the park." The TDX dog must contend with many more variables and a higher degree of difficulty than in the basic Tracking (TD) Test. The track is longer (up to half a mile) and older (at least three hours old); there is only one flag to indicate a starting point, and the dog must determine the direction of the track from that point. An article is left at the start. The handler may let the dog pick up a scent from the article in order to identify the track. Many handlers consider this unnecessary; others do use it.

The track will pass through various types of cover and terrain, and should have at least two obstacles or definite challenges to the dog; these could be a fence, a paved or dirt roadway, ravines, woods, fallen timber, plowed ground, a hedgerow or even a stream or creek. Five or more turns is usual. In addition to the article to be found at the end of the track, there are two other articles along the track that must be found. There are also two places where the track is crossed by the paths of two other people walking together; the dog must follow the primary track, although an indication of the crosstrack is acceptable. As in basic Tracking, the handler may restrain but not guide the dog in any way; that would be a fast way to get "whistled off" by the judge. In advanced Tracking, however, if the dog requires assistance to get over an obstacle such as a fence, the handler may give it. On a few occasions

"Mikey" has no titles appended to his name, but he does have certain duties. Chief among them is that of companion and playmate for young Kathryn Thompson, escort duty in the car, and finishing up anything edible that hits the floor.

the handler has needed assistance as well, such as the very heavy lady who needed a boost from both judges in order to make it up the side of a deep ditch! One can readily see that in advanced Tracking both dogs and people need to be in very good physical condition.

Tracking folk are a distinct variety of dog people, and may be unique in that they really do want each dog to pass. Tracking is a noncompetitive sport—there are no prizes for "best," or placements, only a "pass" or "fail." For those who do pass, finding that glove at the end of the track is full reward enough. For those who hear the judge's whistle signifying a failure, there's always the determination to succeed "next time."

Tracking is also unique in that this is one endeavor where the dog gets to call the shots: Since the handler has no idea where the track may go, she must trust in her dog. Good Tracking handlers develop a very keen sense of what the dog is doing, even thinking, expressed as "reading" the dog. The dog's body language enables the handler to know whether the dog is working scent, or casting about for it, and whether the dog is confident and really "locked in" on the track, or unsure and tentative. Good Tracking dogs will indicate clearly, often pulling strongly into the harness.

Watching a really good Tracking dog work is a thrill; and being on the end of the long line behind a competent tracker is unlike anything else you may do with your dog. We really have very little idea of *how* a dog tracks; we cannot teach dogs how to track, we can only channel natural abilities and give them the opportunities to develop that talent. This is an area where the dog knows far more than we do, and a good handler will never try to out-think the dog, just try to understand what the dog is "saying" and follow along with confidence in the dog.

The next development in Tracking is the Variable Surface Tracking. Because TDX requires quite extensive areas of land, the **VST** (official as of September 1995) is designed as a means of utilizing suburban and urban areas rather than rural ones. A track on various types of terrain including pavement or gravel could be a real test of a dog's abilities. The presence of buildings with their array of scents and air currents, and of other people, adds several degrees of difficulty. At present, this proposal is still in an investigative stage. Based on what police tracking dogs have done in urban areas, possibilities do exist for the development of very useful urban Tracking dogs.

HUNTING TESTS

The Hunting Test program came into being in the early 1980s as a means for ordinary retriever owners to display their dogs' retrieving abilities in an organized program designed to more closely resemble a day's actual hunting. The Hunting Test, like Obedience, is based on a standard scoring system and a pass/fail determination rather than on competition between entrants. All dogs who pass earn a qualification toward the appropriate level title, and there are no placements.

There are three organizations offering Hunting Tests: the AKC, UKC (United Kennel Club) and NAHRA (North American Hunting Retriever Association). Each has three levels of participation, which are roughly similar, although there are slight differences. The following is a description of the AKC tests:

The **Junior** tests are basic tests for dogs who have not had extensive training. Natural abilities are most important at this level. The dog must complete two single land marks and two single water marks. Distances are reasonable, and dogs may be held by the collar or by a slipcord when on line. Four qualifications earns the title of Junior Hunter (JH).

Senior tests are considerably advanced from Junior. The dog must be steady and able to honor (stand by) while another dog works. The dog is tested in at least four hunting situations, including a land blind, a water blind, a double mark on land and a double mark on water. One of these situations should include a walk-up, and a "diversion bird" may be used. Judges often set up very interesting tests simulating different hunting situations. The Senior Hunter (SH) title requires five qualifications at Senior level, or if the dog has earned a JH, four at Senior level.

Master tests are the top level. Dogs are to be tested in a minimum of five hunting situations, these to include multiple marks on land, on water and a combination of land and water. Both land blinds and water blinds are required. Diversion birds and shots may be used, and greater use is made of natural hazards, obstacles and equipment such as blinds and boats. The tests are often very complex and challenging. Dogs who are good at the Master level could likely run Qualifying stakes at Trials, and many have competed in Amateur or Open stakes. The title of Master Hunter (MH) requires six qualifications, or five if the dog has earned an SH title.

The AKC is adamant that there be no placements or awards based on scores at Hunting Tests, believing with good cause that such competition

Goldens like to do fun things, too! "Ziggy" (Gayhaven Heritage) models his Arabian Horse trappings donned for a parade.

would soon push Hunting Tests into the same spiral of competitiveness that has made Field Trials far from actual hunting, or anything in which the ordinary dog owner can hope to participate.

Sheba, first Golden to earn the **MH,** was trained in the suburbs of Houston, Texas, by her owner before leaving for work each morning. She practiced blinds across lawns and hedges, and water marks in the ponds at the park. Work with a gun had to wait until the weekend—the neighbors would not appreciate gunfire at daybreak!

WORKING CERTIFICATE TESTS

As early as 1950, a Working Certificate provision was published in the GRCA's Yearbook, at the same time as the "star system" for champions was initiated. A blank certificate was printed in the Yearbook; if a show champion Golden completed the requisite tests at a licensed or sanctioned Field Trial, the owner could have the certificate signed by the judges at the Trial and send the certificate to the GRCA. The required tests were a double mark on land, of at least forty yards in moderate cover, and "back-to-back" singles in swimming water. The dog was required to not be gun-shy, and to be soft-mouthed. Completion of the double mark was to demonstrate memory, and the back-to-back water retrieves to show that the dog would re-enter water as required. Placement in a sanctioned Field Trial would also qualify the dog for a Working Certificate (WC), and the designation * could be placed after the dog's name. Only champions were eligible for this, a system designed on the same pattern as in England for show champions earning the Field qualifier required for designation as a full Champion rather than solely Show Champion. A few dogs qualified under this provision, but records are very skimpy.

A more structured program was developed by the GRCA and approved at the Club's Annual Meeting in the fall of 1964, at the 25th Anniversary Specialty; now any Golden could run for a **WC**, not just champions. The meeting was held the night before the Field Trial, and several members asked that a WC test be held the next day, to be the first official GRCA WC test. The judges were Forrest L. Flashman (owner of Dual Ch. Craigmar Dustrack) and Reinhard Bischoff (owner/breeder of Ch-AFC Lorelei's Golden Rockbottom UD). Certainly the WC program could have had no more appropriate judges. The next day, eight dogs ran in the test (with birds and gunners scrounged from the Field Trial), and four passed. One of these was Ch. Kyrie Jaen Cobi (later UD), owned by Marcia Schlehr.

The popular WC program has been held not only at the GRCA Nationals and Regionals but also by many local Golden Retriever clubs. Regulations have been refined and clarified by the standing committee on WC/WCX, and a booklet is available with comprehensive information. The basic requirements for WC have not been changed appreciably since the original in 1950, although much detail and clarification of procedures have been added.

About 1978, a higher level, the Working Certificate Excellent (**WCX**), was added. WCX dogs must complete a land triple mark with a shot flyer, and a water double with honoring. Distances and difficulty are greater than in WC, and the dog must be steady and must deliver to hand. Judging is similar to Derby stakes. While the WC is basically an aptitude test, the WCX is also a test of qualities that can be brought out only by training, such as steadiness and memory on the triple mark. All tests in WC and WCX are marking tests, and no handling is allowed, so once the dog is sent, he must work on his own.

The GRCA's WC program was so successful that it was adopted, with some variations (two land singles rather than a double, and the dog must deliver to hand), by the Golden Retriever Club of Canada, and the first Canadian test was run in 1971. **Ch. Kyrie Jaen Cobi,** then nine years of age, also qualified at that test, making her possibly the first Golden to earn both American and Canadian WCs. Later, the GRCC added a WCX that included a blind retrieve. The Labrador Owners Club also organized a WC program, and it was not too many years before the Canadian Kennel Club took notice and officially recognized the Working Certificate program (although they did not make recognition of titles retroactive). Because the Canadian WCX was several steps more difficult than the WC, the **WCI (Working Certificate Intermediate)** was added. In Canada not only the five retriever breeds we know may run in WC/WCI/WCX but also Irish Water Spaniels and Standard Poodles—and of course the native Canadian, the Nova Scotia Duck Tolling Retriever.

AGILITY AND FLYBALL

Agility competition has been a fixture in England for some time. It is something like horse show jumping brought down to dog size, with various jumps and other obstacles along a set course. The scoring is a combination of time faults and jumping faults. The dog works off-lead; the handler may give commands and direction both verbally and by signals but may not touch the dog or the obstacles. Jump heights are set according to the dog's height, with class divisions according to jump height. In this country, all dogs over twenty inches at the shoulder jump twenty-four inches.

The obstacles and jumps can include A-frame, dogwalk (actually a catwalk!), see-saw, open tunnel, a closed tunnel of fabric, pause table, weave poles, hurdles, a tire or window jump, bar jump, broad jump and other variations. Dogs who fail to negotiate an obstacle, or who knock down a jump or leave the course, or a handler who touches a dog or an obstacle, will be failed. There are also other point deductions for errors or faults.

There are three classes: Novice Agility (with A and B divisions), Open Agility and Agility Excellent in increasing level of difficulty. Three qualifications in each class earns the titles of Novice Agility Dog (**NAD**), Open Agility Dog (**OAD**) or Agility Dog Excellent (**ADX**). A dog who has earned the ADX and qualifies ten times more in Agility Excellent class is designated Master Agility Excellent (**MAX**). The first official AKC Agility Trial was held in August of 1994.

Flyball is another very active sport for dogs. Teams of four dogs race down a straight course over jumps to a mechanism that releases a tennis ball when the dog pushes a foot pedal. The dog catches the ball and returns over the jumps to the handler, when the next dog leaves. Each of the two teams running simultaneously has its own jumps and flyball box. Dogs get very excited with flyball, and with the crowd cheering, dogs barking and handlers screaming encouragement, everyone seems to have a good time.

There is a North American Flyball Association that sets rules and awards titles for dogs who compete and qualify, but it is not affiliated with the AKC, and flyball remains an unofficial demonstration sport that its participants enjoy a great deal.

SERVICE DOGS AND GUIDES FOR THE BLIND

Goldens have been used as guide dogs for blind people for many years. Goldens are useful guides particularly because of their stable, sensible temperament; they are often required to remain quiet and inconspicuous in the office, classroom or restaurant, then become instantly alert and working when needed. Their size and strength are appropriate.

Several guide-dog organizations utilize Goldens, and several also use Golden people as volunteer workers in evaluating and fostering puppies, providing stud service or caring for brood bitches. Guide Dogs for the Blind in California and Guiding Eyes in Smithtown, New York, have had their own extensive breeding programs including Goldens (as well as Labradors and German Shepherd Dogs) for many years. Leader Dogs in Michigan also uses Goldens, most donated although some are bred at Leader Dogs. Seeing Eye in New Jersey and other schools have also used some Goldens. The schools that breed also place puppies in volunteer homes for socialization and basic home training; and the young dogs return to the school for specialized training sometime after a year of age. After an extensive checkup on health, soundness and temperament, the young dog is put into training. This work, with an experienced trainer of guide dogs, may take four months or so, and then there is another month working under close supervision with the blind person to whom the dog has been assigned, before the new team is ready to face the outside world.

A good guide dog may be working for eight to ten years. They learn not only to take directions such as "Right," "Left" and "Forward" but also are able to guide the blind person around obstacles such as street repairs and overhanging tree limbs; navigate through traffic, into elevators, and up and down stairs; and much more.

Golden breeders should always keep in mind that a stable, balanced temperament, willingness to work, and sound structure are qualities of great importance to the breed, as these qualities enable the dog to be useful far outside the narrow limits of "competition."

Service Dogs and Assistance Dogs are those who assist handicapped people with daily life. Their training is tailored to suit the needs of each individual; the dog may learn many different tasks such as pulling a wheelchair over curbs or up ramps, opening doors, operating light switches, and retrieving dropped objects including coins and keys. They may carry messages or learn their own special tasks, such as the Golden who takes clothes out of the dryer for her owner.

Canine Companions for Independence is one of the best-known organizations that train service dogs, and Goldens have been a strong source of good workers and breeding stock. Paws with a Cause is another organization, and Assistance Dogs are also trained by local groups and by individuals. There is now a national organization for advancing the interests of Assistance Dogs and the people who use them.

THERAPY DOGS AND OTHER POSSIBILITIES

Therapy Dogs and Social Dogs are used not for physical assistance but for emotional and social support. Most are visitors to hospitals and nursing homes, either individually or as part of programs such as Therapet™ in Ann Arbor, Michigan, sponsored by the Humane Society of Huron Valley. A stable, friendly, relatively calm temperament is of great value. The dogs must work in surroundings that are often crowded and confusing, with strange equipment, noises and scents. Therapy dogs are more than just pleasant visitors: often they serve as a means to establish communication with withdrawn or disturbed patients, and they offer invaluable emotional support and affection. As would be expected, Therapy Dogs must meet high standards for health, temperament, basic training and grooming.

One of the most unique potential uses for dogs is in the medical field. Some dogs have shown an ability to foretell the onset of epileptic seizures in people they know well, often even before the person herself realizes that a seizure is imminent. The dog's actions give the person a chance to get to a safe place or to summon help before the seizure occurs. Another use being investigated is teaching a dog to indicate the presence of certain malignancies, such as some types of skin cancer, or lung cancer. It is well known that dogs can easily discriminate among individual people—couldn't they also discriminate between normal skin cells and malignancies? An experimental program in Florida is working with at least one Golden concerning this intriguing possibility.

LAW ENFORCEMENT, SEARCH AND RESCUE

While the Golden does not show aptitude for police work involving attack or biting because of the breed's very strong bite inhibition and ready socialization to humans, there are other areas in which the Golden's abilities are of great value. Tracking is one, of course; many Goldens are used by law enforcement for that purpose. Because Goldens are not thought of by the general public as "police dogs," they are particularly sought for tracking children and others who might be afraid of a German Shepherd Dog, and for use where it is desirable that the dog not be recognized as part of law enforcement. One might call them "plain-clothes police dogs." A number of Goldens are used in airports and customs locations for detecting contraband, including narcotics, and for firearms and explosives.

The training for detection of narcotics or other drugs does *not* involve any kind of addiction of the dog to the substance to be sought. All training is done on a reward basis, usually starting with retrieving an object scented with something similar to the substance to be found. Very soon the dog is taught to indicate rather than to actually retrieve. The trainer may not want the dog to actually come in direct contact with the substance, which could be injurious to the dog or possibly destroy valuable evidence. A proper indication gets the dog a reward in the form of retrieving a special toy, or a good game of tug with a rolled-up towel. The form of indication varies depending on what is appropriate for the substance and for the situation. Scratching or digging might be appropriate in some cases; in others, a prompt sit and "pointing" with the nose to indicate exact location is preferred.

Search-and-Rescue Dogs are not strictly tracking dogs, as they often use air scenting to find their quarry. They are taught to cover an area and seek out any human they can find, particularly people who are sitting or lying on the ground, or hidden in some way. Whether they work on or off lead, the dogs are always under complete control. They must be in top physical condition (as must be the handlers), as they may be required to cover miles of wild terrain or be transported in aircraft or boats. Dogs who are taught to find people trapped in earthquakes or avalanches also make use of their scenting abilities, and often something more: Many can indicate whether the person is alive or dead. These dogs encounter some of the roughest, most difficult conditions in which a dog is ever asked to work; sound structure, stable temperament, endurance and prime physical condition are absolutely essential.

COMPANION AND FRIEND

Often the term "pet quality" is used in a less-than-favorable sense, as if a dog who is good for nothing else at all would be all right as a "pet." We beg to differ.

A dog who is to share one's life as companion and friend must be more than a warm, furry body. While the somewhat arbitrary details that will win accolades in the show ring are not essential to a companion, soundness and basic breed characteristics are. Temperament is of great importance in a dog who lives with people, meets people, encounters other dogs—in short, lives in the real world. "Competition dogs" who spend the biggest part of their lives in a chainlink run *might* be "successful" in their specialized endeavors in spite of serious flaws of temperament, but a dog who has to contend with children and modern family life had better be stable and reliable.

Trainability is also important. Maybe family dogs won't need to learn the scent discrimination exercises, but these dogs must be properly housetrained and abide by the rules of the house (with a minimum of effort on the part of the owners), or the "zero" they earn on their "scorecard" may be a fast trip to the animal shelter or a call to the local rescue group (if they're lucky).

Behavior problems are the primary reason dogs are given up or destroyed. Granted, in many cases, the person has no idea how to teach the dog in the first place, but dogs who are difficult to teach have a strike or two against them to start with.

The ease of socialization, stable temperament, willingness and general good-will that a typical Golden should have make the dog a wonderful companion. Soundness, good basic structure and health make the dog serviceable and relatively trouble-free. A proper, functional coat helps make the dog practical and easily maintained, a definite consideration in these days of crowded schedules and limited time. Dogs from every litter bred are going to have to live "in the real world," and these qualities cannot be ignored.

Even the American Kennel Club recognizes this and has made available a **Canine Good Citizen** test in which the owner of *any* dog, purebred or otherwise, may demonstrate the dog's suitability for living with people. Very little formal training is needed, but the dog must be properly socialized, behave properly in the presence of people and other dogs, accept some handling from another person and respond to very simple Obedience commands such as "Sit" or "Down." Many dog clubs and humane societies sponsor enjoyable get-togethers where dogs and their owners may participate and earn recognition that they are, indeed, Canine Good Citizens.

Every successful breeder has stories about wonderful Goldens who may never have set foot in a show ring or gone to line at a Field Trial—yet they are as worthy as any champion. Dogs like Mo, who every school day morning escorted his family's children to the school bus stop, and met them every afternoon; dogs like Rosie, gentle companion who brought so much happiness back into a lonely widow's life; and Woody, best friend and confidant for a bewildered teenager, always there for fourteen years. There are many, many wonderful Goldens fulfilling their destiny whose names will never appear in any record books, and their tasks are fully as important as any other.

This dog appears in a painting by George Stubbs, 1789. It is a large spaniel, red-gold in color, about 20–22 inches tall. Except for the beautiful spaniel ears, the dog shows many characteristics that are present in the breed we call the Golden Retriever. The tail has been shortened slightly, common practice in working spaniels.

chapter 2

The Creation of the Retriever

BEGINNINGS

All of what we now consider the retriever breeds are relatively recent, having been created in the 19th century from various types of dogs used for sporting or working purposes. None of the retrievers can be considered "old" breeds, or primary types, in the sense that some of the sighthounds or mastiffs could be. Dogs of those sorts are shown in archeological relics from thousands of years past, whereas the earliest retrievers date no farther back than the early 1800s, and the breeds of today were then considered only "varieties" of retrievers, and not differentiated for official Kennel Club purposes until about 1912.

Before firearms were used for the taking of feathered game, birds were most often captured by the use of a net; the dog indicated the position of the birds by crouching or "setting," keeping the birds immobile and allowing the net to be drawn over. This setting spaniel later developed into the several varieties of setter. Spaniels were also used to find and to roust out small game, both feather and fur, for Greyhounds to course, and for the falconer's hawks to kill. In neither case was there any need for the dog to retrieve the game, it being already close at hand.

When guns were developed to the point of being useful for small game, they were still slow and cumbersome. Single shot, muzzle-loading shotguns and black powder were inefficient, not to say unsafe, and a hunter looking to fill his pot had no compunctions about shooting birds on the ground or perched in trees (hence the term, "pot-shot"). Downed birds could be found by the hunter (or by the servant who came along to reload and carry the spare gun, powder, shot and other appurtenances) or located by the spaniel or setter, if necessary. Often the hunter preferred not to have the dog retrieve shot birds, as the dogs, not being well schooled in that art, did not improve the bird's table worthiness. And if the dog was, perchance, trained well enough to retrieve with a soft mouth, one did not need a specialist dog for that purpose.

With the development of the breech-loading shotgun in the mid-19th century, and concurrent improvements in cartridges and "smokeless" powder, the art of wingshooting became sport and was taken up by the aristocracy and the landed gentry, those who had the resources to keep and to develop dogs for sporting purposes. The gentleman's dogs, usually trained and worked by a gamekeeper or huntsman, kept the larder supplied, as well as providing sport; and nearly every proper country house had a kennel of setters, spaniels or pointers, and possibly hounds and terriers as well. Gamebirds were located by dogs followed by hunters on foot, accompanied by loaders, dog handlers and friends. They might also, while "walking up," flush a covey forward over a hedgerow behind which others waited; this developed into the driven shoot, where a line of "beaters" flushed and drove the birds toward the gunners.

This procedure demanded something far better than the muzzle-loaders with their slow, laborious, dangerous reloading. It also provided the opportunity and the need for a dog who would remain quietly in position during the shooting, marking the falls of the birds, and then be sent to retrieve when opportunity allowed . . . the specialist retrieving dog.

Estates and their land were carefully designed and managed for the propagation and hunting of gamebirds. The expansion of the railroad system, and the patronage of royalty, also contributed to the development of shooting. House parties at country estates became prominent social events. The railways enabled easy travel for a "long weekend," with three or four days of shooting for the gentlemen. Huge numbers of birds were bagged, and the best shots became "star attractions," even as landowners competed for the honor of putting on the best shoots. Now there was a real need for the nonslip retriever who would remain quietly at heel, if walking-up, or in the blind at driven shoots, until released on command to fetch the fallen birds. A dog was quicker, and far better, at finding a bird in heavy cover or across water. As a day's shoot might produce hundreds of shot birds, the dogs' work quickly became an integral part of any successful shoot.

A soft mouth—the ability to carry game tenderly so as not to render it unfit for the table—was essential. Also necessary was the ability to accept training (biddability) so as to be reliably steady, to work when and where commanded, to find fallen game by sight or scent as needed, and bring the game promptly back to the handler. Any dogs fulfilling these requirements were called retrievers, regardless of what breeds were among their antecedents.

SPANIELS, SETTERS AND SO FORTH

Long before the retrievers of today, there were spaniels: Indeed, dogs of spaniel type are evident in paintings and tapestries of 1500, and there are sculptured dogs from Roman times that resemble spaniels. The basic spaniel type is drop-eared, with feathered legs and tail, sturdy in build, and in size varying from small to moderately large. Always they are associated with the hunting of game birds or waterfowl. Their antiquity and bird-hunting aptitudes are behind very many of our modern sporting dogs.

A number of these early spaniels were of a solid yellow or reddish coloring, very similar to that of today's Golden Retreiver. Many early examples of art depict dogs strongly resembling medium- to large-size spaniels, with dropped ears, feathered coats, stocky build and fringed tails carried level. While one could not assign them a specific breed, they are recognizably spaniel in type, just as other dogs in the illustrations are recognizable as scenthounds, sighthounds and mastiff types. One late-16th-century weaving shows large red or yellow spaniels doing the work of retrievers, fetching birds for hunters.

In the 16th century Johannes Caius (John Keyes) described the sorts of dogs that were generally known at the time. Chief among them under the heading of "a gentle kind, serving the game" were the *Acupatorii*, for the pursuit of fowl, comprising *Index* (because the dog indicated or pointed out the game), or setter, which "findeth game on the land," and *Aquaticus*, or spaniel, which "findeth game on the water." Many researchers believe that the setter is nothing but "an improved spaniel," developed from the early basic type.

These very early spaniels were used in either of two ways: to find gamebirds with active searching, rousting the birds out of their hiding places, to be taken by the falconer's hawk, or to find the birds and creep upon them, freezing into stillness while the huntsmen surrounded the birds and drew the net over them, or perhaps shot them on the ground. From these different means of working developed the flushing spaniels and the setting spaniels, later called setters.

Of early paintings, one by Van Dyke (1635), *The Children of Charles I*, includes a red or light brown dog that has been claimed to be an early red setter; in shape and coat, it also resembles some of the early retrievers (though retrievers, as such, were not known in the 17th century). Probably it is a large spaniel of the sort that was the progenitor of setters, and of possible other ancestors of retrievers as well. Similar dogs appear in other paintings—large spaniels, twenty inches in height, often with heavily coated spaniel ears but the head and body shape of a moderately made retriever.

Both spaniels and setters share the same types of coloration: the characteristic shades of yellow to red, black, and liver, each with or without white in various degrees from solid white through particolor, roans, ticked or flecked, and with or without the bicolor pattern that creates "black-and-tan" or "tricolor" in the classic pattern of tan markings above the eyes, on the muzzle, chest, legs and under the tail. The variety may seem confusing, but what is relevant is that in the retrievers, all coat-color combinations have been eliminated except the self-colored black, liver (chocolate) and/or yellow-red.

As late as the 1920s, there is a photo in Ash's *History and Development of the Dog* of Mrs. W. M. Charlesworth's "Golden Springer Spaniel," Noranby Nell, retrieving. A solid yellow or red Springer is quite unheard of these days but certainly has historical reason for being.

From the spaniels, it is likely that Goldens also received much of their eagerness to work afield and to retrieve, as well as a happy and forgiving temperament. Admittedly, many of the spaniels of two or three centuries ago were impudent, harum-scarum, incessantly busy and often over the edge of uncontrollable, but a good part of this could be due to the rather rough-and-ready methods of schooling used in that era, which would probably have ruined (and eliminated) a more sensitive, less forgiving canine.

The spaniel's contribution to the Golden Retriever was indirect, being mainly through the use of setters used to develop the Wavy-Coated (Flat-Coated) Retriever, but there is also the likelihood that descendants of the large, self-colored land spaniels could have contributed to some of the many unregistered or "pedigree unknown" dogs who were used in early years. If a dog looked like the breed and had working qualities to contribute, the lack of a recorded pedigree was of no consideration.

The threads are tangled and often broken or mended, yet they all together make up the tapestry that is our modern dog. These early examples do show that certain type characteristics of size, shape, coat and color that exist in today's Golden Retriever, were evident in a number of sporting dogs long before formal recognition of the breed.

One is invited to read further on the development of spaniels in William Pferd III's excellent book *The Welsh Springer Spaniel,* and C. Bede Maxwell's *The Truth About Sporting Dogs.* Both books are out of print, regretfully, but can sometimes be found at booksellers specializing in rare and out-of-print books on dogs.

The Setters

The "setting spaniel" served as forebear of the modern breeds of setters, which have been distilled from a quite diverse array of varieties and lines. As was common with most breeds, the setters had many varieties or families, often defined by geography or by specific lines kept by the gentry or aristocracy. Of particular interest to retriever history is that setters were quite commonly crossed with types such as the Newfoundland and the Water Spaniel to produce the earliest retrieving dogs. The engraving in Hutchinson's *Dog Breaking* (1848), illustrating the results of such crosses, is well known.

Fashion in the 19th century called for retrievers to be solid color, most preferably black; other colors occurred but were not generally in favor. (One writer stated plainly that "I have no fancy for other than black Retrievers, nor do I think that they will ever be in general favor." Well.) This would indicate that whatever setters were used were most likely self-colored. Using dogs with large amounts of white would probably result in offspring with undesirable amounts of white marking.

So what solid-colored setters were there? We all know of the red Irish Setters, of course, although the beautiful, deep red, silky coats are a fairly modern development. Early, there were many white-and-red setters, and also the "red" was considerably lighter in shade. One writer in 1847 notes that Irish Setters were "usually of a dun or yellow color. These are the genuine, unmixed descendants of the original land-spaniel." Selection for depth and richness of color over many generations led to the spectacular reds of today's showdogs, but lighter shades of chestnut and golden red still occur, too.

There was also the black and tan Gordon Setter, which even today occasionally throws a solid red pup. Vero Shaw in the 19th century writes of black and tan coloring in Wavy-Coated Retrievers as resulting from Gordon Setter in the ancestry, and black-and-brindles as showing evidence of their "Labrador extraction." There were lines of solid black setters; both the Duke of Buccleuch and Lord Home, well-known in Labrador history, were known to have solid black setters. There were solid livers, both light and dark, and at least two or three families of cream-colored setters.

There is a much-reproduced illustration that depicts a blocky headed setter with a thick wavy coat and a bushy tail, on point. Most of the hand-colored plates that retain enough of their original color show the dog to be a light yellow or deep cream color. Rachel Page Elliott, Golden Retriever historian, identifies this as a Featherstone Castle setter. It has a strongly "retrievery" look to it. Gilbert Leighton-Boyce in his book *A Survey of Early Setters* says it "has as a setter something about his body and coat which is almost too close to a forecast of the modern Golden Retriever, though not, I hasten to add, the sort that Mrs. Charlesworth showed in my youth!" He also mentions other lines of cream-colored and "light fawn" setters that could have contributed genetic material to the formation of the Golden.

Featherstone Castle is in the Border country of England, as are the seats of the Buccleuch and Home families. The Featherstone Castle strain was described as powerfully built, deep and broad in the chest, very strong in forequarters, "beautifully feathered on the forelegs, tail and breeches; easily broken, very lofty in their carriage, staunch, excellent dogs and good finders."

These colors of black, liver and yellow ("light fawn" and cream) correspond exactly with the recognized retriever colors.

This old engraving is said to greatly resemble the "Featherstone Castle setter" bred in the Border country in the mid-19th century. In many prints the dog is colored a pale yellow or what was then called "light liver." In build it is similar to the Wavy-Coated Retriever.

So we have black setters who certainly contributed to the development of the Wavy-Coated, then the Flat-Coated Retrievers, from which the occasional yellow "sport" was whelped. We will see that at least one red setter was used in forming the first line of Golden Retrievers. And there is the possibility, even likelihood, that some now-extinct line of cream or pale yellow setters also contributed—perhaps not only coloring, but other characteristics as well. The fringed ears, prominent occiput and square-lipped muzzle; perhaps some ranginess and flat-ribbed build, all characteristics that show up (less now than in earlier years), particularly in unselective breedings in Goldens; nose and birdsense; the tendency to range and quarter ahead of the gun; even the occasional dog who will flash-point game—may owe something to setter ancestors, directly or indirectly.

The Water Spaniels

The dogs called Water Spaniels and Water Dogs have existed in Britain since before any author decided they were worth specific attention, perhaps of such ubiquity, or such minor status, that they never received any specific designation, somewhat as the common American farm dog has never been named or developed into a "pure" breed.

Johannes Caius in the 16th century named the *Aquaticus*, or "spaniell," which "findeth game on the water." Gervase Markham in 1621, in *The Arte of Fowling by Water and Land*, described the Water Dog as black; "lyverhued," "pyed or spotted" although he "may be of any colour and yet excellent." His hair was "long and curled, not loose and straggled; for the first shewes hardnesse and ability to endure the water, the other much tendernesse, making his sport grievous." As for conformation, "his Brest like the brest of a Shippe, sharp and compact, his shoulders broad, his fore legs straight, his chine [brisket] square, his Buttokes round, his ribs compassed [rounded], his belly gaunt, his Thyes brawny, his Cambrels [stifles] crooked [well angulated], his Pasterns strong and dewe clawed, and his foure feet spatious, full and round, and closed together to the cley [webbed], like a water Ducke, for they beeing his oares to row him in water, having that shape, will carry his body away faster."

Even given the quaint language and casual spelling of the period, the preceding is a reasonable description of retriever type in general, even the warning against the "loose and straggled" coat—a pretty good description of an "open coat," so undesired in a water-working dog (although we must not misinterpret the reference to ducks' feet!).

The matter of coat quality was still being discussed two and a half centuries later, when a prominent breeder of Water Spaniels condemned coats "woolly in texture, and too open and long; will hold as much water as a blanket . . . simply a nuisance" and in muck, briars or snow and ice were rendered quite useless. Nor has the problem of coat quality yet been solved today, with some show judges and exhibitors ignoring incorrect coats.

The Large Water Spaniel (Bewick, 1789), which was subsumed into other breeds such as the various retrievers by the late 19th century. The Small Water Spaniel differed only in size. Unlike the modern Irish Water Spaniel, this variety has a smooth face and legs, and a relatively short coat.

As is a natural course of events, different areas evolved varying sorts of dogs for the same general purposes. Perhaps they used different types from which to breed; also, the environment in various areas often demanded different qualities: The dog used on rough, rocky coasts might quite reasonably need somewhat different characteristics than the dog used in still lakes and marshes, for instance. Function and ability were the criteria, not pedigree, and the best workers naturally were bred from more often than poor ones.

The dog writer Stonehenge classes Water Spaniels as English or Irish, "besides which there is the Tweedside breed, which resembles a good deal in appearance a small ordinary English retriever of a liver color." Of the Irish varieties, the Southern variety is the type most familiar to us today as the Irish Water Spaniel, with his long ears, short-haired face surmounted with a topknot, rat tail and unique dark liver coat of long curls. He describes the Northern dog as having "short ears, with little feather either on them or on the legs, but with a considerable curl in his coat" and generally liver in color. The Northern variety is also known as "the old brown Irish Retriever"; They were about twenty inches tall. A gravestone in Ireland for "Drake, a brown retriever dog, died 31 March 1876" carries a profile carving of a dog exactly of this description, a dog closer to what we would think of as retriever rather than spaniel in appearance. This Northern type, with the close curly coat, short ears, legs smooth on the fronts and with a feathered tail was fairly well known up until about the 1850s, but by the end of the century had disappeared or been absorbed into other breeds and varieties.

The English Water Spaniel may have been developed from water-loving spaniels of the sort mentioned earlier, or perhaps by crossing the "large Water Dog" with some sort of setter, or perhaps spaniel. The large Water Dog was a sturdy rather awkward-looking dog with a rough shaggy coat, with long coat on face and all around the legs, somewhat like an unclipped poodle. The Rough Water Dog, or Barbet as it is called in Europe, and the Poodle probably shared some common ancestry; the Portuguese Water Dog is of this type as well. Crossing dogs of this sort with a setter might well result in a dog with smooth face and legs and less length of coat, while retaining a distinct curl and the water-loving temperament. Today the two types are quite distinct—one rough with shaggy face and legs, and the other with a smooth face and feathering only on the backs of the legs.

The English Water Spaniel

The English Water Spaniel was higher on leg than the Springer of the day, and with a coat of crisp tight curls "like Astrakhan fur" everywhere except on the face, which was short-haired. There was no topknot. The dog writer Stonehenge mentions that "his powers of swimming and diving are immense, and he will continue in it for hours together, after which he gives his coat a shake and is soon dry." Rawdon Lee describes Mr. Phineas

Bullock's "Rover," one of the few English Water Spaniels to be shown, who took a second prize in 1869 at the Birmingham show and earlier a Gold Medal at the Paris (France) show. Other well-known dog men of the time also admired Rover:

> A beautiful bright chestnut-red in colour, with a very deep, square body, which was not long, legs straight and about twice as long as the fashionable field spaniel . . . beautiful flat bone . . . without being lumbersome. . . about 48 lb.; . . . tail shortened a bit but . . . rather long; his neck was simply grand, and sprung from the very best of working placed shoulders.

Alas, the English Water Spaniel and other similar varieties, useful as they were in their time, were by the end of the 19th century almost universally replaced in Britain by the retriever breeds, into which the water spaniels were absorbed. They did leave in their descendants not only their working capabilities, but also the curly or markedly waved, very water-resistant coat.

While these Water Spaniels are no longer extant in Britain, very similar types do remain elsewhere. The Wetterhoun (Water Dog) in the Netherlands is almost exactly like water spaniels painted in the late 1700s and is still used for hunting in that country. In North America, a sturdy working spaniel was developed from combining the English Water with curly-coated retrievers and small land spaniels. In areas of Minnesota and Wisconsin, the American Water Spaniel became the indigenous retriever, in use from at least the mid-19th century even though it was not officially recognized for registration and showing until much later by the American Kennel Club.

The Tweed Water Spaniel

The painting by John Charlton now in the GRCA archives, which is believed to represent a Tweed Water Spaniel, shows a dark brown dog of indeterminate size, though giving the impression of being large enough to be quite useful. The smooth face and legs with only slight feathering on the backs of the legs are similar to that of the American Water Spaniel; the ears are shorter and less feathered, giving a look more like retriever than spaniel.

The Tweed, we will find, is important to the history of the Golden Retriever, as at least two, possibly more, were used by Lord Tweedmouth in laying the foundation for his strain of yellow retrievers. His Tweeds were obtained from David Robertson of Ladykirk, near Berwick on the Tweed, a cousin of Sir Dudley. There's a reference to the Tweedside dog in Richard Lawrence's *The Complete Farrier and British Sportsman* (1815): "Along the rocky shores and dreadful declivities beyond the junction of the Tweed with the sea of Berwick, Water-Dogs have received an addition of strength from the experimental introduction of a cross with the Newfoundland dog," going on to say that the Water Spaniels were of different colors, but

Artist's depiction of Belle, a Tweed Water Spaniel (c. 1865). "Light liver" in color, probably 20–21 inches tall, with close coat, somewhat curled, smooth legs and face. Bred to the yellow retriever Nous in 1868, Belle produced the first litter of Dudley Marjoribanks' (Lord Tweedmouth's) yellow strain.

"the liver-coloured is the most rapid of swimmers and the most eager in pursuit." We should clarify that the term "liver" in the 19th century was used to describe varying shades from pale sandy to dark brown coat color, and the "Newfoundland" of this early date was *not* the giant dog we think of today but one of the smaller types called the Lesser Newfoundland or the St. Johns Dog, which were also the forebears of the Wavy Coated/Flat Coated Retrievers and the modern Labrador.

Mr. Skidmore, the Irish Water Spaniel breeder, around 1870 thought the Tweed Spaniel almost extinct; he describes them slightly differently; "from their appearance, close coat, sparseness of feather, and style of head, I always thought that there was a dash of Bloodhound in their veins . . . heads are, or were, conical, lips heavily flewed, ears set on Bloodhound-like, whilst they were all light in color." It is entirely possible that the Tweedside dogs varied in coat and head type, just as Goldens today can show the same degree of variation in these qualities. The reference to light color should be noted.

A reference in Dalziel's *British Dogs*, 1881, describes the Tweed Spaniel as "very light liver-color, so close in curl as to give me the idea that they had originally been a cross from a smooth-haired dog; they were long in tail, ears heavy in flesh and hard like a hound, but only slightly feathered—forelegs feathered behind, hind legs smooth, head conical." Other references to the Tweed Water Spaniel breed are difficult to find.

Mr. Stanley O'Neill was a well-known breeder of Flat Coated Retrievers in England, and one of Elma Stonex's correspondents on the origin of the breed. As a young man, he often accompanied his father, who was Superintendent of Grimsby Fish Docks from 1899 to 1906, and visited every port where fish was landed in England and Scotland. Young Stanley had the opportunity to observe hundreds of Water Dogs used as ships' dogs, and it was "well known" that they had been used as a cross to improve the water-retrieving talents of the Curly-coat as early as 1800. Mr. O'Neill says:

I had an uncle who bred Curly-coats . . . (at) Grimsby I went—a small boy—into what seemed a world of Curlies. Every third or fourth ship still had one. The fishermen told me theirs weren't Curlies, they were Water-Dogs. I said the Water-Dogs were Newfoundlands. They said there couldn't be dogs that were more Water-Dogs than Water-Dogs. And so the argument went on. In 1903 from Newcastle and Shields we went on to Blyth . . . and at a stop further up the coast, probably Alnmouth, I saw a man netting for salmon. With them was a dog with a wavy or curly coat. It was a tawny colour but, wet and spumy, it was difficult to see the exact colour, or how much was due to bleach and salt. Whilst my elders discussed the fishing I asked these Northumberland salmon-net men whether their dog was a Water-Dog or a Curly, airing my knowledge. They told me he was a Tweed Water Spaniel. This was a new one on me. I had a nasty suspicion my leg was being pulled. This dog looked like a brown Water-Dog to me, certainly retrieverish and not at all spanielly. I asked if he came from a trawler, and was told it came from Berwick.

A friend from a family long established in Berwick later told Mr. O'Neill that the Tweed Water Spaniel was the same as the water dogs to be seen along the east coast of England from Yarmouth to Shields (most of the east coast), the only difference being that in the Border area (Berwick and River Tweed) the browns *and yellows* predominated.

It seems logical then that Sir Dudley Marjoribanks would choose dogs of this sort from his cousin living near Berwick to contribute to the breed of yellow retrievers he was intent on developing, both for color and for aptitude in retrieving and swimming.

Interestingly, the Tweedside area is not far from the breeding grounds of the early Labrador Retrievers, the Duke of Buccleuch's Drumlanrig, the Earl of Home's Hirsel, and Sir Richard Graham's Netherby. The head gamekeeper to the Duke of Buccleuch wrote about 1897 of the early imports from Labrador: "They were kept pure for many years, but the difficulty of getting fresh blood arose, so they became crossed with other breeds, especially with flat-coated retrievers and Tweed water spaniels." This shows both that the Tweed Spaniel was known to dog men in the area and that all of the retriever

"Brush, a celebrated retriever," from a painting by A. Cooper, R.A., is typical of the early St. Johns Dog and its derivative, the Wavy-Coated Retriever. The black-and-tan coloring and the touches of white marking were not uncommon.

varieties were not only interrelated, they were the next thing to inseparable. The Tweedside dogs were known among keepers and practical dog men of the area, even if not to the writers who expounded at great length upon "purebreds" and Kennel Club topics.

Stanley O'Neill, writing in 1957, further describes the Tweeds that he saw:

> Just to give yourself a personal idea, imagine a dog halfway between a Curly and a Chesapeake; clean in head, inclined to be clean in front of leg and shoulders with great bone. Bone was a feature. In describing the curl . . . I called it "tight." This might be misleading. I certainly didn't mean "close" or curling pinched-like to a small curl. I meant firm and hard. The water ran off them from the oiliness and strength of hair as it did off the Labs 50 years ago. Ears were smallish. Some had far more curls than others. . . . I think the whole of the Retrievers and Newfoundlands get their aquatic side of descent from these dogs. One of the fundamental differences between the Curly and the Water Dog, as I realized later, was the Water Dog's broader skull. He was also broader in front, and tended to be lower in front than behind, like the early Labs. In breeding to the broader skull than the Flat-coats of the 1907–14 period, the Golden breeders would be true and correct to their Tweedmouth origin.

This description of coat is interesting, as a similar coat occasionally occurs in Goldens of unblemished ancestry even today. The three or four I have seen had a curled coat, which in the smooth areas as on the head and legs is hard and almost waxy to the touch, with a dense jacketing that is nearly impervious to water and is also toughly resistant to brush and briar. To a lesser degree, some of the qualities of the Tweed's coat may also be evident in the flat wave and firm springy texture of topcoat of some excellent Golden coats today.

Unfortunately, the craze for an absolutely straight coat in the show ring (completely contravening the Breed Standard's equal consideration for straight or wavy) has much diminished the number of equally correct wavy coats in show-bred Goldens.

A soft, curly coat without a protective undercoat, on the other hand, is a curse, as burrs and stickers will penetrate to the skin and cause terrible tangles. Nor is it protection against wet and cold, and it carries a burdensome amount of water.

THE DOGS FROM THE NEW WORLD

While the spaniels, setters and water spaniels had been long established in Great Britain, most researchers agree that a very large part of the foundation for our modern retrievers were dogs imported from the part of the New World now known as Newfoundland. Beyond that very general statement, there are endless arguments and discussions both as to just what the dogs who came from Newfoundland were, and what *their* antecedents might have been.

We will see how the Golden Retriever breed, as other retriever breeds, came into being. Like the Labrador, it was developed privately by aristocratic families, using genetic contributions of the dogs from the New World combined with other breeds or types. Richard Wolters has detailed admirably the genesis of the Labrador Retriever in his book *The Labrador Retriever; The History, The People.* Golden Retriever history has many parallels.

What dogs might there have been in Newfoundland whose descendants crossed the Atlantic to be sold at Poole Harbor with the fish caught on the Grand Banks? What were these dogs who were bred with native British varieties to be the foundation for the modern retrievers? Here we enter an area of much conjecture and little solid record, and perhaps one person's surmise is as good as another's.

The first record of dogs in Newfoundland is archeological. At a burial site at Port au Choix in northwestern Newfoundland, dated about 3,930 years ago, were found the remains of two dogs probably forty-five to fifty-five pounds in size, well muscled, probably hunting dogs. The careful placement of the dogs with human remains and possessions indicates a strong relationship between the people and their dogs.

There were contacts by Norse voyagers about A.D. 900 and also unrecorded contacts by English pirates and privateers, seamen adrift on the

Atlantic, and possibly some fishermen, before the arrival of John Cabot, the explorer. Later explorers found the local Beothuck Indians "altogether harmless," scraping by on bare subsistence. At that time they had neither dogs nor boats, although they lived in a land with a variety of wildfowl, deer, "buffles" (moose?), bears, wolves, foxes and other furbearers.

By 1583, when Sir Humphrey Gilbert audaciously took possession of the harbor of St. John for England, the Portuguese, French and English had already been fishing the Grand Bank for many years. The Basques had established a whaling factory on the south coast of Labrador as early as 1450. The English began fishing about 1498, the French and Portuguese a few years later. The settlements (if one could grace them with that term) were without formal government of any kind, being only temporary summer stations to dry and salt the fish caught.

By 1650 probably half the population was deserters and their families. What little law there was on the island was that of the British marines; there were no courts, no police, no schools or churches. Life was hard and grim, no less so for the unfortunate Beothuck Indians, who were often hunted for sport, if they hadn't succumbed to the diseases brought by the Europeans. The last Beothuck died in 1829.

The British gained full sovereignty in Newfoundland in 1713, although other nations continued to fish offshore. There was always a degree of commerce between workers of the different nationalities, particularly when crews came ashore for supplies and for recreation.

All this time, dogs were being used both on the land and in the fishing boats. They were used for hunting wildfowl and small game; they served as draft animals to pull firewood and supplies; they retrieved fish that slipped off the barbless hooks of the long ganglines, or equipment that fell overboard and they swam carrying lines between boat and shore. And, no doubt, they also served as companions in a bleak and heartless land. In fact, their usefulness was such that ships' captains soon had a fair trade going taking these animals back to sell at Poole Harbor on the south coast of England, and Greenock on Scotland's west coast. By 1800, the dog from the New World had become known in England as a useful gundog and retriever, and had also been much crossed with British dogs to produce different varieties.

THE DOGS OF NEWFOUNDLAND

And what kinds of dogs were sent from Newfoundland? Here is an area of great confusion. The terms "Newfoundland dog," "Labrador," "lesser Labrador" and "St. Johns Dog" are used most confusingly; and the definition of what was the "original type" is the subject of interminable discussion, which continues even today. Rather than try to trace all the intricacies and arguments, we can make some points and assay some logical conclusion.

First, if the native Indians did not have dogs at that time, as most sources indicate, then any dogs in Newfoundland must be the result of importation from the European countries that were represented in the area: England, Portugal, France and Spain (including the Basques). What dogs might they have brought with them? From England, and from France, any of various hunting dogs: hounds of several sorts, including the black St. Hubert's hound; large and small spaniels; Mastiffs; Greyhounds. From Portugal, the long-coated Water Dog, shorthaired pointing dogs such as the muscular Perdigueiro or the all-purpose Castro Laboreiro (country worker, or "farmhand"). From Spain, heavyset pointers, sheepdogs, large guarding dogs; and the Basques' herding dogs and Pyrenean Mountain dogs. No doubt there were also others of vanished types or breeds not known to us today.

Because Newfoundland was an area rich in many types of wild game, and because these wild creatures provided a large part of the diet for both settlers and crewmen, various sorts of hunting dogs such as hounds and spaniels certainly would have been brought. Dogs showing facility in the water would be useful to both fishermen and to hunters. Large, strong dogs such as the mountain dog of the Pyrenees, who could pull a sledge with firewood or dried fish and also guard the dwellings, would be valuable as well.

How these dogs might have interbred and combined, there is no record of. While dogs left to their own devices tend to breed indiscriminately, we can surmise that only the sturdiest survived the rigors of life in Newfoundland in those years when even the settlers barely managed to subsist. Often dogs were left to live on their own when crews left the islands. Dogs neither useful enough to be fed and cared for in some rough fashion, nor clever and strong enough to survive on their own, had little chance of surviving and perpetuating their genes. This is perhaps some explanation of the retrievers' tolerance of pain and hardship, and ability to thrive on small amounts of food—and to put on weight when fed abundantly!

One of the earliest descriptions of dogs of the island is in Capt. Peter Hawker's 1814 *Instructions to Young Sportsmen*, which has been so often quoted in books on retrievers. Well, we shall present it once again, as perhaps there may be a slightly different interpretation of this statement, which might help shed a little light on matters.

Newfoundland Dogs: Here we are a little in the dark. Every canine brute, that is nearly as big as a jackass, and as hairy as a bear, is denominated a *fine Newfoundland dog*. Very different, however, is [are?] both the proper Labrador and St. John's breed of these animals; at least, many characteristic points are required, in order to distinguish them.

The one is very large; strong in the limbs; rough haired, small in the head; and carried his tail very high. He is kept in that country for drawing sledges full of wood, from inland to the sea shore, where he is also very useful, by his immense strength and sagacity, among wrecks, and other disasters in boisterous weather.

The other, by far the best for every kind of shooting, is oftener black than of another colour, and scarcely bigger than a pointer. He is made rather long in the head and nose; pretty deep in the chest; very fine in the legs; has short or smooth hair; does not carry his tail so much curled as the other, and is extremely quick and active in running, swimming, or fighting.

He then goes on to state that "the St. John's breed of these dogs" is used on the coast by fishermen, and also has such discrimination of scent and aptitude that "for finding wounded game, of every description, there is not his equal in the canine race; and he is a *sine qua non* in the general pursuit of wildfowl." Later, he uses the term "Newfoundland" inclusively, as if referring to either of the types described above. Well, both were dogs of Newfoundland.

The inference drawn from the first paragraph quoted is that the huge, hairy dog called Newfoundland in England is *not* the dog then found in Newfoundland, but one that had been modified from the "original"—one guess would be, by crossing with some sort of Mastiff in order to produce a large, imposing dog. Hawker then describes two types of dogs found in Newfoundland (by which reason they may both be called Newfoundland dogs), but which he differentiates as the "proper Labrador" (a very large, strong dog) and the "St. John's Dog." The second dog, "oftener black than of another colour" fits our conception of a Labrador Retriever rather well. The reference to the hair being "short or smooth" can be taken to include both the familiar short coat and a somewhat longer coat with some development of ruff, breeches and tail plume, differentiated from a curly or a rough shaggy coat. Paintings of early St. John's dogs do show this type of coat, with a brush tail and the suggestion of fringes on legs and ruff. (As late as the early 20th century, some Labradors were criticized for carrying too much brush on the tail and breechings.)

Well, if the dogs are from Newfoundland, how did the "Labrador" tag become attached? The area called Labrador, the easternmost point of the mainland of Canada, is a part of the *province* of Newfoundland. The *island* of Newfoundland, which is only *part* of the province, contains the great bulk of the population. One theory about the name is that the workers at the Portuguese fishing stations on the south coast of the mainland peninsula were called *lavradors* or *labradors*, meaning laborer or worker; the term was then used to denominate both that area and the working dogs. It's also intriguing that the native working dog of Portugal is the Castro Laboriero, a medium-size dog similar to today's Labrador in shape and coat, and which comes in colors of fawn, brindle and sable-gray—perhaps an explanation of the "tabby" markings on some of the early dogs?

Early depictions of dogs from Newfoundland show the larger types as being commonly white with markings of black or red. The smaller sorts were most often dark in color, black or black and tan, sometimes with white markings on feet, chest and face. Landseer painted a "Labrador dog" named Cora in 1823: She looks more like a combination of Border Collie–retriever, with her high-set small ears, snipey muzzle and the white markings on a glossy black coat definitely somewhat feathered.

Back to Britain

So various dogs called Labrador or Newfoundland or St. Johns Dog (after the town of St. Johns; in Newfoundland they were called simply Water Dogs) were brought to England and Scotland. They were sold for various purposes and later bred with local dogs as there was no conception or thought of keeping them a "pure breed." People who wanted a large, imposing dog for draft purposes (dogs were used to pull carts until 1850 in England), as a benevolent watchdog or decorative item for the country estate, bred them with dogs of the Mastiff type.

For use as gun dogs or for other sporting purposes, they were crossed with setters and water spaniels of various sorts. The well-known engraving of "various retrievers" used as the frontispiece in Hutchinson's later editions of *Dog Breaking* (1848) shows several of these crosses, which represented types used in the development of the Wavy-Coated and Curly-Coated Retrievers. In 1844, Charles Darwin discusses changes in the English dog over a century, saying that the Newfoundland dog is "so much modified" that it no longer resembles "any existing native dog" of Newfoundland. No wonder that dog writers and breeders in the late 1800s were heatedly debating what was the "true" and "original" Newfoundland or Labrador dog!

The St. Johns Dog; the Water Dog of Newfoundland

The particular blending that we are interested in here is that which produced the Wavy-Coated Retriever, which was the forerunner of today's Flat-Coat and also a major stem of the Golden Retriever. The chief combination was the St. Johns Dog, the smaller import (usually dark in color with a "short or smooth" coat—that is, short like today's Labrador, or thick and brushy or slightly feathered), crossed with any of various setters, large spaniels or water spaniels . . . whatever promised to fulfill the purpose intended.

There are enough references in writing before the Kennel Club to note that the "English Retriever" in both smooth (or wavy) and curly coats was well known as a development from the Newfoundland Retriever, Labrador or St. Johns Dog. The short-coated variety we now call Labrador was still almost unknown to dog writers, so closely kept were they by the aristocratic families who had them for personal use and never sold them. The wavy- and curly-coated varieties were more commonly known, although as types of retriever rather than as distinct breeds; indeed, they were often mentioned only slightingly, as if too *common* a sort to be ranked with the real "bluebloods" of the dog world.

Mid-19th-century retrievers were designated "Wavy-Coated" or "Curly-Coated." The one on the left shows the Newfoundland influence. Curlies of that era, as on the right, often had longer coats than modern Curly-Coats, with some feathering.

The Curly-Coated may be the oldest of the retrievers, possibly predating the New World imports. Perhaps the characteristic coat came from early curly-coated spaniels, and it may possibly have been helped by an infusion from the Barbet or the Poodle—or perhaps not, as neither of those breeds have the naturally short coat and smooth face of the Curly-Coated Retriever. Any crossings with setter or St. Johns Dog would probably greatly diminish any tendency to curl. Even today, it is difficult to get and to keep the ideal coat with small inward-turning ringlets covering the body from ears to tail. Very early writers state clearly that the Curly-Coated does not admit of any cross-breeding and still remain typical.

The St. John's Dog may be considered the basic stem from which the other various named varieties (now breeds) of retriever were developed. Crossings with setters emphasized the feathered coat and an affinity for feathered game, and gave a certain elegance of line to the appearance of the retriever later designated as the Wavy-Coated, then Flat-Coated Retriever. The original imports with a little outcrossing, plus a dash of pointer and of foxhound, kept the shorter, smoother coat in the variety to be known as Labrador, developed by the aristocratic families of Malmesbury, Home, Buccleuch and a few others. The St. John's Dog combined with water spaniels gave a hardy, curled-coat retrieving dog, delighting in water work; one variety was the Tweed Water Spaniel, another the also-now-extinct Northern Irish water spaniel variety.

Even the American development, the Chesapeake Bay Dog, was built upon the progeny of two "Newfoundlands," almost certainly the Lesser Newfoundland or St. Johns Dog, brought to the shores of Maryland's Chesapeake Bay in the early 19th century. The breed's history parallels that of the British breeds as far as being developed for function, with outcrossings to native dogs of varying sorts. A notable difference is that the Chesapeake was developed not by aristocrats but by Americans who kept practical hunting dogs for sport, particularly at kennels connected with exclusive hunting clubs, and by market hunters of the Chesapeake Bay. Many of the latter were not gentlemen, by any stretch of that term, and the Chessie owes at least part of his tenacious and sometimes protective nature to that part of his history.

All the retriever varieties in Great Britain were interbred on occasions, rather freely during the 19th century when all were still in development and function was of primary importance, and decreasingly less after recognition by the Kennel Club, when they evolved into separate breeds.

THE QUESTION OF COLOR

As previously mentioned, by the middle of the 19th century, the more popular types or strains called retrievers were most often black in color. Occasionally, other colors occurred, but they were generally not welcomed. Any one might have a touch of white on toes or chest. Brown, liver, sandy and red colors were mentioned, plus the odd yellow or white.

One must keep in mind that terminology for color and some other matters as well was quite casual at this time. "Brown" could be almost anything that wasn't black, white or gray. "Liver" could include anything from a light pale tan through sandy and yellow shades to deep rich brown. Think of the Chesapeake in all possible shades from pale to dark, and you may have some idea of the colors that could be called liver. Whether the term was used only for dogs with basic brown skin pigment, or included those with black skin pigment, is uncertain. At any rate, "liver" could be used to include coat colors we would think of today as yellow or red, as well as brown.

Genetically, a black retriever can carry recessive factors for brown (now called "chocolate" in the Labrador) and for yellow/red, or for both. Recombining these factors can produce offspring of four different phenotypes (though of nine different genotypes). The four phenotypes are black coat with black skin pigment, yellow coat with black skin pigment, yellow coat with brown skin pigment, and brown coat with brown skin pigment. These four types are most common in Labradors. The Chesapeake has eliminated the black skin pigment and coat. The Flat-Coat and Curly-Coat are only black or brown according to the breed Standard, but those pesky yellows (creams) do manage to turn up on rare occasions, as they do in Newfoundlands. The Golden Retriever has the yellow coat and black skin pigment as a trademark, and because the yellow factor in Goldens is recessive, the dominant black coat has been eliminated.

While black parents can produce yellows from two recessive yellow genes, black puppies do not occur in yellow-to-yellow matings in today's purebred retrievers. (Yellow-to-yellow matings in other breeds that have different genes causing a yellow or red coat color *may* produce black puppies.) Wholly black puppies born to Golden Retrievers are the result of mismating with a dog of another breed somewhere along the line. The only other possibility is that of a true mutation, where the gene for yellow mutates to the dominant black form. While this is theoretically possible, it may be discounted for all practical purposes.

So when we read of Lord Tweedmouth's yellow dog Nous (said to be the only yellow in a litter of black, Wavy-Coated Retrievers) being bred to a "liver" Tweed Water Spaniel to produce yellow offspring, then we must surmise that TWS Belle quite likely was a yellow-coated bitch who may have had either brown or black skin pigment. The prevalence of brown noses and amber eyes in many early Goldens certainly points to that possibility—as well as to the possible later use of brown-pigmented dogs, of course. From their photos, Nous definitely had black pigmentation, as did Ada and Crocus, two of the offspring.

Early and continued selection for dark eyes and the much more attractive black eye rims and noses has nearly eliminated brown skin pigment in Goldens, but it is the rule in the Nova Scotia Duck Tolling Retriever, a red-coated (yellow) dog in which selection has been against any black skin pigmentation.

While the "ordinary English retriever" was common enough to be known to most dog writers of the 19th century, the term was often used for any nondescript middle-sized canine who would serve the purpose of picking up dead game. The finest strains of working retrievers were all kept privately, by the landed gentry and the aristocrats who could afford the luxury of large private estates and game preserves. Dogs were given to friends and relatives but rarely sold, as there was no market and no buyers. Retrievers were not dogs the lower classes would keep, simply because they had no occasion to use such a dog and certainly would not keep any dogs who didn't earn their keep.

A few retrievers were exhibited at the shows that began late in the 19th century; indeed, the Flat-Coated Retriever variety became popular, in large part, due to the dogs developed and exhibited by S. E. Shirley of Ettington, first president of The Kennel Club.

In the hands of the landed families, definite strains of retrievers were developed. Some faded out and disappeared; others persisted and grew, making use of desired qualities from other lines or strains. Some, in time, became firmly enough established to warrant recognition as a breed. Among these was the line of yellow retrievers developed by Sir Dudley Marjoribanks, first Lord Tweedmouth.

chapter 3

The Golden Established as a Breed

In 1854 Dudley Coutts Marjoribanks, age thirty-four, bought the estate of Guisachan, located in the Scottish Highlands southwest of Inverness, from William Fraser, whose family had been there for some 300 years. The Marjoribanks (pronounced Marshbanks) family was Scottish, taking that name in the days of Robert The Bruce. Edward, Dudley's father, went to London in 1796 and became a lifelong partner in Coutts Bank, one of the largest in England; even members of the Royal family went there for discreet loans.

Nous, born 1864, near Brighton, England. Nous was the sole yellow in a litter of Wavy-Coated Retrievers bred by Lord Chichester. A keeper gave the dog to a cobbler in payment for a debt, in the summer of 1865; Dudley Marjoribanks (later Lord Tweedmouth) saw the young dog and bought him. Taken to Scotland, Nous produced at least two litters from the Tweed Water Spaniel, Belle, and it's also likely that he was bred with other bitches owned by friends of the Majoribanks family.

Like many of the gentry, young Marjoribanks much enjoyed shooting sports and had been leasing the Guisachan forest for deer stalking for several years before buying it. Guisachan, meaning "Place of the Firs" in Gaelic, consisted of some 20,000 acres in the wild Scottish highlands. A definite amount of social status was involved in owning such a magnificent property, and certainly few could fail to be taken with the great beauty of this wild region. Marjoribanks was also a gentleman with a deep appreciation of the aesthetic; his collections of paintings and books, his advancements in animal breeding and his restorations of other Scottish properties were to be well known.

In the next few years Marjoribanks made great changes at Guisachan. The century-old manor house built by William Fraser of Guisachan was replaced by a grand new house of gray granite, with a large sunlit dining room, sixteen bedrooms for family and fifteen for servants, and a glassed-in conservatory, surrounded by a trim lawn with a highland brook at its foot, and set about with great trees. Guisachan Home Farm had a magnificent granite cattle barn, stables for riding horses, a dairy, a brewery, a meal mill, a laundry and other necessary buildings. To house the many workers associated with the estate, Tomich village was built, with tidy stone cottages replacing the shabby crofts; the more than 200 inhabitants consisted of those employed on the estate and their families. A good-sized country house such as this required dozens of servants in the house and out, plus farm managers and workers, gamekeepers, stalkers, huntsmen and kennel boys. It was essentially a self-contained community. The whitewashed stone kennel was home to pointers, deerhounds, spaniels and retrievers, in addition to the Cairn and Skye Terriers who pattered through the rooms of Guisachan House after the Marjoribanks children.

His granddaughter Lady Pentland writes that DCM, as she called him, was "devoted to animals and sport of every kind." Educated at Harrow and Oxford, he became a barrister and a member of Parliament. The family resided at Brook House in London when Parliament was in session. In 1866 Marjoribanks was made a baronet, and in 1881 raised to the peerage, taking the title of Baron Tweedmouth as a compliment to his constituency of Berwick, on the Tweed River in the Border country. He was also a shareholder in Meux Brewery, at one time a director of the East India Co., and in the 1880s invested in cattle ranching in Texas and North Dakota. His wife, Isabella, was the daughter of Sir James Weir Hogg, a baronet, chairman of the East India Co., and also a Member of Parliament. Her brother was a baron.

Prominent among Lord Tweedmouth's many interests was the breeding of animals, with an eye to improving both appearance and practical use. His purebred cattle included Aberdeen Angus and shaggy red Highland. He crossed the sturdy, surefooted Highland ponies with thoroughbreds to provide excellent riding horses; his pointers were well known for their achievements on the grouse moors and fanciers of Golden Retrievers are forever indebted to him.

Marjoribanks had had retrievers in his kennel since at least 1842; most were the ordinary black retrievers, probably wavy coats; there was at least one Irish spaniel. His kennel record notes a retriever bitch named Gypsy when he was leasing Guisachan. In 1855 the kennel expanded to include three retrievers, Gypsy and Paddy, who produced a litter in 1858, and Boatswain. In 1863 Tweed, of "Ladykirk breed," was given by David Robertson, a cousin of Marjoribanks who lived at Ladykirk, on the Tweed River near Berwick, but no pups from him or her are noted.

In 1865 Marjoribanks was visiting Brighton, that seaside resort so popular with vacationing Britons. One Sunday he and his eldest son Edward, then about fifteen years old, went walking upon the downs north of the town. Along the way they encountered a man leading a handsome young retriever, a dog with a thick coat the bright color of a gold coin. Certainly Marjoribanks' eye must have been caught by the unusual color, and the good looks of the dog, with a sturdy build and nobility of expression. Upon questioning, the man said he was a cobbler and had been given the dog in payment of a debt owed him by a keeper on a nearby estate. The dog had been the only yellow pup in a litter of black Wavy-Coated Retrievers owned by Lord Chichester. As the cobbler had no use for a retriever, an agreement was quickly made, although because it was a Sunday the actual sale was put off until the next day. And so Nous was acquired, and traveled the length of Britain to Guisachan in the Scottish Highlands to found a dynasty.

Cowslip (left), Crocus (center) and Ada (right). Sired by Nous out of Belle. Cowslip was retained by Lord Tweedmouth and was a keystone of the Guisachan retriever line. Crocus belonged to Edward Marjoribanks and contributed to both the Tweedmouth and Ilchester strains. Ada, owned by the fifth Lord Ilchester, was the progenitress of a long line of Ilchester retrievers. Their descendants no doubt are also behind many of the unregistered dogs who enter into early pedigrees.

Recorded breedings of retrievers in the Guisachan kennel record, 1850-1890.
Dudley Coutts Marjoribanks (Baron Tweedmouth) died in 1894. His son and successor, Edward
Marjoribanks, 2nd Lord Tweedmouth, left no written records but the names of several of his
yellow retrievers are known, including Rock, Comet, Conon, Ginger, Haddo, and Lucifer.

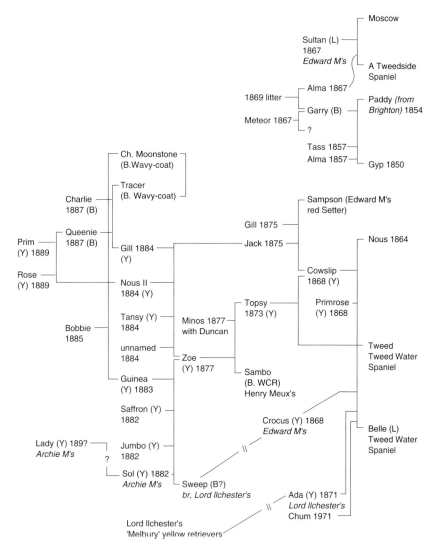

Sultan (1867) was shown as a 'Russian Retriever' about 1869. The three Tweed Water Spaniels
were all from David Robertson of Ladykirk, near Berwick. B=black. Y=yellow. L=liver. Archie
M(arjoribanks) and Edward M. were sons of 1st Lord Tweedmouth, and the 5th Lord Ilchester was
his cousin, as was David Robertson.

The year previous to the purchase of Nous, two bitches had been acquired: Alma, born May 1867 (from "The Hall, Bushey"—the home of DCM's brother Edward), and Belle, born 1863, another Tweed Water Spaniel from David Robertson of Ladykirk. Although Alma produced a litter by Garry (son of Paddy x Gypsy) in January 1869, it was the breeding of Nous to Belle that was the proverbial "gold mine." Four yellow puppies were born to Nous and Belle in June of 1868; two bitches, Cowslip and Primrose, were kept, and a male, Crocus, was given to DCM's brother Edward at The Hall, Bushey. The fourth puppy is usually assumed to be Ada, who went to another cousin, Henry Edward Fox-Strangways, 5th Lord Ilchester, but evidence is strong that Ada was born in 1871 from a second mating of Nous and Belle. Ada's gravestone on the Ilchester estate carries the birthdate of 1871 and is inscribed "ADA with the golden hair." Although the birth of the 1871 litter was not noted in the kennel record for that year, in 1873 there is a listing of Chum, born 1871, from Belle, which would be the litter that also contained Ada. Also, Ada's photograph in Mrs. Charlesworth's book (1933) is captioned with the date 1871.

The Tweedmouth kennel record is often spoken of as a "stud book." However, it really appears much more like a simple inventory of dogs made at the end of each year. Some litters are noted; others are not. Some deaths or transfers are noted; many are not—the record is frustratingly incomplete. Even Nous' death is not noted; he simply fails to appear in the 1873 listing.

In 1872 another "Tweed" from David Robertson appears, and in 1873 was bred to Cowslip to produce Topsy. Cowslip was also bred later to a red setter, Sampson (noted as red, *not* as Irish), owned by "Edward"; whether this was DCM's brother Edward or his son Edward, is not clear, as DCM's son also lived at Bushey Hall . . . so "Bushey breed" could well have meant either. Jack and Gill were kept from the Sampson x Cowslip breeding.

In 1877 Minos and Zoe were kept from Topsy's litter sired by Harry Meux's Sambo (presumed black wavy-coat). Minos, like several other dogs, was sent to another shoot (leased property), but Zoe was bred to Sweep, a dog acquired in 1881 from Lord Ilchester's line of retrievers descended from Crocus (one of the first Nous x Belle litter). Sweep was probably a black, carrying the yellow coat factor, as he produced Sol, Saffron (both yellows) and Jumbo in March of 1882. Lord Ilchester did use black dogs in his breedings, usually well-bred wavy-coats, but always kept yellows. In 1884 Sol was given to DCM's youngest son, Archie, and went with him along with another yellow retriever to the Rocking Chair Ranch in Texas where he died some years later.

"Lady," photographed in Ottawa, about 1894. Lady was owned by Lord Tweedmouth's son, Archie Marjoribanks, at that time Aide-de-Camp to the Governor General of Canada. She was from Guisachan breeding and is said to be the granddam of some of the earliest Goldens registered with the Kennel Club.

Further linebreeding on Cowslip produced three yellow pups from her granddaughter Zoe, whelped at Duns Castle, another Tweedmouth property. The three were Nous (Duncan's), Tansy and Gill. Gill was later bred to a black wavy-coat, Tracer (son of the very well-known Zelstone and brother to Ch. Moonstone), and a resulting black daughter, Queenie, was bred back to Gill's brother, the second Nous. From Nous x Gill came Prim and Rose, the last litter noted in the Tweedmouth record. More breedings were made, and dogs kept, but the records, if any, have not come to light. The yellow dogs remained at Guisachan after first Lord Tweedmouth's death in 1894, until the estate passed into the ownership of the Earl of Portsmouth about 1905. A few dogs also went with Duncan McLennan, son of the Duncan McLennan who had been stalker at Guisachan since the age of eighteen, when he left Guisachan about the turn of the century.

The aforementioned dogs are the best-known part of the Golden Retriever's foundation breedings. Of course there are other contributors; DCM's cousin, the fifth Lord Ilchester, kept a line based on breedings from ADA, one of the keystone Nous x Belle offspring. The sixth Lord Ilchester (born 1874) kept the line going up until the late 1930s, although few of his "Melbury" Goldens were registered with the Kennel Club. Lord Stavordale (Lord Ilchester's oldest son) was a Patron of the Golden Retriever Club. Their dogs were kept for work.

The sixth Lord Ilchester, Giles Stephen Holland Fox-Strangways, wrote two articles in the magazine *Country Life* in 1952 and 1953 detailing the background of the Golden, which caused no little furor among those who believed in the romantic story of Russian circus dogs, which had been accepted, and endlessly reprinted, until that time. As early as 1938 A. Croxton Smith, well-known dog writer, had published the story of the purchase of the yellow retriever from Brighton who became the foundation sire for the Tweedmouth strain; he had been told this by DCM's grandson, Dudley Churchill Marjoribanks, third Lord Tweedmouth. Few people, it seemed, were really willing to accept this version, especially as other writers and breeders, notably Mrs. Charlesworth (who wrote the first published book on the breed), so vigorously promoted the story of a troupe of Russian circus dogs supposedly purchased by Lord Tweedmouth.

While it is sometimes said that the first Lord Tweedmouth never parted with yellow bitches except to his cousin Lord Ilchester, certainly both Edward Marjoribanks' Bushey line and the Ilchesters' Melburys had descendants who were bred from. On the death of Edward, second Lord Tweedmouth, a number of dogs did go to others, notably Lord Portsmouth and Sir Lewis Harcourt.

Edward, second Lord Tweedmouth, was a popular and well-liked figure in the British government, rising to the position of First Lord of the Admiralty. He had married in 1873 Lady Fanny Churchill, third daughter of the seventh Duke of Marlborough and sister of Sir Randolph Churchill (whose son Winston was to surpass them all in renown). Edward's son Dudley Churchill Marjoribanks was the same age as Winston, and both attended Harrow. Fanny, "who looks such a fragile Victorian," according to Elma Stonex, was "a real tough and shot with the best." She was well-loved by all who knew her, and especially by Edward, who was crushed by her death in 1904. Distraught and in financial difficulties, he sold Guisachan, Brook House in London, and his father's exceptional collections of books and paintings. His health having failed rapidly, he died in 1909.

Newton Wallop, sixth Earl of Portsmouth, who acquired some of the yellow retrievers as part of the Guisachan estate, had earlier often been a visitor at Guisachan as a friend of Edward and as a member of the government. (Edward was First Lord of the Admiralty, Portsmouth Undersecretary for War). Known familiarly as "Porty," he seems to have been rather an eccentric; he was said to have tied up his luxurious red beard in a cloth bag in order to keep the dust out of it when motoring.

Guisachan passed into the ownership of the Portsmouths, who kept it primarily for sporting purposes. Parts of the estate were sold, piece by piece, and parts leased for various purposes (including, at one point, a youth camp). But no one wanted to purchase Guisachan House with its heavy burden of maintenance, its thirty-one bedrooms with but five bathrooms, its antiquated Victorian amenities a long twenty-three-mile drive from the nearest railway station. Then just before World War II, the house was bought, for a pittance, and to avoid taxes, the owner had the roof removed and left the house to the assault of Highland weather. Its stately ruins have captured the imagination of Golden devotees for years.

LADY—FROM TEXAS TO CANADA TO ENGLAND

Lady is one of the well-known individuals in Golden history, from her several photographs in the Golden Retriever Club archives provided so graciously by Lady Pentland (DCM's granddaughter). By the evidence available, Lady was possibly the daughter of Sol (Sweep x Zoe, 1882) and an unidentified bitch taken to Texas by Archie Marjoribanks. Archie was the superintendent of the Rocking Chair Ranch (a cattle company underwritten in part by his father DCM and Lord Ilchester) in Collingsworth County, Texas, from 1883 to 1893, when he went to Ottawa as aide-de-camp to his brother-in-law, Lord Aberdeen. There are several photographs showing Lady, Archie and the Aberdeen family. Lady appears to be a sturdy sort, with the typical broad Guisachan head, a mild and benign expression, medium color and a fairly smooth coat. Archie married a young lady from Tennessee in 1897 and returned to England; in failing health, he died in 1900.

Lady may well be called the first "American bred" Golden Retriever. Born in Texas before 1892, she was young enough on her return to England to produce a litter, possibly sired by a Guisachan or Ilchester dog, and whelped at Kerrow House, not far from Guisachan. At least one was kept by Duncan McLennan and was the dam of two who went to Lord Harcourt near the turn of the century and helped found the Culham kennel of yellow retrievers. Regretfully, McLennan destroyed all his records and correspondence upon preparing to go into military service in 1914.

Other Guisachan dogs were known at the time. There is a photo dated 1903 showing Comet, Conon and Ginger; Conon's name appears in some early pedigrees. All three are quite good-looking dogs, with attractive heads and strong builds. Lucifer, a Tweedmouth dog, sired Don of Gerwn, a name

An oil sketch by Wright Barker, prominent English painter, of three of Col le Poer Trench's yellow "Russian Retrievers": St. Hubert's Czar, St. Hubert's Prince and St. Hubert's Peter. A larger finished version of the painting is in England.

Eng. Ch. Noranby Campfire, the first Golden officially recognized as a Champion. Owned and bred by Mrs. W. M. Charlesworth, by Culham Copper (Culham Brass x Culham Rossa) out of Normanby Beauty (pedigree unknown). Campfire was born July 24, 1912, and earned his field qualifier at age 9. He was an intelligent, sensible worker who remained strong and hearty well past his 13th year, and contributed a great deal to the then newly recognized breed.

well known to Flat-Coat historians as winner of the International Gundog League retriever trials in 1904.

Remember that at this time (before 1913) what were to be "Goldens" were still registered as Wavy- or Flat-Coated Retrievers, and all were considered to be one breed, with differing colors. Not until 1913 were the yellows allotted their own registry, as "Retrievers (Yellow or Golden)." In about 1920, the breed became simply "Retrievers (Golden)," as they are today. Indeed, all retrievers were considered varieties, not separate breeds, for many years. As varieties, they were allowed some degree of interbreeding by the Kennel Club, under controlled circumstances.

There were blacks, browns, yellows and reds, and occasionally other colors such as black-and-tans and whites. There were short coats and long coats, in flat, wavy and curly. When ability and working aptitude were the essentials, color and coat were matters of taste and preference. Only after the establishment of the Kennel Club registry, and the sense of orderliness that insisted on separation, did the concept of "pure" breeds proscribe what dogs might contribute to development of the retriever. In the early years of the Kennel Club, some interesting situations developed from the rather free and easy means of deciding upon "breed"; for instance, a Cocker might have a littermate competing as a Field Spaniel, and a son or daughter as a Springer!

Surely one cannot fully understand any retriever breed until one recognizes what all retrievers have in common, and what each has contributed to others. The ties are closer than most people might think.

THE "RUSSIAN TRACKER" AND OTHER POSSIBILITIES

The early story of the Golden Retriever's origins was the romantic tale of a troupe of Russian dogs that supposedly appeared in a circus at Brighton; they so appealed to Lord Tweedmouth (then Sir Dudley Marjoribanks), it was said, that he purchased the entire group of eight, as the Russian trainer was unwilling to break up the troupe, and transported them to his Guisachan estate. There they were used for tracking deer. After some years, says Mrs. Charlesworth in *The Book of the Golden Retriever* (1933), "Not being able to obtain more of the strain, and finding the type deteriorating through inbreeding, he very wisely cast around for an outcross which would carry on the tracking qualities, and decided on the Bloodhound."

She describes the Russian dogs as "pale biscuit, cream, or sometimes nearly white, with curly or wavy coats and a long and exceedingly curly tail. These coats were very dense, with a thick undercoat, which of course was their protection against the rigors of the Russian winter. . . . In conformation these dogs were decidedly long in the back, but had powerful loins and quarters, beautiful bone and feet; the head was broad, the nose and eyelids generally black, as was the skin. The tail was long and frequently curled over the back." The Bloodhound cross was supposed to have resulted in dogs "of a smaller size, more 'houndy' in type, varying in color from biscuit to dark golden. In some cases the noses, lips and eyelids were, and still are, 'smudge' or brown . . . in rare cases the colour is pink, which is very ugly."

For many years this version of the Golden's origin was accepted unquestioningly. No matter that no one ever found any record of a troup of eight performing dogs from Russia displayed at Brighton, nor is there any note of such a group in the Guisachan kennel records, which begin in the 1840s. Mrs. Charlesworth's book has a photo of "keepers and dogs at Guisachan"; only one dog in the photo could be taken to be a Golden. This is the dog later identified as "Nous" by Lady Pentland, Lord Tweedmouth's granddaughter, and the date is given as 1870–1872. In the 1933 edition of Mrs. Charlesworth's book, there is a photo of "Ada, b. 1871; the property of the Earl of Ilchester. She was the daughter of Lord Tweedmouth's original dog." Original *dog?* What happened to the other seven? Ada looks not the least "bloodhoundy"; indeed, she is a very attractive retriever with tidy, well-set ears. If she was born in 1871, a daughter of the "original dog," then where are the several generations of inbreeding that supposedly resulted in the "deterioration" of type? Perhaps cannily, Mrs. C. gives no date for the supposed purchase of the eight Brighton dogs, only that it was before Dudley Marjoribanks became Lord Tweedmouth (1881). The date of purchase has been given in other writings to be as early as 1858, or as late as 1868. It would seem that with a gene pool of eight animals to draw from, as intelligent a breeder as Tweedmouth could avoid deterioration due to inbreeding in the twelve years or so before the supposed bloodhound cross in the 1870s. Indeed, the Guisachan kennel record shows clearly that he did develop a uniform strain on the basis of an equally limited number of individual dogs used to found the Nous-Belle strain.

In support of the "circus dog" story, quoted in Mrs. Charlesworth's 1947 book, is a letter from Duncan MacLennan, at one time Head Keeper on the Guisachan estate. The letter was written sometime after World War I and is quoted as follows:

. . . I am taking the liberty of enclosing some photographs for your inspection.

The group of dogs belonged to the late Colonel le Poer Trench, who, with his brother, is seen in the photograph; this was taken in 1903.

I must say they were beautiful dogs, and true to type, with the heavy head and shoulders of the older type. They were very wise and beautiful workers on all kinds of game.

In his last letter to me Colonel Trench said he was setting out for a remote part of Russia in Asia, where these retrievers come from originally, and I believe he succeeded beyond a doubt in proving the origin of the breed. Later he sent me a letter with a short account of his journey.

Now that the question of the origin of the Guisachan [dogs] has cropped up, I cannot tell you how sorry I am for destroying many letters I had from Colonel Trench during 1906 to 1911, in which he described conversations between himself and the first Lord Tweedmouth (then Sir Dudley Marjoribanks), all pertaining to the Golden Retrievers. They would be interesting and valuable at the present time. Unfortunately, I destroyed everything before I joined up in 1915.

My mother has got an old photograph of the first dog, and the finest, of the group of dogs bought by the first Lord Tweedmouth between 1860 and 1870, from a party of Russians who were performing with them at Brighton.

Duncan MacLennan refers to Nous as "the first dog, and the finest" of the group. What of the others? Were they bred, kept, given away before reaching Scotland? Or did they never exist? One does wonder. Indeed, it would be interesting to read Col. Trench's account of his "conversations with Lord Tweedmouth, then Sir Dudley Marjoribanks," since if the conversations took place before Marjoribanks took his title in 1881, Trench had not yet acquired his first yellow retriever. One must conclude that Col. Trench was rather embellishing his connection with Lord Tweedmouth; Lady Pentland has said that she thought it highly unlikely that her grandfather had ever met Col. Trench.

The 1939 Yearbook of the Golden Retriever Club of America gives the "AKC Official History of Retrievers (Golden)," elaborating upon the circus dog story, with the supposed date of purchase as 1860 and the Bloodhound cross as 1870. The same history is repeated in the 1948 Yearbook.

OTHER THEORIES

The first mention in the U.S. of an origin other than the "circus dog" story may have been in a slim book published in 1947, titled *Bob Becker's Dog Digest*, in which Joe MacGaheran offered a short chapter on Goldens. Here is sketched the version told by the third Lord Tweedmouth—the story of Nous, bought in Brighton, the one yellow pup in a litter of black wavy-coats. MacGaheran was a Vice President of the GRCA and wrote an article on "The Golden Retriever in North America" in that same 1948 Yearbook, yet no mention is made there of the third Lord Tweedmouth's recounting of Nous's origin. One wonders whether there might have been opposition from certain parties to straying from the "official" history of the breed. Not until the 1957 GRCA Yearbook does an article by Rachel Page Elliott, based on researches by the sixth Lord Ilchester and Elma Stonex, present the later findings based on the Guisachan kennel record as the official origin of the breed.

Well, what of these Russian dogs? What credence, if any, might there be in the tale of the "Russian Tracker"? Is it all a fairy tale, a myth, a conjecture?

One of the staunchest supporters of the Russian theory was Col. the Honorable William le Poer Trench. An article by Arthur Croxton-Smith in *Country Life* magazine in 1914 featured the "St. Huberts" kennel of Col. Trench, with numerous photographs. Col. Trench had earlier exhibited Irish Water Spaniels with success from about 1880–1890. He acquired a yellow retriever as early as 1883, "Sandy," bred by the fifth Earl of Ilchester; Sandy's portrait reproduced in *Country Life* is of a modern-looking dog with a very appealing expression. Col. Trench reportedly said (although there is some doubt) that he had met Lord Tweedmouth in the Park in London, and Tweedmouth, upon examining the dog Sandy, declared him "the exact counterpart of the originals." Well, little wonder, as he was bred by Ilchester, whose line began with Ada, bred at Guisachan by Tweedmouth! Some years later Trench acquired from a ghillie in Scotland a dog given the name of St. Hubert's Rock, and after some searching, a bitch, St. Hubert's May. At first Trench hesitated at breeding from her, as she was "an albino"; that is, she had light eyes and a pink nose. Someone, however, assured him that this was no fault— quite the contrary, it was a mark of pure breeding (!)—and so she was bred to Rock. Several litters resulted, some twenty-seven puppies, it is said, none of whom inherited the dam's lack of pigmentation.

Many of the St. Hubert's dogs' photographs appear in the *Country Life* article; some appear large, heavy and loosely put together, with very heavy coats. Some are distinctly curly. Several are more Golden-like than others, and the youngest group, appearing to be probably eight to nine months of age, very much so. Color appears to range from very pale, even cream, to mid-gold with light shadings.

The story also goes that Trench journeyed to Russia about 1911 or 1912 (different sources say he went to the Caucasus, or maybe to Siberia—no matter that they are thousands of miles apart!) in order to acquire additional stock, but as it was the wrong time of year, all the dogs were still up in the mountains. An agent was delegated to pursue the subject, but the dogs were lost, either eaten by wolves or perishing in some other way.

Col. Trench did succeed in getting official Kennel Club recognition for the "Marjoribanks and Ilchester Breed of Russian Yellow Retrievers." A standard was drawn up, supposedly based on consultation with Lord Tweedmouth and Lord Ilchester, but this is highly unlikely. Dudley Marjoribanks, first Lord Tweedmouth, died in 1894, long before the Russian Yellow Retrievers received the blessing of the Kennel Club; and the Lords Ilchester (both the fifth, who died in 1905, and sixth) *never* called their dogs "Russian."

It is true that there is mention of various "Russian" breeds or varieties in old dog writings. It's also true that "Russian" was attached to various dogs who might or might not have been imported. The allure of the exotic was even stronger in the 19th century than today, and a dog might then have won a class for foreign breeds much more easily than as a plebeian "home-grown" specimen. Many unregistered dogs were shown and bred, and in fact many earned their way into the Stud Book strictly on the basis of achievement rather than on pedigree. In those early days a certain degree of flexibility, even permissiveness, was necessary, and helpful, allowing for the use of various types and bloodlines in order to form the lines that have evolved into our modern breeds.

One writer mentions a show in 1863 (long before Col. Trench's "Russians") where "The Russian retrievers formed a miscellaneous class of all sorts and sizes, and all rough with one exception. We do not pretend to criticize these animals, of which we know nothing." Possibly their owners knew little more about them.

Some mentions of the "Russian Retriever" describe a dog with a heavy, matted coat and hair overhanging the eyes. They are criticized as being heavy, slow and cumbersome, and often surly or quarrelsome in nature, and pretty much useless in the field. The physical description, as well as an illustration in Hutchinson's *Dog Encyclopedia*, published about 1933, fairly shouts "Komondor!" It would not be unlikely that, if some specimens of this type happened to arrive in Great Britain, then sportsmen would try them out

Lord Harcourt's dog, Culham Brass, about 1908. Brass and his offspring Culham Copper and Culham Bronze are very important in early Golden pedigrees.

as sporting dogs . . . after all, they were not dissimilar in looks from the large Rough Water Dog, or the Barbet of France and Germany. But almost certainly they would have lacked the bird sense and retrieving instinct, and the field aptitude of the Water Dogs, and may be discounted as having any part in the Golden Retriever's origins.

The St. Hubert's "Russian Retrievers," however, were quite different, some looking rather like Pyrenees, others just like very large Goldens. A dozen or so were registered by Col. Trench with the Kennel Club, and a few by other people in the years 1910–14, but as a breed, disappeared into oblivion upon Col. Trench's death.

There is the small matter of Edward Marjoribanks' dog Sultan, a liver-colored retriever, born in 1867, exhibited in 1871, by Moscow, also liver-colored, out of a Tweedside Spaniel, according to the KC studbook listing. Sultan? Moscow? Odd names for a retriever . . . and who was *this* Edward Marjoribanks? It might have been Lord Tweedmouth's eldest son, born 1849, or his brother, both named Edward. Both lived at Bushey, in Hertfordshire; and from Bushey came the bitch Alma, whelped May 1867. Alma's parentage is not noted, only that she was of Edward's breeding.

The dog Sultan might quite possibly be from that same 1867 litter. Alma whelped a litter in 1869 by Lord Tweedmouth's Garry, but no further mention is found of Alma, or of Sultan, in the Tweedmouth record. Could "Moscow" have been the Russian dog whose arrival led to the story of the Russian circus dogs? Might he, or his parent(s), have been brought back by an officer serving in the Crimean War, as has been intimated by some writers? We have only conjecture.

CLOSE RELATIVES OR THE REAL THING?

In a book titled *Dogs and People*, by George and Helen Papashvily, there is mention of the dogs of George's youth, "Basar, Juliko and Murka, golden trackers, buried in a mountain valley on the southern slope of the Caucasus."

This must have been just before World War I, as George Papashvily, born in Russian Georgia, served in the army before emigrating to the U.S. There are many references to the "yellow Caucasian sheepdog," or of Owtchar, which is one of the several varieties of Owtcharka (variously spelled Aftcharka, and so on) are of differing colors and coat types. They serve not as herding dogs in the sense of a Collie-type dog but as guardians living and traveling with the flocks, and protecting them as part of the dog's "adopted pack," exactly as the Russian Tracker circus dogs were said to do. The same service is performed by the Great Pyrenees and other large dogs of the mountains: The Tatra Mountain Dog (Poland); the Maremma Sheepdog (Italy); the Akbash, Karabash and Anatolian Sheepdogs (Turkey) and other regional types or breeds.

The Caucasian Owtcharka is now a very rare breed. They are in size twenty-five inches tall or more, with a very dense, thick coat with ruff, heavy breechings and tail plume. Color is often the "wild" color (agouti)—that is, a cream or beige with black bands or tipping on the outercoat. There are lighter shadings without blackening on the underside, and often a dark mask on the face. Light-colored cream or yellow dogs also occur. The ears are small and dropped, although often cropped extremely short in their native land.

There are other Owtcharka varieties; some are of the coat type with long hair on the face and all around the legs, similar to a Bearded Collie. In their natural ungroomed state, they are generally heavily matted, similar to a Komondor, and like some of the descriptions of the "Russian Retriever" mentioned previously.

THE HISTORIANS: ELMA STONEX, LORD ILCHESTER, RACHEL PAGE ELLIOTT

Elma Stonex of the Dorcas kennels in England began before 1950 researching early pedigrees of Goldens. The sixth Lord Ilchester, whose father had owned Ada from Tweedmouth's Nous x Belle, wrote some articles in 1952 and 1953 on the origins of the breed. He disavowed the popular story of the Russian circus dogs, as had Croxton Smith as early as the 1930s, yet the romantic myth had persisted in popular writings and even in the Kennel Club's offical history of the breed. Lord Ilchester's articles, complete with facsimile of Lord Tweedmouth's own handwritten notes, created rather a stir, particularly with some breeders who stoutly endorsed the "circus dog" origins. One of these was the outspoken and redoubtable Mrs. Charlesworth, and one gets the impression that there was no love lost between these two oldtimers in Goldens! Mrs. Stonex always spoke of Lord Ilchester, then in his eighties, as a true gentleman, a historian, and particularly careful with the truth. And indeed, hardly anyone else was as qualified to speak on the matter as this son of the fifth Lord Ilchester, who in 1953 could still remember his father's Ada as an elderly dog, along with many dogs of the subsequent generations bred from her at their home.

Both Mrs. Stonex and Lord Ilchester corresponded with Marjorie, Lady Pentland, granddaughter of the first Lord Tweedmouth. Through her graciousness, Mrs. Stonex was able to examine first-hand Lord Tweedmouth's original kennel record, and many photographs and other memorabilia. Much of the information she laboriously copied by hand, and she was able to have some of the photos duplicated and sent to Mrs. Elliott for her historical collection. Mrs. Elliott and Mrs. Stonex kept up a lively correspondence for years, with Pagey gathering much on the development of the breed in North America, and their researches contributed immeasurably to the accepted history of the breed.

THE MISSING YEARS: 1890-1912

Lord Tweedmouth's kennel record ends in 1890 with the litter containing Prim and Rose, born 1889. While the record may have ended, certainly the keeping, working and breeding of the yellow retrievers did not. Edward, second Lord Tweedmouth, was "a most active sportsman, a keen rider, a good shot, and an enthusiastic fisherman," as was his wife Fanny, daughter of the seventh Duke of Marlborough and sister of Winston Churchill's father. Retrievers remained at Guisachan, and litters were born. Some of the dogs undoubtedly were given to friends and quite likely were not only used for work but were bred. On occasion they were bred with black retrievers and quite possibly setters or other types.

The fifth Lord Ilchester maintained his line of yellow retrievers starting from Ada (1871), and we know that he bred often to blacks, including Montague Guest's Sweep, "a smooth coat" (that is, flat, not a curly coat) who was used for more than one litter and sired "the best of our second generation." He also had descendants of Edward Marjoribanks' Crocus, a male from the 1868 litter of Nous x Belle. One of them, Robin, was painted (along with a deerhound from Guisachan) about 1880. The portrait shows a dog with the deep stop and broad skull we associate with the "English type" even today, although perhaps a bit hard in expression. The sixth Lord Ilchester wrote in 1952 that Robin was a "first-class worker, with a beautiful nose and mouth, and a splendid water dog. The picture of him does not do him justice."

Both black Wavy-Coated and, later, yellow Labrador sires were used by the fifth Lord Ilchester. He also acquired a retriever from Lady Breadalbane about 1895 (the Breadalbanes had extensive properties in Scotland, including deer forests and shooting properties), but the small, reddish dogs, though good workers, were not good breeders, and that strain died out. While Ilchester never bred to the Bloodhound, he did have some dogs from that cross, which was done elsewhere. His son, the sixth Lord Ilchester remembered these dogs as large and extremely powerful, used for tracking wounded deer. One story was of tying a rope to the dog "Mars" and sending him after a stag that was mired in a swamp; the dog seized the stag in his teeth, and dog and deer were dragged out together by the keepers.

The original Ilchester strain, according to the sixth Lord Ilchester, died out during World War I when the breeding of dogs was drastically curtailed, the keeping of dogs being thought detrimental to the war effort. There were again yellow retrievers at Melbury after the war, brought in from other breeders, and the sixth Lord Ilchester did have Goldens in the late 1930s; again, the dogs were kept solely for work, not for showing, and were not registered with the Kennel Club. Mrs. Charlesworth, founder of the Golden Retriever Club, dedicated her book on Goldens to the Countess of Ilchester "with affection and gratitude by all Golden Retrievers."

Other aristocrats had the yellow retrievers, but as they were kept very privately and not shown nor registered with the KC, it is very difficult to trace them. Every now and then traces of them will pop up, often in family portraits.

Speaking of portraits, "Idstone" (The Rev. Thomas Pearce), in his 1872 book *The Dog,* has this comment about "liver coloured and sandy Retrievers":

> They are the sort which "always were kept," people tell you, "in our family," and possibly one or more of the breed, or the head of one with the squire's hand on it in a full court-dress, is hung in the picture gallery, so much being introduced because the painter had not room for more of the animal in his kitcat portrait. I know of no family priding itself on this coloured species just now, but I have heard that they are not uncommon in Norfolk.

By 1872 Dudley Marjoribanks had bred several litters of yellow retrievers, but the strain was still kept very privately. Like his contemporaries writing about dogs, the Rev. Pearce apparently had little knowledge of the aristocratic families and their specific lines of retrievers.

There are other mentions of yellow or red retrievers, and very occasionally one runs across an old photograph of such, all the more frustrating because of a lack of information. One may also find references to dogs appearing in Labrador pedigrees who were almost certainly Goldens. Indeed, a dog bred by Lord Ilchester, "Sam," was owned by the oldest son of the Duke of Buccleuch (later well known for a major strain of Labradors) and photographed in 1886.

THE KENNEL CLUB (ENGLAND), DOG SHOWS AND REGISTRATIONS

It may be useful to touch briefly on the role of the Kennel Club, as it has so strongly affected the development of the whole concept of the purebred dog. While there had been dog shows of a sort before the formation of the Kennel Club, they were haphazard affairs, without rules or regulations except what the promoters of each show might lay out. The shows were largely commercial, primarily for the purpose of drawing paying spectators. Dogs and litters of puppies were displayed for sale. Sometimes individuals both judged and exhibited at the same show. Because there were few or no written Standards, the judging and placements were often controversial. There was an obvious need for a central regulatory body.

The Kennel Club was formed to alleviate this situation. A registry was formed, and dogs could be registered with whatever information the owners chose to provide. Pedigrees were sometimes noted, though many entries were of the sort of "Bob, #1780," registered as a Retriever, "Bred by Mr. Davis of Southampton from a pure breed of Shannon water spaniel." Sometimes pedigrees were deliberately not given: Mr. Gorse, who had many noted retrievers, both wavy- and curly-coats, withheld pedigree information on many of his retrievers—perhaps fearful of giving away "trade secrets"?

One of the headaches of tracing early registrations is the duplication of names; there are many different Sailors, Jets, Wyndhams, Belles, and so on. A dog might change names with a change of ownership or be registered with one name after having been shown under a different name. Dogs could win their way into the Stud Book, which was a separate entity from the registry, by placing at Field Trials or in shows, or by virtue of having produced a trial or show winner.

Before 1912 all retrievers were thrown together in registry and Stud Book; color and coat type might, or might not, be noted. Parents' names and breeders' names were often inconsistent even between littermates. Color might be inferred from the name—Sambo, Sweep and Midnight were probably blacks; Lucifer, Comet, Ginger, and Chrome were yellows; but what of Dusk and Smut? And a "liver" dog might be anything from pale yellow to dark brown.

After the various retrievers were registered separately starting in 1912, puppies born in litters of "mixed" ancestry could be registered as whatever variety they most resembled. This soon proved unsatisfactory, producing the somewhat comical situation of littermates competing as different breeds; and in 1916 a system was introduced whereby those of combined background could be registered as Interbred Retrievers. After three generations bred back to the same variety, the offspring could be registered as purebred. In this way, the variegated pedigrees of these early dogs could be accommodated and used to the benefit of the breed. In later years it also served to allow for the occasional outcross, such as the breeding done in 1929 by the Haulstone Kennels, with one breeding to the yellow Labrador FTCh Haylers Defender. This is the only interbred line that is of any importance in Golden Retrievers. Several of the interbred Haulstones achieved success in the field, notably FTCh Haulstone Bob, a second-generation Interbred. His son FTCh Haulstone Brock was registered as a Golden, being the third generation down from the Labrador infusion. A daughter of Bob, Haulstone Patsy, was imported to the U.S. by John K. Wallace and was the first Golden to place in a U.S. Field Trial; she also won show points, including WB at a GRCA National Specialty.

Although recognition was gained in 1912, the war years, 1914–18, severely affected the development of purebred dogs and organized competition. Breeding and the raising of puppies were so heavily proscribed by the government as to effectively terminate many breeding programs. Certain bloodlines were lost as a result. Field Trials and shows were held in abeyance. Additionally, the loss of many younger men killed in the war had an effect on the development of dogs for sport and exhibition. The 1920s and 1930s, however, saw a resurgence of activity, at least in part due to the activity of the Golden Retriever Club formed in 1911. Sport and the organized activities of dog showing and Field Trials were turned to with much relief by a generation wearied by the war years, even if economics of the postwar era had much diminished the standing and estates of the gentry.

Before curtailment of shows due to the war, several Retrievers (Yellow or Golden), as they were then known, earned the three Challenge Certificates toward a championship. Of this group, only Noranby Campfire, owned by Mrs. Charlesworth, also completed his field qualifier, which earned him the title of Champion at the age of nine years in 1921. Undoubtedly the lack of Field Trial activity during the war years prevented many of the others from completing the full title. They are recognized, however, as Show Champions retroactively from the establishment of that title in about 1962.

INGESTRE

One of the most influential retriever kennels at the turn of the century was that of Ingestre. Ingestre Hall was the home of the Earl of Shrewsbury, one of the highest-ranking Earls. It was his keeper, Mr. D. Macdonald, who was the actual breeder and person responsible for the Ingestre retrievers. The dogs were, above all, workers, and some were shown; but it is as foundation stock that they are important to us. The Ingestre kennels held retrievers of several colors who can be found in old pedigrees of both Goldens and Flat-Coats. The breeding of Ingestre Scamp and Ingestre Tyne was particularly important to Goldens, producing Sh. Ch. Klip and two important brood bitches, Beena and Yellow Nell, as well as Ingestre Dred and Ingestre Luna. These last two siblings, when bred together, produced Sh. Ch. Noranby Dandelion, another major contributor to early Golden pedigrees.

The pedigree of Ingestre Scamp and Ingestre Tyne is not very revealing, although Ingestre Tyne's sire Wavertree Sam (also shown on pedigrees as Faithful Sam) was sired by Lord Tweedmouth's Rock. Rock's exact pedigree is not known, as the second Lord Tweedmouth left no record, but it is certainly Guisachan breeding, and others behind the Ingestre dogs may well have been of similar background.

The first Golden to earn the distinction of Dual Champion (bench show and Field Trial championships) was Mr. R. Hermon's DCh. Balcombe Boy, born in 1919. He was a gift from his breeder, Lord Harcourt, to Mr. Hermon. Boy's sire, Culham Tip, was of Culham and Ingestre breeding. His dam, Culham Amber II, was of similar background.

LORD HARCOURT AND THE CULHAM RETRIEVERS

About 1904 the Honorable Lewis Harcourt acquired a pair of yellow retrievers, said to be the grandpups of Archibald John Marjoribanks' Lady, who had traveled from Texas to Ottawa to England with Archie. It is not known which of Harcourt's originals were Lady's grandpups, and it's quite likely that others of his numerous dogs were of Guisachan descent as well, though not necessarily all.

Lewis Harcourt, born in 1863, succeeded to the estates of Stanton Harcourt, of Nuneham-Courtenay, and others, in 1904, upon the death of his father, the Right Honourable Sir William George Granville Vernon Harcourt. This was the year Lewis is said to have acquired his first yellow retrievers. The dogs were used primarily for work, and the well-known photo of Culham Brass shows him retrieving to a keeper at Nuneham Park.

"Lou-Lou," as Lewis Harcourt was familiarly called, followed his father's example with his own career in government, being a member of the Cabinet. His wife was an American, Mary Ethel Burns. Elevated to the peerage in 1917 as the first Viscount Harcourt, he suffered declining health and died in 1922.

An article was published in *Country Life* in 1910, with photographs of several of the Culham retrievers, including Brass, Flame, Rossa and Copper. Rossa and Brass appear to be very attractive, with good wavy coats of rich gold with lighter shadings—well-made and strong-looking dogs. They are the parents of Bronze and Copper. Copper's photo is not a good one; the dog is standing very awkwardly. He has shaded coloring and a definite white strip down the center of his muzzle, and what appears to be a white frill on his chest and white toes, common at that time.

Arthur Croxton-Smith wrote in the *Country Life* article that the dogs were "absolutely true to type and color, and were fine workers, being very tractable and easily broken . . . also delightful companions and had very soft mouths." Harcourt also acquired dogs from Lord Portsmouth, almost certainly dogs of Guisachan breeding. The young dogs in the group photos accompanying the article are consistent to type—even more so than in the 1920s and 1930s when an increasing population brought in varying types. Like many of the Ingestre dogs, most of the Culhams were registered before 1912 under "Retrievers" as Flat-Coats. Those exhibited at shows competed in special classes for Flat-Coats of "Any other color." Some dogs were re-registered as Retrievers (Yellow or Golden) after 1912, some remained in the Flat-coat registry, and any of their progeny who happened to be black would have been able to register as Flat-coats, at least until 1916 when the regulations were tightened.

Culham Brass's son, Normanby Balfour (out of Normanby Beauty), was sold to Mr. W. S. Hunt in 1914 and contributed heavily to Hunt's Ottershaw line, a large kennel that was prominent until the late 1930s. Balfour also sired Rory of Bentley, the sire of that premier producer, Ch. Michael of Moreton. Culham Copper made his contribution by siring Ch. Norandy Campfire, the first Golden Retriever champion.

Another very strong line from the Culhams was that of the first Dual Champion, Balcombe Boy, whelped in 1919; although parents of his dam, Culham Amber II, were unregistered, his sire, Culham Tip, was by Culham Copper out of Beena, another of the Ingestre Scamp x Ingestre Tyne combination. Balcombe Boy was a very influential sire in his own right.

BETWEEN THE WARS

During the 1920s and 1930s, there was little disagreement that the Golden Retriever was to be, before anything else, a dog suitable for hard work as a retriever in the field. However, there was some difficulty in maintaining physical type. There was considerable variation in size, coloring and coat, and in head type. Some of the dogs of the early 1920s were decidedly Flat-Coat in make and shape, if not color. While there were many dogs of a "middle-of-the-road" type, there were also dark settery-looking dogs with straight, flat coats, and in the 1930s, a lighter-colored, more broadly built type with a heavier, sometimes wavy, coat. For a while there was a definite preference for the darker shades, what we would call red—not the deep mahogany of the Irish Setter, but a rich chestnut. There were, to be sure, some *very* dark dogs, and even a few who appeared to be liver. White markings on head, chest and toes were not uncommon. Joan Gill of the Westley **kennels** began showing in the late 1930s with Speedwell Dulcet, a small dark bitch, a year old, from Mrs. Evers-Swindell. Although a bit disappointed in her looks, Joan said, "she had won several puppy classes so I supposed I was wrong and that was how Goldens should look." In 1938 Joan went to the big Crufts show, where Ch. Chief of Yelme was Best of Breed; he was a big, light-colored dog with a strong head and plenty of bone—she thought he was lovely. At another show, Ch. Anningsley Fox was Best of Breed. He was very well named, a small, darkish, light-boned dog and a very good mover. Joan says "I was very confused and wondered which was supposed to be right." Variation in type is not a late development! Both of these dogs, however, were well-made, useful retrievers and within the range allowed by the breed Standard, although tending toward opposite ends of the range.

Although there were wide differences of type, the good dogs of the time were honest, well-balanced retrievers without exaggeration. Exhibitors of today might quibble that they lacked the fancy points, seeming too plain, ear too large, coat too short, perhaps more up on leg than what we see today. The poorer dogs were often ill-balanced and lacking soundness; weak, straight rears and loaded fronts were not uncommon. How much was inherent and how much due to less than optimum nutrition and/or rearing is unknown.

The best dogs of that time, however, were certainly worthy examples, combining type, balance and beauty with athleticism, working ability and suitability for use, characteristics too often laid aside by the modern breeders and judges in favor of eye-catching coat and showmanship.

THE FOUNDATION PEDIGREES

Mrs. Elma Stonex's interest led to a great deal of research in Golden Retriever pedigrees, through which she eventually pinpointed four breedings to which some 99 percent or more of all Golden Retrievers after World War II may be traced. These were the following:

Pedigree A: Ch. Heydown Gunner x Onaway, 1924 (produced Ch. Cubbington Diver and Cubbington Fionn); his is often shown as two pedigrees, designated here as A1 and A2, as several siblings of Gunner and Onaway were also very important.

Pedigree B: Binks of Kentford x Balvaig, 1921 (produced Ch. Cornelius and Ch. Flight of Kentford)

Pedigree C: Rory of Bentley x Aurora, 1924 and 1925 (produced Ch. Michael of Moreton and Ch. Noble of Quinton)

While there were other bloodlines as well, you will not find a pedigree after 1940 that does not have the preceding dogs in them, often many times over.

Pedigree A1. Ch. Heydown Gunner, born 1921, sire of Ch. Cubbington Diver (1924: sire of 5 champions), owned by Mrs. Cottingham, and Cubbington Fionn, owned by Mrs. Morgan. **Also Ch. Heydown Grip,** born 1927, (sire of Dual Ch. Anningsley Stingo and Ch. Anningsley Fox); **Heydown Gurth,** sire of Ch. Birling James of Somersby.

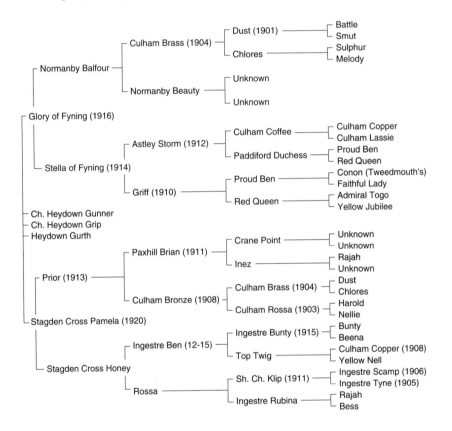

Culham Copper by Culham Brass x Culham Rossa. Conon (or Conan) by Felix x Ranee (or Rennie) was 2nd Lord Tweedmouth's; he appears in a 1903 photograph taken at Guisachan. Yellow Nell was by Ingestre Scamp x Ingestre Tyne, same as Sh. Ch. Klip and Beena. Ingestre Scamp by Sailor x Duchess; Ingestre Tyne by Wavetree Sam (a son of Lord Tweedmouth's Rock), x Corrie II.

Pedigree A2. Onaway (1922), dam of Ch. Cubbington Diver and Cubbington Fionn; **Ch. Haulstone Dan** (1922); **Amber Dimple** (1922), dam of Ch. Sundawn Dancer; **Balcombe Pride** (1925), dam of Eng. Am. Ch. Marine of Woolley; and **Haulstone Rusty** (1922), granddam of Gilder***.

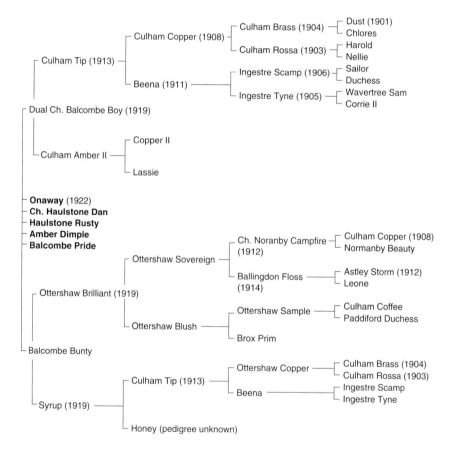

Pedigree B Ch. Cornelius (dog) born June 1921, owner Mrs. Evers-Swindell; (wins at trials, sire of 2 Chs., 1 FTCh.) **Ch. Flight of Kentford (Indian Dual Ch.)** (dog) owner the Hon. Mrs. Grigg. (Wins at trials. Sire of 3 Chs., 1 Sh. Ch. Exported to India, became Ch/FTCh.)

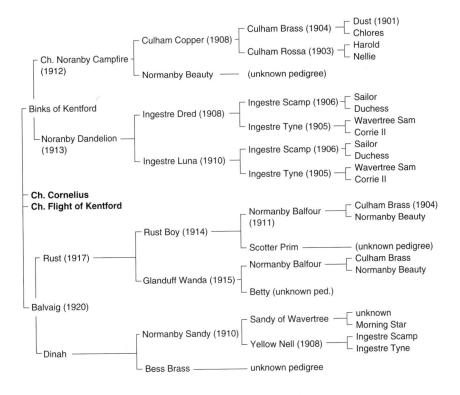

Pedigree C. Ch. Noble of Quinton (dog) born May 1924, owner H. Woodhouse
Ch. Michael of Moreton (dog) born Feb. 10, 1925, owner R.L. Kirk
Winner of 17 Ccs, winner at fields trials; sire of 7 champions.

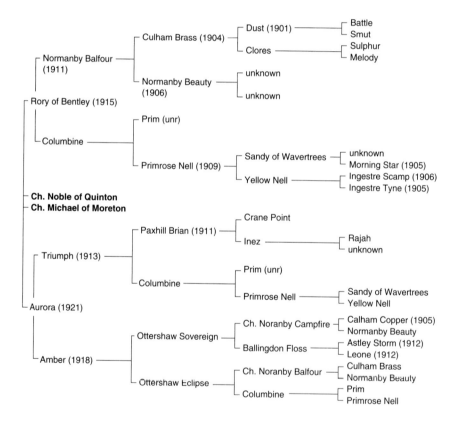

Gilder, bred by E. Needham-Davies and owned by H. Wentworth-Smith, was truly an exceptional sire. Born in 1929, he was still producing at thirteen years of age and sired no less than nine full champions in England. Gilder and his offspring were of great importance in modifying type. Given the linebreeding evident in his pedigree, perhaps it is not surprising that he was so dominant.

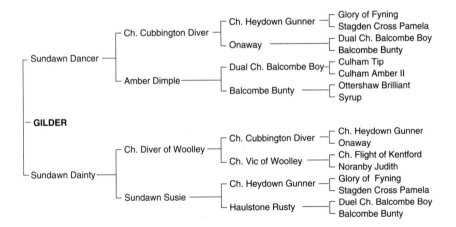

The 1930s in England were a period of steady growth in the breed. Numbers of dedicated breeders helped develop a good-looking dog capable of excellent work in the field. There were Mrs. Charlesworth (**Noranby**), pioneer in the breed since 1906; and Major and Mrs. Wentworth-Smith, whose suffix **of Yelme** was a force to be reckoned with in show and field, and whose sires Gilder and Buffworth put their stamp on the breed. Gilder, born 1929, produced no less than nine full champions before WWII. There were the Honorable Mrs. Grigg, whose **Heydown** kennel was headed by the redoubtable Ch. Cornelius and the remarkable sire Ch. Heydown Grip; and Mr. and Mrs. Evers-Swindell, whose **Speedwell** Goldens included the very influential export, Am. Can. Ch. Speedwell Pluto. There were also Mr. Jenner, whose **Abbots** prefix graced some very beautiful Goldens; the Rev. Needham-Davies, breeder of Gilder, who, oddly, did not carry the Reverend's **Sundawn** prefix and Mr. and Mrs. Eccles' **Haulstones**, a force in the field that could not be ignored. And there was Mrs. Nairn's large kennel of **Stubbings**, based on the elegant dog Ch. Birling James of Somersby. Sir George Bowyer, who used the prefix **Wilderness** (and sent Wilderness Tangerine to Sam Magoffin as a foundation bitch for the **Rockhaven** kennels), was so taken with his Goldens

Eng. Ch. Cornelius, born 1921, one of the true founding sires of the breed. Owned by Mrs. K. Evers-Swindell, Speedwell kennels, he was a full brother to Ch. and Indian Dual Ch. Flight of Kentford. Their pedigree is the one designated Pedigree B by Mrs. Stonex, one of those to which all present-day Goldens can be traced.

Eng. Ch. Michael of Moreton, born 1925, won a record 17 Challenge Certificates before WWII, and was a renowned sire, with at least five English champions, plus Am. Can. Ch. Speedwell Pluto, foundation sire in North America.

that when he was created Lord Denham, a Golden Retriever was made a part of his coat of arms. Starting before the war, and active after it as well, were Elma Stonex's beautiful **Dorcas** line, founded on Sally of Perrott (double granddaughter of Ch. Michael of Moreton, and also linebred on Dual Ch. Balcombe Boy and Ch. Noranby Campfire), which was so strongly influential in many other prominent kennels as well; Mrs. Parson's **Torrdales**, based on her lovely Ch. Dukeries Dancing Lady; and Joan Gill's dual-purpose Westleys, started with Simon of Brookshill. The Gilder son, Ch. Hazelgilt, owned by Mr. and Mrs. Cyril Walker (**Hazelfax**), quite likely would have completed his Dual title, but the war ended his career.

There was considerable variety among the dogs but just one function and purpose: They were working gundogs. Not all ran in Field Trials, but most were used at least for "picking up" at shoots. Two dogs had achieved the distinction of earning both Champion and Field Trial Champion titles: Dual Ch. Balcombe Boy, bred by Lord Harcourt and owned by Mr. Hermon; and Dual Ch. Anningsley Stingo, whose breeder/owner was H. Venables-Kyrke, from the Anningsley kennel that collected titles in both show and field competition.

On the eve of World War II, the Golden in Britain was just on the brink of greatness. There were some very good dogs and dedicated breeders, and interest was high. And then came the war.

MRS. W. M. CHARLESWORTH
AND THE NORANBY KENNELS

Mrs. W. M. Charlesworth says in her 1933 book: "In the early days . . . the then Lord Tweedmouth gave away certain dogs and puppies to relations and a few friends. These were very jealously guarded and never sold. It was purely luck, and the influence of that great sportsman the late 'Parson Upcher'

Normanby Beauty, born 1906, drawn from an early photograph. If anything was ever known of her pedigree, it was never revealed. Nearly all today's Goldens can be traced back to Beauty's sons, Normanby Balfour (by Culham Brass) and Ch. Noranby Campfire (by Culham Copper). Mrs. Charlesworth's affix was originally *Normanby*, but after 1911 became *Noranby*.

(as he was affectionately called in Norfolk) that enabled me to get my first Golden. . . . Noranby Beauty, destined to become famous through the progeny of her two sons Noranby Balfour and the late very deeply lamented champion Noranby Campfire." The implication is that Beauty was of Guisachan stock, although whatever Mrs. Charlesworth may have known of Beauty's background was never published.

Mrs. Charlesworth says that Beauty was "one of the cleverest retrievers I have ever owned. She retained the nose, sagacity, hardness of constitution, and untiring energy of the original Russian dog, combining with these qualities, pace, style, and refinement, that made her invaluable as a worker and a brood bitch."

Perhaps it should be explained here that the original spelling of the kennel name was "Normanby," and the first dogs of Mrs. Charlesworth's breeding carried that spelling. Then, through an error and a disagreement with the Kennel Club, the decision was made to use the spelling "Noranby." And that they remained for nearly fifty years. Noranby Balfour, Beauty's son by Lewis Harcourt's dog Culham Brass, became a very major influence in the breed, as he was sold to Mr. W. S. Hunt (Ottershaw) in 1914 and sired two pillars of the breed, Rory of Bentley and Glory of Fyning.

From Beauty's 1912 litter by Culham Copper (Culham Brass x Culham Rossa), Noranby Campfire was to take his place in history as the first Golden Retriever Champion.

Campfire bred to Sh. Ch. Noranby Dandelion (Ingestre Dred x Ingestre Luna) sired Noranby Daybreak, Rufus of Kentford and Binks of Kentford, each of whom proved to be extremely influential, and Noranby Judith, first in the "J" line, which carried the very dark coloring and the working capabilities of the Ingestre lines.

Noranby Daybreak's dam, Noranby Dandelion, was an inbred Ingestre combination, her sire and her dam being full brother and sister by Ingestre Tyne x Ingestre Scamp. Dandelion was bought in 1912 by Mrs. E. D. Grigg and became the foundation of the Kentford kennel. However, Mrs. Charlesworth took back the bitch Noranby Daybreak from Dandelion bred to N. Campfire, and this was the beginning of the "D" line of bitches that culminated in Dual Ch. Noranby Destiny, wh. 1943. A study of Destiny's pedigree shows clearly Mrs. Charlesworth's determination to maintain quality in both field and bench through careful linebreeding and judicious outcrossing.

Normanby Sandy (by Sandy of Wavertree x Yellow Nell), owned by Mrs. Charlesworth, was the first recorded Golden Retriever to place in a Field Trial. A writer in 1915 says of him: "Normanby Sandy ran well . . . and was awarded a Certificate of Merit, quite a triumph considering the quality of the entry, and . . . was splendidly handled; he showed initiative, proved that he had a good nose, and showed no fear when asked to face rough covert."

Normanby Sandy also carried Ingestre lines, his dam Yellow Nell being from the Ingestre Scamp x Ingestre Tyne combination; Sandy's paternal grandsire Fox of Melbury carried Lord Ilchester's suffix, connecting back to the original Guisachan dogs.

Mrs. Charlesworth, or "Charlie" to her friends, was a unique character. Possibly the first woman to train and handle her own dogs at retriever trials, she was strongly opinionated and quite outspoken. She never minced words and had as many opponents as friends. Joan Gill recollects that "She was, indeed, a formidable lady. Her marriage lasted one week, so we are told. She always wore a man's jacket and a collar and tie. Women didn't wear trousers in her day, but when she was sitting at a table, with her skirt out of sight, and her hair cropped short, she was always addressed as 'sir.'"

She always upheld the story of the Russian circus dogs as the foundation for the breed and did not waver even in the face of later confirmation of the Wavy/Flat-Coat Retriever–Tweed Water Spaniel breedings. Her book on the breed, first published in 1933, credited the "circus dog" story and admitted nothing of any other contributing lines, nor did she modify this in later editions even in spite of certain knowledge that the Ingestre lines so close behind her own breeding were clearly of Flat-Coat breeding.

Normanby Campfire, the first of the breed to achieve recognition as a champion, was whelped in 1912. Today he would be considered light-boned and not "pretty." However, his pictures taken later in life show a very sound, muscular, clean-cut dog, with wonderful legs and feet. In 1925 he was still active and in excellent health at over thirteen years of age.

His more substantial half-brother, Normanby Balfour, became grandsire of Ch. Michael of Moreton and Ch. Noble of Quinton. Michael became an exceptional winner and producer, not least as the sire of Can./Am. Ch. Speedwell Pluto, who went to North America and became a keystone of the breed there.

Noranby Tweedledum (Sandy of Wavertree x Yellow Nell, born 1909) won a Certificate of Merit at Field Trials about 1912. In spite of his good structure and working ability, Mrs. Charlesworth never bred from him, terming him "a throwback to the old type" because of his light color and his very wavy, almost curly coat.

The Noranby bitches were notable. Chs. Noranby Diana, Daydawn and Jeptha all placed in Field Trials, Jeptha coming very close to the Dual title. A dozen or so Noranbys placed in Field Trials, and several won Challenge Certificates. A number were exported to the U.S. and Canada, including Destiny's brother, Am. Ch. Noranby Baloo of Taramar.

The Noranby Goldens were always known as fine workers, sensible and intelligent, and Mrs. Charlesworth believed adamantly that Goldens must be workers and must adhere to breed type. On the subject of breeding to type, she said:

> If the type is not adhered to by some breeders it is their own fault, but the type is there, and always has been, if people would only breed to it, and not follow the "Will o' the Wisp" which lures so many kennels to destruction, of "Mating a Champion to a Champion to breed a Champion." This way madness lies, and not only that, but the ruin of the breed.
>
> It is only by very careful, selective, and what I term slow breeding, that a few of us have managed to keep the right type on top.

Her words are as applicable today as they were more than sixty years ago.

The Golden Retriever Comes to North America

EARLY DAYS IN CANADA

The first Golden Retrievers were in Canada long before the Canadian Kennel Club recognized or recorded them. Sam Magoffin, as well as other early owners, said that he "had heard of" Goldens brought to Canada by retired British Army officers, as early as the turn of the century. This is borne out by photographs in the GRCA Archives, showing dogs of distinct Golden type. A large, wavy-coated dog appears in a photo dated about 1912, in British Columbia. Another pair of photos, dated 1903, shows unidentified dogs of somewhat more medium size in a setting that suggests the western part of North America.

Lord Tweedmouth's daughter Lady Aberdeen and her husband John Gordon, seventh Lord Aberdeen, had in about 1891 purchased property in Canada near Coldstream, British Columbia. Christopher Burton, a friend of Sam Magoffin's, at one time visited the Coldstream ranch or farm and said that he saw a photograph on the wall in the office which he believes showed Coutts Marjoribanks (Lady Aberdeen's brother) with a yellow retriever. An earlier photo of Coutts taken in North Dakota shows him with a black, Wavy-Coated Retriever type dog lying at his feet. Certainly it is reasonable that Coutts, like his brother Archie in Texas, should bring one or more of the family retrievers along for both sporting purposes and companionship. Coutts had earlier been employed at the Horse Shoe Ranch in North Dakota, a smaller spread than Archie's Rocking Chair Ranch in Texas. Unfortunately, these dogs were too early to have had any influence on the breed; so distantly separated from their origins, with no dogs of similar type to breed to, and no effort to record them even privately, their lines disappeared into oblivion. But they may well have left a memory of Golden character and traits.

This photograph, identified only with the date 1903, is in the GRCA's Archives. It appears to have been taken in the Western U.S. or Canada. Might the dog perhaps have been one of the dogs brought over by the "retired British Army officers" mentioned in some early writings? Could it have been bred from dogs brought over by Archie or Coutts Marjoribanks, Lord Tweedmouth's sons? Likely we shall never know.

In Canada, as in England, the earliest CKC records only refer to "Retrievers," the varieties or breeds not being distinguished until about 1927. The imported dog Foxbury Peter (Eng. Dual Ch. Balcombe Boy x Wonham Duchess), born Sept. 18, 1927, bred by Mr. MacIntosh, owned by Mrs. Alex MacLaren of Buckingham, Quebec, was the first champion to be published as a Golden, in 1928. In 1930 the bitch Dame Daphne (Speedwell Nimrod x Guiding Star) was imported in whelp, having been bred to Eng. Ch. Haulstone Dan before export. Dame Daphne later, in 1931, became the first Golden bitch to complete a Canadian championship. Among her litter bred in England but whelped in Canada, on April 28, 1930, were Can. Ch. Saffron Peter Boy, Saffron Penelope and Saffron Chipmonk. The two bitches, Saffron Penelope and Saffron Chipmonk, were owned by Samuel S. Magoffin and became integral to the Rockhaven foundation stock and hence to the basis of the breed in North America in the 1930s.

By 1926, possibly earlier, there were Goldens in the Gilnockie Kennels of Bart Armstrong in Winnipeg, including the first Golden Retriever registered

Can. Am. Ch. Speedwell Pluto, owned by S. S. Magoffin, was a keystone of the breed in North America. Sired by Eng. Ch. Michael of Moreton, Pluto carried some of the foremost bloodlines in England. Not only the first Golden to win a Best in Show, he was also an experienced and useful gundog.

as such with the Canadian Kennel Club: Judy of Westholme, wh. May 8, 1926. However, Armstrong had earlier imported a male, Noranby Eventide, wh. 1922, a double grandson of Ch. Noranby Campfire. Eventide had completed the requirements for championship in Canada, but when the championship certificate arrived, it bore the designation "Retriever—Wavy." This did not sit well with Bart Armstrong, and some lively correspondence with the CKC ensued, with Bart extolling the virtues of the Golden above other retrievers and spaniels. One of his letters read, in part:

April 18, 1927

To Mr. J. D. Strachan, Esq.,

Secretary, Canadian Kennel Club:

Incidentally, it will interest you to hear that I had my dog, Ch. Noranby Eventide, in the Assiniboine River on Saturday the 15th and Sunday the 16th. As the papers will indicate, this river was going through its annual stage of the break-up of ice which flows down from hundreds of miles of territory, and it is quite a sight to see this torrent with the river swollen far beyond its usual size, and almost over-flowing its high banks.

He went into the water without any special urging, and this indicates the hardihood of the breed to go into a swift river with ice running, and off the high banks up which he had to return. It indicates also that he likes ice-cold water. I have experimented with various breeds of Retrievers, and the Springer Spaniel also, and I find the Golden is the best of them all in this regard. This is very important in sizing up the Golden Retriever, and the purposes for which it is required. It is especially interesting that he is considered an equally good dog for upland shooting.

Bart Armstrong

After due consideration by the Board of Directors of the Canadian Kennel Club, a new championship certificate was issued, properly designating Noranby Eventide as a Golden Retriever and giving recognition to the breed itself. So, while Foxbury Peter is the first Golden Retriever published as completing the Canadian championship, in 1928, it seems that Noranby Eventide was actually the first Golden to earn the title (1927), even though originally published as a Wavy-coat.

Bartle Mahon Armstrong was an ardent sportsman, active both in sporting dog clubs and in horse racing; his business in insurance and construction enabled him to travel to Scotland and England regularly. He had other sporting dogs as well as Goldens but preferred Goldens "on account of their tractability, courage, disposition, size, hardihood for standing cold weather and cold water, and above all for their appearance, as they are decidedly better looking than any of the other breeds."

First registered with the Canadian Kennel Club in 1922, Bart Armstrong's Gilnockie kennel name is the oldest still in use in Golden Retrievers in North America. It is also the name of Gilnockie Tower in the border country of Scotland, stronghold of Johnie Armstrang, Laird of Gilnockie, hanged by King James' men in 1530. Bart Armstrong's parents both came from Scotland, and whether or not they were of Johnie Armstrang's descendants, the name of Gilnockie was used for Bart's dogs. Upon Bart Armstrong's death in 1932, his kennel name was transferred to his friend, Samuel Shelby Magoffin, and was used for the kennel established in Colorado by Sam and his brother, John Rogers Magoffin. Then, when Sam Magoffin died in 1959, the name was transferred to Eliesa Enloe of Colorado, who carried it until her death in 1995.

Col. Samuel Shelby Magoffin is one of the men who first put the Golden Retriever "on the map" in North America, yet without his friendship with Christopher Burton, the history of the Golden might be quite different. Born in England in 1898, Chris had been a dedicated sportsman since a small boy and often hunted with a yellow retriever belonging to his brother-in-law. After serving in World War I, Christopher Burton settled in Winnipeg, Manitoba, where he met Bart Armstrong. Later, he and his wife lived several years in the interior of British Columbia, then moved to Vancouver where he became very good friends with Sam Magoffin.

Samuel Shelby Magoffin of Vancouver, BC, pictured with one of the
Rockhaven Golden Retrievers.
Magoffin's Rockhaven and Gilnockie kennels were based on
the darker-coated dogs popular in
England during the 1930s; he imported a number from well-known
English bloodlines.

When Sam Magoffin was looking for a useful gundog in 1930, he asked
the advice of Christopher Burton, as he had been "a dedicated Golden man
since I was knee-high." He cabled his brother-in-law in England about finding a "well-broken Golden Retriever male not over three, with points according to Kennel Club regulations." After some cable correspondence back and
forth, and a three-week journey by rail, steamship and then rail again across
the breadth of Canada, Speedwell Pluto arrived in Vancouver. By Eng. Ch.
Michael of Moreton x Eng. Sh. Ch. Speedwell Emerald, Pluto had placed in
a Field Trial as well as a conformation show. When Pluto stepped out of his
traveling box, so handsome and impressive a dog was he that Chris Burton
said he thought Col. Magoffin "would burst into tears" at the sight of this
"wonderful dog." And indeed, Pluto lived up to all his early promise, becoming not only the first Golden to go Best in Show (1933), with wins in both
the U.S. and Canada, but a hard-working, courageous gundog and one of
the foremost sires in the breed.

Chris Burton had one of the first dogs bred at Rockhaven: Rockhaven
Beau Brummel, by Am. Can. Ch. Speedwell Pluto x Saffron Chipmonk, was
Mr. Burton's personal gundog and the first of three generations of Goldens
in direct male line from Pluto. Beau Brummel had won at Field Trials *before*
the CKC officially recognized them or awarded Field Trial championships.
His two first places in all-breed Retriever Trials would have given him the
title if these wins had come after official recognition. Beau's grandson, Vic's
Winsome Beau York, died in 1971 at age fifteen, remarkably only the third
generation from Ch. Speedwell Pluto, who was born in 1929!

Ch. Rockhaven Rory, bred by Sam Magoffin and owned by Henry B. Christian of Goldwood Kennels, was Best of Breed at Westminster in 1936. He was a strong, well-balanced dog of exceptional quality for his time and was said to be a very powerful swimmer, perhaps due in part to his excellent forequarters.

Mr. Burton in his later years became very interested in the early history of the breed, and much of his research is maintained in the Archives of the GRCA and the GRC of Canada, of which he was a founding member. He attended the 25th Anniversary of the Golden Retriever Club of America in 1964, and those who were there will remember the distinguished British gentleman with the silvery hair and the courtly manner. He always felt that regardless of beauty—and success in the show ring—the Golden breed must be given the opportunity to fulfill its original purpose. To this end, he staunchly advocated both Field Trials and other retriever tests such as the Puppy Stake and the Working Certificate Tests for those who might not be able to afford pursuing licensed Field Trials. Honored with Life Memberships in both the Golden Retriever Club of Canada and the Golden Retriever Club of America, Christopher Burton died in 1983.

ROCKHAVEN

Samuel Shelby Magoffin's Rockhaven kennels were in North Vancouver, British Columbia. Randolph Hall, kennel manager, was largely responsible for the well being and success of the Rockhaven dogs; Charles Bunker trained them in field work and ran several in trials. The Gilnockie Kennels at Englewood, Colorado, were overseen by Sam Magoffin's brother, John Rogers Magoffin, until his death. Both kennels were based on Ch. Speedwell Pluto

Eng. Am. Ch. Bingo of Yelme***, born 1933. Owned by John K. Wallace of Whitebridge Kennels, St. Louis, MO. Bingo completed his championship in 4 shows undefeated and competed honorably in Field Trials owner-handled. He is the sire and grandsire of field and show champions. This photo shows particularly good neck, shoulder and upper arm construction. Overall proportions are correct, with proper leg length and depth of body. His head is excellent and well illustrates the demands of the breed standard, with a powerful muzzle capable of easily handling large water-fowl. His coat is of a practical sort, dense and with an acceptable wave. Hindquarters could be more strongly developed, but they are at least as good as many of today's champions, whose legs are disguised in massive amounts of hair.

and carefully chosen bitches such as the sisters Saffron Penelope and Saffron Chipmonk, and imports that included Wilderness Tangerine, later Am. Can. Ch. (by Speedwell Barley out of Eng. Ch. Wilderness Maud). The Rockhaven prefix occurs on eighteen of the first thirty-five Canadian champions; adding Pluto, Tangerine and four Gilnockie dogs makes a total of twenty-four of the thirty-five from 1928 to 1949.

THE CENTRAL FLYWAY:
WHERE GOLDENS WORKED

Samuel S. Magoffin (1899–1959), an engineer by profession, had made a peculiarly providential choice in marrying Margaret Boalt. Both her brothers, the twins Ralph and Ben Boalt, and a brother-in-law, Henry B. Christian, acquired Golden Retrievers from the Rockhaven-Gilnockie breedings, and with the addition of bloodlines from a few more well-chosen English importations, established Golden Retrievers in the upper Midwest of the United States. In the 1940s and 1950s, this was *the* area of the Golden Retriever. The dogs proved their sporting capabilities in the cornfields and croplands of North Dakota and Wisconsin, the wide rivers and lakes of Minnesota, the broad expanses of Wisconsin's Horicon Marsh and other centers of gamebird hunting on the flyways of the central U.S.

An exceptional pedigree. Of this litter, born Jan. 2, 1940, Nitro Express qualified for the National Retriever Trial every year from 1942 to 1947, after winning the Country Life Trophy for top Derby Dog in 1941. Superspeed, a dog who well deserved his name, qualified for the National five times and sired Ch. Czar of Wildwood, six-time Best in Show winner. Katherine produced four show champions, notably Ch. Gold Button of Catawba**, foundation bitch for Torch Flinn's Tigathoe kennels in Connecticut. Vee and Victor (a bitch, in spite of the name) went to Canada and produced well there: Victor as the granddam of Can. Dual Ch. Byrcober Sir Alexander CD. Shur Shot sired Ch. Golden Knolls Shur Shot, CD, 14 times Best in Show and sire of many champions, including the record-breaking Ch. Golden Knolls King Alphonzo.

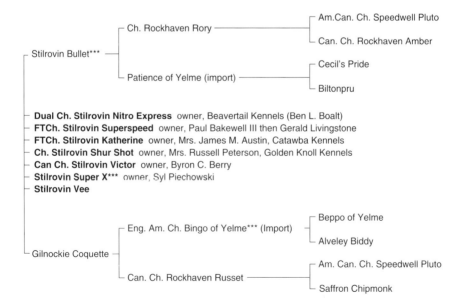

Stilrovin Bullet***
- Ch. Rockhaven Rory
  - Am.Can. Ch. Speedwell Pluto
  - Can. Ch. Rockhaven Amber
- Patience of Yelme (import)
  - Cecil's Pride
  - Biltonpru

- **Dual Ch. Stilrovin Nitro Express** owner, Beavertail Kennels (Ben L. Boalt)
- **FTCh. Stilrovin Superspeed** owner, Paul Bakewell III then Gerald Livingstone
- **FTCh. Stilrovin Katherine** owner, Mrs. James M. Austin, Catawba Kennels
- **Ch. Stilrovin Shur Shot** owner, Mrs. Russell Peterson, Golden Knoll Kennels
- **Can Ch. Stilrovin Victor** owner, Byron C. Berry
- **Stilrovin Super X***** owner, Syl Piechowski
- **Stilrovin Vee**

Gilnockie Coquette
- Eng. Am. Ch. Bingo of Yelme*** (Import)
  - Beppo of Yelme
  - Alveley Biddy
- Can. Ch. Rockhaven Russet
  - Am. Can. Ch. Speedwell Pluto
  - Saffron Chipmonk

THE BOALTS

Ralph G. Boalt's kennel name of Stilrovin is one of the best known of that era—and dog generations later. Twin brother Ben's kennel name was originally Beavertail, then Gunnerman, and is still to be found in pedigrees of fine working dogs. These prefixes were carried by many standout dogs from the 1930s into the 1960s.

One of Ralph's early notables was Stilrovin Bullet*** from the imported Patience of Yelme bred to Ch. Rockhaven Rory. Bullet did well at Field Trials, but it is as the sire of a remarkable litter out of Gilnockie Coquette that he left his mark on Golden Retriever history. From this litter whelped in 1941 came a Dual Champion, two Field Champions, a show Champion and others with field placements. Several of the litter became exceptional producers in both field and show competition. Gilnockie Coquette also produced the first U.S. Dual Champion, Stilrovin Rip's Pride, (by F.Ch. Rip), and set an unequaled record as an Outstanding Dam: two duals, two Field Champions and three conformation champions.

Ralph Boalt's brother Ben first used the kennel name Beavertail, which was later changed to Gunnerman after the original kennel name became the subject of some hilarity. The Gunnerman name was active well into the 1960s. Twins, Ralph and Ben always had a jocular rivalry, which included some interesting practical jokes. Ralph also liked to name his dogs after characters in the "Steve Canyon" and "Terry and the Pirates" comic strips—hence Luke Adew, Tuppee Tee, Savannah Gay, Chum Fun, Terry Lee and others.

With Stilrovin in Winona, and Beavertail/Gunnerman in Milwaukee, the Boalt brothers were well known at Field Trials across the Midwest. They were also active in the Tri-State Hunting Dog Association, which bred dogs with the prefix Tri-Stada, notably FCh Tri-Stada Upset, Ch. Tri-Stada Sir Mickey***, and Ch. Tri-Stada Autumn Hugh***.

GOLDWOOD

Goldwood, owned by Henry B. Christian, was established at White Bear Lake, Minnesota, near Minneapolis–St. Paul in 1933. Henry Christian owned Ch. Rockhaven Rory and the imported Ch. Sprite of Aldgrove**, who placed in Field Trials. Bred together, they produced Ch. Goldwood Pluto***. Sprite, bred to Rockhaven Tuck** (Am. Can. Ch. Speedwell Pluto x Saffron Chipmonk), produced FTCh. Goldwood Tuck, an exceptional sire of working Goldens. Also from this kennel came the first and second UD titlists, Goldwood Toby UD and Goldwood Michael UD, a double grandson of Ch. Rockhaven Rory. Goldwood Kennels has been in operation as a boarding kennel for many years under the management of Peggy Hilton, Henry

Christian's daughter, and her husband Frank. Frank and Peggy ran Goldens in Field Trials into the late 1960s, among them Goldwood Bingo*** and Stilrovin Target of Goldwood***. Although not as active in competition now, Goldens are still very much a part of Goldwood.

REMINISCENCES

by Peggy Hilton,
Goldwood Kennels

"Our Goldens were housed in a beautiful six-run kennel with hardwood tongue and groove paneling; large wooded exercise area where there was an open-sided, roofed lounging area for shelter if needed, and an office/trophy room. We had a 'kennel man' by the name of Bob Bruce, very devoted to the Goldens. His only job was to exercise and groom the dogs, and fix and serve the special formula food for the Goldens; and the puppy care too, of course. So much was research and experimentation; food quality and nutrition was not what it is today, so health, coat quality, etc., was a more difficult job. . . .

I do recall that when my uncles [Ralph and Ben Boalt] (and others) came for Field Trials and training they brought their Goldens, most of whom also were running around inside our house. Fortunately we had a very large house. We, as children, were always surrounded by Goldens and I recall we *never* had any dog 'altercations.' All the dogs were very congenial—wonderful dispositions. . . .

When I was just a couple of months old there are pictures of me and my twin brother lying next to a Golden Retriever. I can't imagine life (or death for that matter) without one around."

THE MISSISSIPPI VALLEY

From the mid-1930s, through the 1940s and 1950s and into the 1960s, the majority of working Goldens came from the upper Midwest. St. Louis was another area of exceptional importance, as here were the Wallaces.

John K. Wallace (Whitebridge) owned Goldens as early as 1935, first as personal shooting dogs. One of his first was Speedwell Tango, a granddaughter of Eng. Ch. Cornelius and Eng. Ch. Michael of Moreton; she produced two field champions, Whitebridge Wally (by Eng. Am. Ch. Bingo of Yelme) and the immortal Rip (by Speedwell Reuben), first Golden Retriever to earn the title of Field Trial Champion. Rip's sister Queen Mary K produced bench show winners, including Ch. Whitebridge Sally (a Westminster winner). Wally's sister, Whitebridge Judy, became the granddam of FCh/NFCh Beautywood's Tamarack. In these days there was no differentiation between

FC Whitebridge Wally (Am. Can. Ch. Bingo of Yelme*** x Ch. Speedwell Tanngo) shows a fast return and a soft-mouthed carry at a Field Trial in 1938. Bred by John K. Wallace and owned by S. Cupples Scudder. *Photo courtesy J. K. Wallace Jr.*

"show" dogs and "working" dogs—there were just Golden Retrievers, who might hunt on Saturday and show on Sunday, if there wasn't a retriever trial being held.

In the years before World War II, John and Mahlon Wallace imported at least a dozen Goldens from England, most from the Yelme Kennels of Mr. and Mrs. Wentworth-Smith, and also bought from the Rockhaven Kennels. The Yelme dogs were brought over specifically as dual-purpose working/show/breeding stock from a kennel well known for working dogs who won on the bench; most were offspring of the well-known sire Gilder or of the dog Buffworth, a working Golden from old lines. One of the best of the imports was Eng. Ch. Bingo of Yelme, a handsome, sound and well-balanced dog.

Bingo earned his American championship in four shows, undefeated, to become the first English-American champion. Amateur-handled by Mr. Wallace at Trials, he was the first Golden to achieve All-Age status. He also became a cornerstone of American Goldens by siring the premier dam, Gilnockie Coquette, dam of dual, bench and field champions, as well as FTCh Whitebridge Wally, a National contender. An advertisement for Whitebridge Kennels in a 1938 show catalog states that Bingo was "Best of Breed every time shown in America (including Westminster, Boston, Chicago and St. Louis)." Shows were few and far between in those days, and earning a championship often entailed long, arduous days of travel on the train and equally arduous days at the lengthy shows, which sometimes lasted three or four days.

Paul Bakewell III and the first Field Trial Champion Golden, Rip, at an early trial in 1939. Rip has just completed a retrieve from the Mississippi River. In today's trials, dogs are not expected to sit in front when delivering the bird, but often go directly to Heel position in order to be ready for the next retrieve. *Photo courtesy J. K. Wallace Jr.*

Bingo placed several times in Amateur All-Age stakes, but at that time no points were given in those stakes and there was no title of Amateur Field Champion (AFC). Bingo's photographs show him to be a sound, workmanlike dog with good substance and a very attractive head. He was obviously a great favorite of John Wallace, who ran Bingo in trials himself; Bingo's picture appeared on the Wallace's Christmas cards, and his portrait in color still hangs in John Wallace Jr.'s home.

Mr. and Mrs. Mahlon B. Wallace Jr. (Audlon) owned Golden Girl of Audlon (whelped 1932) and Haulstone Patsy, both bred in England, and bred several litters from Golden Girl. Patsy ran well at trials and also had show points. Another trial competitor was Golden Prospect of Yelme (Buffworth x Amber Blush), a particularly good-looking dog with a beautiful head and expression. While his activity in Goldens lessened during the war years, in 1948 Mahlon bought Ready Always of Marianhill. While the name "Ready Always" was particularly appropriate for this small dog with the heart bigger than he was, he was more familiarly called "Lucky." He eagerly broke ice to make retrieves in freezing water that many Labradors and Chesapeakes refused to enter. His photograph shows a well-made, beautifully moving dog of functional retriever structure and type. He won the Open Stake at the GRCA Nationals twice (1950 and 1952) and the National Retriever Championship in 1951. Mrs. Wallace handled Lucky in Amateur stakes, and Billy Wunderlich in Open competition. He finished his career with 53.5 points in

Ch. Tonkahof Bang*** in a classic water entry. Owned by Henry Norton and Joe MacGaheran, Bang was a Best in Show winner with Field placement in the 1940s, and sire of the first bitch to earn the Dual Champion title, Tonkahof Esther Belle.

Open stakes and 26.5 in Amateur, for a total of 80 points, putting his total for years second only to that of FC/AFC Oakcreek's Van Cleve's total of 124.5.

Pink Lady of Audlon**, bred by Mahlon Wallace out of an imported dam, was sold to Ralph Boalt. Bred to Stilrovin Bearcat, a dog of good field breeding but of no recorded achievement, she produced some of the foremost field dogs of the 1960s, including the three Stilrovin Field Champions: Tuppee Tee, Luke Adew and Savannah Gay. Pink Lady was sired by AFC-Ch Lorelei's Golden Rockbottom UD out of Masaka of Wynford, a full sister to Eng. FTCh Mazurka of Wynford who is behind so many of the Holway/Wynford Field winners. This may be a hint as to why Pink Lady's descendants "nicked" so well with the Holway Leo and Holway Barty bloodlines later on in the 1970s and 1980s.

FTCH RIP

Rip was the puppy no one wanted. A leggy, awkward youngster with a splash of white on his long nose, he was the last of the litter from John Wallace's Ch. Speedwell Tango. For the sum of $35, Rip went to a young man named Paul Bakewell III and in a few years set the retriever world on its ear. In an era when nearly all serious trial dogs were run by professionals, Rip was owner-handled. Born in November of 1935, Rip first placed at a licensed trial in April 1938, second in an amateur Novice stake. Eighteen months later he completed a Field Trial Championship, the first Golden Retriever to do so. Two years after that, he had totaled sixty-three points in Open or Limited All-Age stakes; if there had been an Amateur Field Champion title, he'd have had that as well. The big, burly, long-legged Rip was a dynamic dog to watch; some thought him "jittery" on the line, but he won in an era when steadiness and birdsense were of great importance. Rip and Paul were a superb team; it was calculated that Rip had retrieved under judgment no less than 236 consecutive birds without a miss. Rip won the Field & Stream Trophy for top winning retriever (any breed) in both 1939 and 1940, and qualified for the National Championship Trial in 1941, earning six placements in less than two months that spring. But his amazing career was cut short by death in August, before he was six years old, an age when most field competitors are in their prime. While Paul Bakewell continued with retrievers, both Goldens and Labradors in his Deer Creek Kennels, Rip must have been that truly once-in-a-lifetime dog.

The Midwest has always been a center for Field Trial activity. While there were some Trials on the East and West Coasts, Goldens were particularly strong in the Midwest. At many Trials, the numbers of Goldens were equal to those of the Labradors; Chesapeakes were also well represented. Most Trial dogs were also used as hunting dogs, and many of them were shown at conformation events as well. The first three Dual Champions Goldens all came from the Midwest.

The first National Retriever Trial championship was won by a Golden, NFTCh/FTCh King Midas of Woodend in 1941. Born in 1937, King Midas was sired by Rockhaven Tuck*** (Ch. Speedwell Pluto x Saffron Chipmonk) out of the imported bitch Glittering Gold. She was a granddaughter of Gilder, the outstanding sire of the 1930s in England. King Midas, owned by Edwin N. Dodge, before October of 1941 had earned just one point in Open stakes; within three memorable weeks in October of 1941 he took two firsts and a third to complete his title, and six weeks later won the National, two days before Pearl Harbor put an end to Field competition for so many.

King Midas, himself a dog of very attractive appearance, left his mark on the breed by producing Giltway Strike***, who in turn sired two noteworthy daughters. One was Am. Can. Ch. Des Lacs Lassie CD*, the first bitch to earn a place in the Show Dogs Hall of Fame, with twenty-two Group placements and a Best in Show, and the foundation of Bart Foster's Des Lacs Kennels. Giltway Strike's other daughter of note was Rock River Sue, unfortunately never shown nor trained, a very good-looking bitch with plenty of working instinct, owned by Bruce Ashby. Both Sue and Lassie were bred to the imported Ch. Gilder of Elsiville and produced champions by him and by other sires as well. Their lines are still behind several quality lines of Goldens today.

OTHER MIDWESTERN KENNELS
STARTING BEFORE 1940

Vernon Johnson of Battle Lake, Minnesota, bred good working dogs from basic Rockhaven/Beavertail/Goldwood lines under the kennel name of Shelter Cove. He bred several times to Ned Dodge's NFTCh King Midas of Woodend. Most prominent of the Shelter Cove Goldens was Dr. Leslie Evans' bitch, National FTC of 1944, Shelter Cove Beauty (Rockhaven Ben Bolt x Happy of Willow Loch). Trained by Charles Morgan, Beauty was a big, rangy bitch, who might have washed out with a trainer less understanding than Charlie Morgan. She was the granddam of Dr. Evans' second National Champion, NFTCh Beautywood's Tamarack.

Tonkahof, the kennel name of Henry Norton (Minneapolis), was derived from his foundation bitch, Ch. Tonkabelle of Woodend (Rockhaven Tuck** x Can. Ch. Rockhaven Judy). Henry Norton believed very firmly in the dual-purpose Golden. His advertisement in the 1939 GRCA Yearbook was repeated in 1950: *"The aim and final test of our breeding is the constant improvement of one type of Golden Retriever who can distinguish himself afield, on the bench, and in the home."* He not only said it, he did it, having produced not only Ch. Tonkahof Bang, the Best in Show dog with Field Trial placements, but also Bang's daughter, Dual Champion Tonkahof Esther Belle (first DCh bitch).

Woodend, owned by Harold Ward, near Minneapolis, held both Goldens and Labradors. Ward's Can. Ch. Rockhaven Judy (Eng. Ch. Marine of Woolley x Can. Ch. Rockhaven Lassie) produced three All-Age qualified offspring by FC Rip, including the sires of Dual Ch. Stilrovin Rip's Pride and FC Royal Peter Golden Boy. Judy was also the dam of FC Banty of Woodend and Ch. Tonkabelle of Woodend (by FC Goldwood Tuck).

Willow Lake and Willow Loch were used by James S. Thompson, Windom, Minnesota. He started with the sisters Rusty Heger and Belinda of Willow Lake, whose parents Speedwell Boine and Onyx of Emley were both English imports. Bred to Henry Christian's Ch. Rockhaven Rory, Rusty Heger produced Ch. Toby of Willow Loch***. Toby ran and placed in Field Trials trained by Orin Benson, and was said to be a tough, hard-going retriever. Jim Thompson thought that Toby might do well in bench shows, so Toby went off to the shows with Orin. Not only did Toby do well, he finished his championship in three shows and went Best in Show at the third, the first American-bred Golden to win Best in Show. Toby sired a number of the Goldwood dogs, including Rachel Page Elliott's Goldwood Toby UD.

Golden Valley belonged to Richard Ryan. He began with two Canadian-breds, Nero of Roedare*** and Golden Beauty of Roedare. Why Nero never achieved titles is a mystery; he is credited with thirteen Open points (ten are required for a Field Championship), including the required first place; had fourteen points in bench shows, and two "legs" on a CD title. Ryan did earn the Field Championship on Golden Beauty, and she whelped Carlton Grassle's FC Pirate of Golden Valley (by FC Goldwood Tuck). Other contributors to American field lines also carried the Golden Valley affix.

Chateau D'Or: Kenneth Bulkley bred seven litters before 1940, all linebred on Ch. Speedwell Pluto through the bitch Gilnockie Lady. Lady had been bred and owned by Bart Armstrong, then passed to the ownership of Sam Magoffin and thence to Mr. Bulkley at seven years of age. Chateau D'Or dogs appear in the far reaches of many present-day pedigrees, as other breeders in Minnesota utilized them.

Beavertail was Ben Boalt's original kennel name. The Rockhaven dog, Ch. Rockhaven Moonshine**, and two bitches, Ch. Rockhaven Glory** and R. Noel Lady, formed the basis of Ben Boalt's line, beginning in 1935. Ch. Beavertail Butch, B. Bruno and B. Beryl were all important producers. Decades later, AFC Gunnerman's Coin of Copper and his sister Gunnerman's Copper Penny, both bred by Ben Boalt, would carry on the lines into a new era of Field winners by producing Shenandoah of Stilrovin*** and Jolly Again of Ouilmette CD***, whose names are not far behind so many of today's field winners.

IN THE EAST

In the Eastern part of the U.S., Golden Retrievers were not completely unknown, even before the Rockhaven/Gilnockie dogs. The first registrations with AKC (1925) were the pair Lomberdale Blondin and Dan Hill Judy, both owned by Robert Appleton of East Hampton, New York. They and a few of their offspring were shown a few times in 1927 and 1928. At this time, the AKC had not separated the retrievers, and usually all varieties of retriever showed together. Labradors and the few Goldens competed together for the points. Even as late as 1941, Labradors and Flat-Coats were lumped together at certain shows.

Dr. Charles Large of New York City was one of the first serious breeders of Goldens in the U.S. From 1930 until his death in 1933, he imported seven Goldens and bred at least four litters. He also championed the Golden Retriever through a column written in the AKC's *Kennel Gazette*, written with insight, covering breed history and stories of early dogs. Among his dogs were Minor of Tone and Sherry of Tone (siblings of the English Field Trial winner, Silence of Tone), Noranby Mica (son of Eng. Ch. Michael of Moreton), Eng. Ch. Anningsley Beatrice, and Ch. Alaisdair of Highstead, a son of Beatrice sired by Eng. FTCh Anningsley Crakers. Dr. Large used the affix Fernova on the dogs he bred. The names of several of these dogs can still be found in some current American pedigrees, if one cares to go back far enough.

After Dr. Large's death, his dogs went to various friends. One of these was Nelson Lee, who continued the column in the Gazette. Mr. Lee, in late 1932, had imported a bitch from W. S. Hunt's Ottershaw kennels in England, who would become Ch. Ottershaw Collette. Eng. Ch. Anningsley Beatrice and her son Michael of Fernova also went to Nelson Lee after Dr. Large's death. Lee put the Ottershaw name on dogs of his breeding, which is the cause of some confusion as the original Ottershaw name belonged to W. S. Hunt in England, who had been breeding since 1914.

Alaisdair of Highstead and Sherry of Tone, as well as Bonita of Fernova, went to Michael Clemens (Frantelle). He later acquired others, including the imported Lady Burns (Eng. Ch. Bruar Scot x Abbots Amber), and finished her championship. Mr. Clemens was dedicated to popularizing the Golden and was active into the 1950s. Ch. Frantelle's Fiddler was a prominent winner in the mid-1940s. In later years he used the prefix Indian Fields.

Natalie Brown's Willow Bank kennels in New York imported Wanden Lad and three siblings of Dewstraw breeding, registered as Headisland Peter, Longisland Redde and Glenisland Caroline (read as "Head Island," "Long Island," and so forth). Caroline produced Ch. Willow Bank Gunner, sired by Peter.

E. F. Rivinus of Philadelphia imported Speedwell Boine and Onyx of Emley in 1933. MacGregor of Three Acres, the first American-bred champion, was their offspring, as were the two foundation bitches who went to James Thompson (Willow Loch) in Minnesota. Mr. Rivinus started writing the Golden column in the AKC Kennel Gazette in 1938 and was one of the few Easterners to run his Goldens in Field Trials both licensed and sanctioned. His Stubbings Golden Melissa had a number of placements in sanctioned trials, and her offspring Sporting Hill Towhead was shown, and placed in the Sporting Group.

In Massachusetts, Mrs. A. W. Smith had imported from England Ottershaw Norma and Donkelve Punch. They produced, in 1935, Ch. Alexander (called Spur) and Ch. Frieda, called Vanity. Shot of Little Hill, sired by Eng. Ch. Davie of Yelme, was brought over in 1941, a refugee from the London blitz. Spur grew to dislike Shot intensely, and for the sake of peace in the household (all were housedogs; there was no kennel), Spur was given to Ted Rehm of the Taramar kennels. Mrs. Smith bred several generations from Vanity (Ch. Frieda), using the affix Little Hill. Many appear in early pedigrees of Eastern dogs. Ch. Frieda was the first Golden to place in the Group at Westminster (1941). Mrs. Smith did not consider herself primarily a breeder, merely an owner with a deep appreciation for the best qualities of the Golden. Her daughter remembers Vanity as a particularly wise and diplomatic Golden, and Spur as a lovable galoot who was often slightly befuddled but always happily willing.

The Smith family lived in Beverly, Massachusetts, and acquired Goldens after Mrs. Smith saw one in England and became enchanted with the breed.

Donkelve Punch (by Ch. Donkelve Jester) was bought by Mrs. Smith in 1932 but not registered with AKC until 1935. Ottershaw Norma, imported in 1934, was a granddaughter of Ch. Cubbington Diver and also traced back directly to the second Lord Tweedmouth's Conon (or Conan). In Mrs. Smith's later litters, the prefix Little Hill was used. From Vanity bred to Widgeon of Fernova came Ch. Little Hill Miranda and others bred into the Little Hill lines, William Harvey's Twin Hill kennel, and Ted Rehm's Taramar line.

William Harvey was a dog man of the old school. He ran his own Twin Hill kennel, and served as kennel man and handler for Ted Rehm and also for Mrs. Smith when needed. Emily Smith Cain remembers him very well:

> He was an exact, proper, clever, kindly, but not effusive person; medium height, medium weight, gray hair cropped close and combed flat on his head. My recollection is that he wore, or very nearly wore, a tie in the kennel; which is to say, he gave the illusion of wearing a tie; he was always in proper slacks, a shirt, etc.; he had the air of a very competent and low-key crafts-man, a professional, which he was. His kennel was comprised of perhaps ten long and sunny, yet shaded and very clean runs; kennels nicely orga-nized; his set-up was very good, just beyond his modest and very neat house.
>
> Our dogs always went to Harvey for whelping, and mother and week-or-so-old babies appeared as if brought by the stork to be adored by us and especially by me. They also went there to board, and also to be shown.

Mr. Harvey handled the Smith and Rehm Goldens at shows. Emily Cain has some fascinating photographs of Mr. Harvey showing Miranda; with them are some of the other early Goldens shown in the East being posed on the judging block, a low wooden platform upon which the dogs stood. When Harvey's son, William A. Harvey Jr., married Ted Rehm's daughter Sanchia, it was felt to be entirely appropriate. Both later became well known as AKC judges.

IN THE WEST

Initially, of course, there were Sam Magoffin's Rockhaven dogs, based in Vancouver, Canada, and registered with both CKC and AKC. Speedwell Pluto completed his American championship in 1932. Wilderness Tangerine and Rockhaven Harold also completed their U.S. titles under Magoffin's owner-ship. In 1935, R. E. Everly of Carnation Farms acquired Can. Ch. Rockhaven Mermaid, who was then bred to her half-brother Harold and to Can. Ch. Rockhaven Rust. Carnation Farms owned numbers of dogs of various breeds, many of whom were used in helping develop Carnation Company's com-mercial dog foods.

Later, Charles Snell's Oakcreek kennel (Hillsboro, Oregon) would be a prominent kennel in the Northwest, with many well-known dogs, including the incomparable trial winner FC Oakcreek's Van Cleve, Can. Ch. and

Am. FC Stalingrad Express, Victorious of Roedare and the imported Toby of Yelme.

In California, Peter Jackson owned the Blue Leader Kennels in Santa Barbara. Blue Leader was a very large kennel with multiple breeds that were shown throughout the country. Eng. Ch. Marine of Woolley was imported at age five, as well as a young bitch from the same kennel, Trace of Woolley. Sam Magoffin bred to Marine, producing Can. Ch. Rockhaven Judy, foundation of the Woodend kennels in Minnesota, and Marine also sired Petan Rip Tide, an attractive dog who can be found behind many California Goldens of the 1940s and 1950s.

THE FOUNDATION IN THE U.S.

These dogs of the 1930s and early 1940s represented a variety of bloodlines. In the Midwest, emphasis was on the Golden as a working retriever. The darker-colored Rockhaven dogs were the most influential, continuing the dark, close-coated, good-working dog who was favored in the 1920s and 1930s in England. Other imports such as those of the Wallaces were also dual-purpose dogs. In a very few years, Richard Ryan could report that some 98 of 267 entries in the fall trial circuit of 1939 were Goldens, and they took 25 of the 57 awards.

In the East, Goldens were of more varied bloodlines and types, and the primary interest was in showing rather than working. Relatively few Easterners trialled their Goldens. For the Midwesterners, work as a hunting dog was primary, Field Trials were to demonstrate working skills, and shows were of less importance. As might be suspected, this made for some dissension between factions in the East and West.

E. F. Rivinus, columnist in the Kennel Gazette, was one Easterner with a broader outlook. He commented in October 1940:

> I feel strongly that we must keep type always in mind. There must not be both a working Golden and a show Golden. . . . No matter how closely we read the Standard, we cannot hope to produce an ideal type unless we understand the work for which our dog must be ideal.
>
> To all members East and West let me say that it is your duty as members of the Golden Retriever Club of America to advance the breed in every way. We have a great working dog bred for years to conform to a standard which in its essence describes the dog most suited for retrieving work. A dog which can take Best in Show is only a worthy Golden Retriever if he will go into December water to get his second duck. A Field Trial Champion is worthless for breeding purposes if he does not conform to the Breed Standard.
>
> The future of the Golden Retrievers in America is now the responsibility of the leading breeders and exhibitors. The kennel names . . . [of] today

will be the foundation for the future, and will mean to coming generations what such names as Noranby and Speedwell mean to us.

We can be eternally grateful to those English kennels that no one name represents a working strain and that no one name represents show stock. This is a trust we must carry on. We still have the Golden Retriever which these breeders have given us. Our opportunities for furthering the breed are unlimited if we make the effort.

More than fifty years later, these words are as meaningful as when first printed.

chapter 5

After the War: The Modern Era in the United States

THE WAR YEARS AND AFTER

World War II affected dog affairs in North America substantially, although not nearly as severely as in Great Britain. Rationing meant that gasoline and tires were difficult to obtain, and travel by train was not an easy option; meat was hard to get, but some commercially prepared dog foods were available. The Americans were never threatened with invasion, nor did they suffer the devastation of bombings as did the British.

Dog Shows and Field Trials continued in a limited way. There were far fewer shows than we are accustomed to, fewer than 100 a year, and shows were considered major events, even if the entry was quite small by today's standards. Many young men first learned dog training as handlers in the Canine Corps, and a number of them continued as trainers after the war, in Obedience, Field work, security or other areas.

Golden Retrievers in the U.S. had been established as a separate breed less than ten years before the start of World War II. In 1941, 183 Goldens were registered with the AKC. However, the main Golden breeders were determined to put the Golden on a firm footing as a working retriever, and in spite of the war, did so. In many Trials, Goldens made up as much as half the entries and sometimes more than half of the placements. Goldens such as the National Champions King Midas of Woodend and Shelter Cove Beauty made Goldens a strong force in the field.

Gilnockie Coquette, Ralph Boalt's daughter of Am. Eng. Ch. Bingo of Yelme x Can. Ch. Rockhaven Russet, wasted no time or effort in shows or trials, but in the whelping box became the cornerstone of Stilrovin and produced show, field and Dual champions as well as outstanding producers. As previously mentioned, foundation kennels such as Goldwood, Des Lacs,

Eng. Ch. Dorcas Glorious of Slat (born 1943) was an influential sire. His descendants include many Goldens throughout the world with high achievements in both field and show. One was Eng. Irish Dual Ch. David of Westley, the only Golden to earn the Dual Ch. title in two countries.

Tonkahof, Woodend, Beavertail (later Gunnerman), Shelter Cove and Golden Valley developed the breed in the Midwest, primarily on the Rockhaven/ Gilnockie lines plus Roedare from Canada, and some of the Yelme imports.

DES LACS

Bart Foster first encountered Golden Retrievers in North Dakota where he was employed by the U.S. Fish and Wildlife Service at the Des Lacs National Wildlife Refuge. Needing a hunting dog, he purchased a puppy sired by Giltway Strike*** from Vernon Johnson's Shelter Cove Kennels in western Minnesota. She was registered as DES LACS LASSIE. A few months later the Fosters were transferred to the Upper Mississippi River Refuge at Winona, Minnesota. By nine months of age, Lassie had placed second in an informal Field Trial against some thirty-five dogs of all ages, and Bart was hooked on Goldens.

The 1946 GRCA National Field Trial and show were to be held in Fargo, North Dakota, and never having seen a dog show, Bart entered Lassie in that as well as in the Derby Stake. The night before the trial, Lassie was ill, so she did not run in the Derby. She recovered enough to place third in Novice bitches at the show, and Bart was approached by a distinguished-looking gentleman

Am. Can. Ch. Des Lacs Lassie CD* was the first Golden bitch to go Best in Show in North America, and the first to win the National Specialty twice (1948 and 1949). She was also a hard-working retriever used both in hunting and in conservation work, and a GRCA Outstanding Dam.

who asked whether the young Golden was for sale. It was Ted Rehm of Taramar kennels in Massachusetts, and the sum he offered was ten times what Bart had paid for Lassie, but the offer was politely refused. She was "family" and not for sale. But Ted Rehm's comments about Lassie's potential for greatness stuck with Bart, and after a few months he contacted professional handler Hollis Wilson to show her. She completed her championship at the 1947 GRCA National and in the next thirteen months won twenty-two Sporting Group placements and a Best in Show—the first for a Golden bitch.

From the yellow ribbon in 1946, to Winners in 1947, Lassie took Best of Breed at the GRCA National in 1948. Best of Opposite Sex went to Ted Rehm's English import, Ch. Noranby Baloo of Taramar. The gracious Ted Rehm offered his congratulations, saying "Remember what I told you at Fargo two years ago? I have watched Lassie's record all the way." To further sweeten this win, Lassie's litter sister Patricia of Rochester, acquired by Bart Foster only days before the show, went Winners Bitch. And in 1949 Lassie repeated her win of Best of Breed at the GRCA National.

Between shows and several stints in the whelping box, Lassie was not only a hunting dog but was also used by Bart at the Wildlife Refuge to find ducklings to be banded. She earned a CD and produced seven show champions, more than any Golden bitch previously. All Des Lacs breedings were

June Atkinson's Wynford and Holway Goldens are a dynasty in working retrievers, accounting for the great majority of English Field Trial Champions since WWII (including two National Championships) and also contributing strongly to US and Canadian performance bloodlines.

based on Lassie and Patricia, combined with the dogs Ch. Des Lacs Laddie of Rip's Pride (grandson of FCh Rip) and the imported English-bred dog, Ch. Gilder of Elsiville. Des Lacs Goldens performed notably in many areas of the country, and also became foundation stock for other breeders.

ACROSS THE COUNTRY

In the 1950s and 1960s, other kennels were established in the Midwest. Merle and Esther Long's Indian Knolls Kennels in Illinois were based largely on Shur Shot and some of the later Rockhaven dogs. Anne Christiansen's Ch. Indian Knoll's Colonel UD*** (born 1953) was one of the first, and few, Ch-UD dogs to become a qualified field dog. Ch. Indian Knolls Roc Cloud, UD, was Bill Worley's first Golden, a notable producer and founder of the Sun Dance lines, now carried on by Bill's stepdaughter, Lisa Halcomb. "Buck," as Roc Cloud was called, bred to Jim Mardis's Sidram bitches from various field lines, produced some outstanding performers. Ch. Sun Dance's bronze was a National Specialty winner.

Jim Mardis of Muncie, Indiana, started with a trim, dark bitch sired by Ch. Zag of Sandywood out of Featherquest Patton (a daughter of Goldwood Toby UD) named Ch. Sidram Shining Star. Both sides of her pedigree were all Minnesota-Wisconsin breeding. Jim later bred to several outstanding Field Champions, producing many good working dogs. Ch. Sidram Sampson CD,

Eng. Ch. Boltby Skylon (born 1951), bred and owned by Mrs. R. Harrison. Important as show dog and as sire, Skylon stamped his descendants with his distinctive style and color, influencing breed type in Great Britain and also quite strongly in Scandinavia and in parts of Canada.

a Group winner, and Sidram Selectric UDT WC, with a Group placement, were sired by Dual Ch. Squawkie Hill Dapper Dexter out of Sidram Selected**, a daughter of NFCh Ready Always of Marianhill. Selectric proved sterile, but other Sidram dogs can still be found in some pedigrees.

As Goldens spread throughout the Midwest—Iowa, Illinois, Indiana, Michigan, Ohio—emphasis was always on the working retriever. Conformation was not neglected, but working ability, whether in hunting or Obedience trials, was paramount. In Ohio, Harold Kaufmann's R. R. (**Rolling Ridge**) dogs were based on daughters of FC Goldwood Tuck. Charles A. Frank in Detroit, Michigan, had three generations of top Obedience winners in his Ch. Duckerbird Atomic UD, D. Atomic II UD and Ch. D. Atomic III UD: The first "Tommy" was Stilrovin/Sheltercove breeding, and Tommy II by him out of an R. R. bitch. Charlie Frank was a fixture in Midwestern Obedience competition for some twenty years; after the Atomics, he campaigned Braewick's Pecos Bill UD and then an American Water Spaniel, Americana Wahoo, UD. Hearing Charlie yell "Wahoooo!" was quite an experience!

In Iowa (she later moved to Idaho), Mrs. Russell S. Peterson's **Golden Knolls** kennel produced quite a few well-known conformation winners, including Ch. Golden Knolls Shur Shot CD and his son Ch. Golden Knolls King Alphonzo. Hollis Wilson campaigned both Shur Shot and King to exceptional show records (some forty Bests in Show between them), and they were a large part of the trend toward very large, rather settery dogs that became of such concern. In spite of this variation in type, many of the dogs retained good working instincts, as witnessed in Ch. Golden Knolls Town Talk CD** (Ch. Golden Knoll's Shur Shot x Ch. Des Lacs Goldie CD**) and King's two *** sons, Ch. Sprucewood's Chore Boy*** and Ch. Sprucewood's Chuck O'Luck***. King himself had some field training with his first owner, Andre Perry. Both Chore Boy and Chuck were out of Maureen and Bud Zwang's Ch. Chee Chee of Sprucewood.

Chee Chee was a very attractive bitch and a good winner in her own right, twice Best of Breed at the GRCA National Specialty and the second bitch to enter the GRCA Show Dogs Hall of Fame. She was bred three times to King Alphonzo, and from the combination came sixteen champions. Chee Chee's granddaughter Ch. Sprucewood's Harvest Sugar would equal that achievement, making the **Sprucewood** name very influential for many years.

In the East, Reinhard Bischoff based his **Lorelei** dogs on Midwestern lines through Dual Ch. Stilrovin Rip's Pride bred to his first Golden, Greenfield Jollye, producing the notable Ch. Lorelei's Golden Rip**. Greenfield Jollye, called Lorelei, was not pretty; indeed, at one show the judge withheld a ribbon from her. However, as the daughter of a Chateau D'Or dog, she carried old basic bloodlines and, bred to Stilrovin Rip's Pride, a grandson of FC Rip, she produced three champions: Lorelei's Golden Rip, Lorelei's Golden Anne and Dufy's Golden Desire. Bisch acquired a bitch he named Lorelei's Golden Tanya, who would prove a tremendous producer. Tanya's pedigree was based on some of the earliest imports to the East Coast, her grandsires being Ted Rehm's Ch. Alexander (Donkelve Punch x Ottershaw Norma) and Ch. Headisland Peter (Eng. Ch. Prince of Dewstraw x Annette of Dewstraw). Tanya later in life went to Bill and Flo Gamble's **Aureal Wood** kennel and can be found in those pedigrees as well.

"Bisch," one of the breed's authentic characters, was active with Goldens for a period of nearly thirty years from the mid-1940s until his retirement and move to South Africa. Among his last Lorelei titlists were Ch. Lorelei's Reza Odu and Ch. Lorelei's Zajac Archer, both sons of his lovely Ch. Lorelei's Fez Ti ZaZa. ZaZa and her sister ZuZu are the only Golden brace to win Best Brace in Show at the Westminster Kennel Club.

From Lorelei Kennels came foundation stock for other prominent Eastern lines such as Marshgrass, Star Spray, High Farms, Feather Fetch, Nerrissida and others. Most well-known of Bisch's dogs is the famed Ch-AFCh Golden Rockbottom UD, the first Golden to achieve this combination of titles and probably the only Field Champion to win a Best in Show . . . and all handled by his owner-breeder.

Midas' Timba was a well-known sire in the East in the late 1940s. His dam was a sister to Goldwood Toby UD, and his sire a son of Ch. Alexander, hence he combined old Midwestern lines with Eastern from imports. Timba produced five champions, including the MacNaught's producer of Marshgrass champions, Ch. Golden Lassie III, and the Best in Show winner Ch. Prince Alexander (not to be confused with his great-grandsire, Ch. Alexander).

The **Taramar** kennel, owned by Theodore Rehm, had been established in Massachusetts since the mid-1930s. Most of their stock was based on the Little Hill dogs of Mrs. A. W. Smith (breeder of Ch. Alexander and Ch. Frieda). William Harvey served as kennelman for both the Rehms and Mrs. Smith, taking care of grooming, handling and boarding, and providing the wise advice of an experienced dog man. In the late 1940s Ted Rehm imported from England the dog (Ch.) Noranby Baloo of Taramar, a litter brother to

Ch. Lorelei's Fez Ti ZaZa, bred, owned and handled by Reinhard Bischoff, was exceptional in a era when bitches seldom took top awards. She had two Group 1sts and two 2nds, and won both a Best of Breed and a BOS at GRCA Nationals, and produced a Show Dog Hall of Fame winner.

Noranby Destiny, who would become the first Eng. Dual Ch. Bitch. Baloo was a very sound, handsome Golden with a lovely personality. He traveled with the Rehms to Bermuda and other places, and went with them when they moved to Arizona. He was used at stud only a little, which is rather a loss as his get were excellent Goldens with strong working capabilities. A Taramar bitch was also the dam of the first Golden in New England to qualify in All-Age Field Trials, Rachel Page Elliott's Tennessee's Jack Daniels***.

Rachel Page Elliott is known to all Golden devotees, and many others as well, for her pioneering work in analyzing canine structure and movement. Her interest in the subject led to her filming a vast number of dogs of all breeds and types; she then developed a series of lectures with slow-motion picture studies, a book and several motion picture/video presentations on different breeds, including the Golden Retriever. The Golden who started Pagey on this path was Goldwood Toby, the first Golden Utility Dog. His descendants proved their worth as practical workers and Obedience titlists. Pagey has also bred and shown a number of Goldens to show championships, with the **Featherquest** prefix.

Josiah and Marilu Semans' **Golden Pine** Kennels' first notable Golden was Ch. Duke of Rochester II, CD. By Happy Rochester x Beauty Valle, Duke was of Midwestern breeding. "Rusty" made quite a splash at the Westminster show in 1952, when judge Beatrice Godsol placed him Best of Breed from the Open class, over the top winning champions of the day. Rusty, through his daughter Ch. Wessala Pride of Golden Pine, will be found in most of the original Golden Pines pedigrees. He was tragically killed in a fire that destroyed the Semans' home. Pride, bred to Rockbottom's son Ch. Little Joe of Tigathoe***, produced some top winners, including Ch. Golden Pine's Brown Bear, Ch. Golden Pines Easy Ace and Ch. Golden Pines Bambi's Lady, the latter two also outstanding producers. Brown Bear died young, before making a mark as a sire. Later Golden Pines bitches combined with Ch. Misty

Right: Ch. Little Joe of Tigathoe*** (by AFC-Ch Lorelei's Golden Rockbottom UD x Ch. Gold Button of Catawba***) winning BB at the 1957 GRCA Eastern Region Specialty, handled by his breeder/owner, "Torch" Flinn. Left is his daughter Ch. Golden Pines Bambi's Lady, BOS, owned by Golden Pines Kennels. Many of today's winners can trace their pedigrees back to these influential Goldens.

Morn's Sunset and his half-brother Ch. Cummings Gold Rush Charlie, creating a vast number of show-winning descendants.

High Farms kennel in Connecticut (Ralph and Ruth Worrest) developed a strong line of bench winners utilizing local lines, largely Lorelei, with some field-bred bitches and an outcross to the English import, Ch. Crusader of Carthew. Ruth's son and daughter-in-law Bob and Ginny Worrest also ran High Farms dogs in Field Trials. High Farms provided foundation stock for several other Eastern kennels, and for Laura Ellis Kling's Laurell kennels (Ohio).

The West Coast was not without Golden activity. Eric Johnson, originally from Minnesota, relocated to California and took with him Ch. Czar of Wildwood, a son of FCh Stilrovin Superspeed out of a daughter of FCh Rip. Czar ran in some Derby Trials in Wisconsin but in California proved to be a smasher as a show dog. For some years he and his descendants ruled the rings in California, and his grandson Ch. Czargold's Storm King was successful on the East coast. Unfortunately, too close breeding on Czar resulted in head type and coat that were not good—with low ears, narrow heads and roman noses very evident, and coats soft and silky in many cases—but they did catch the judges' eyes.

Deerflite Selina (Eng. Ch. Concord of Yeo x Deerflite Pheasant). "Pippa," imported from England and owned by John and Anne Bissette, was an important foundation bitch for their Beaumaris kennel in Colorado.

In the Pacific Northwest, Oakcreek (owned by Charles E. Snell) was a strong force, particularly in Field; the imported Toby of Yelme (a grandson of Gilder and Quick of Yelme) produced FC-AFC Oakcreek's Sir Dorchester, sire of two FCs; the balance of Oakcreek's breeding was based on bitches of Beavertail breeding plus others of similar background. In 1948 Oakcreek advertised no fewer than eight dogs at stud, including Victorious of Roedare, the sire of FC-AFC Oakcreek's Van Cleve, Canadian National Field Trial Champion and record holder for many years for Field points acquired. Unfortunately for the breed, he proved sterile.

A NEW DIRECTION IN THE U.S.

American bloodlines in the 1940s and 1950s had been based primarily on the **Rockhaven/Gilnockie** breedings, with an infusion from **Roedare**. There were a number of English imports also; some blended well with the basic American lines and were maintained; other imports met with indifference or even dislike for being "too different" from the American dogs, who at that time were often tall, dark to very dark (even approaching Irish Setter red in color), sloping in topline, flat-sided and with narrow tapering heads. The English were tending toward the lighter-colored, blocky dog with a level topline. And while there were certainly dogs on both sides of the ocean who fell between the extremes, some of the imported Goldens who could have been used with benefit were either not made use of or simply did not produce.

About 1950 a number of American breeders, members of the Golden Retriever Club of America, voiced their concern about the type of Golden who was dominating the show rings. Some of the winning dogs were very large, far too large to be efficient retrievers. With dogs approaching twenty-seven inches in height winning Sporting Groups, and of a type far removed from the original, useful sort, the GRCA undertook an extended discussion

Eng. Am. Ch. Figaro of Yeo. A very sound dog of exceptional breed type, Figaro won the GRCA National Specialty in 1963. He was owned by Mrs. C. W. Englehard, whose Cragmount kennel was well known in the 1960s.

of the Breed Standard in the Club's publication, the *Golden Retriever News*. Much of this discussion was under the editorship of Bart Foster (Des Lacs Kennels) and Henry Norton (Tonkahof Kennels), men experienced in all areas of Golden Retriever activity, including practical field work.

A survey was made of a number of champion-titled Goldens, gathering various measurements. Several proposed revisions were discussed and eventually resulted in the adoption of a completely rewritten Breed Standard that was much more comprehensive than the original. The revised Standard made very clear what the Golden was to be, while still allowing for a range of variation to accommodate differences inevitable in a country the size of the U.S., with widely varying terrains in which the dog may be asked to work.

With the new Standard, the trend toward the oversized Golden was effectively quashed, although for some time the settery sorts still did considerable winning. There were a number of English imports brought over in the late 1950s and 1960s; they were generally more wisely used than some of the earlier imports, and more breeders developed an appreciation of the type being developed in England. Not all the imports were successful; for example, Eng. Ch. Figaro of Yeo was a dog of truly exquisite breed type and soundness, and while he produced at least eight litters in England, he produced very few litters in the U.S. However, he did serve as a wonderful illustration of what classic Golden Retriever type could be. His English-bred son Am. Ch. Orlando of Yeo produced the fine brood bitch Am. Can. Ch. Beckwith's Frolic of Yeo CDX.

THE GOLDEN RETRIEVER CLUB OF AMERICA

The GRCA was a strong parent club and through the 1950s oversaw the formation of active local groups in various areas. The Eastern Region had an active group in the Northeast, and in the Western Region, Washington and California were centers of activity. In the Central Region, Illinois and Michigan were the first recognized Chapters (1956), then Wisconsin, Nebraska and

Iowa. Within a few years there were Chapters of the GRCA throughout the country, until in the early 1960s the AKC decreed that all Chapters must be autonomous local clubs, earning the right to hold events in their own name. Many local clubs still kept close ties to the parent club, with a high percentage of members belonging to both organizations. The development of the *Golden Retriever News* as a means of communication within the Golden fancy helped this cohesiveness immeasurably, as did the later implementation of the "member club" system, with local clubs appointing delegates to receive and transmit communication between local and parent clubs.

1955 marked the first GRCA National Specialty to be held outside the Minnesota-Wisconsin area; Cincinnati, Ohio, was the place. In 1963 the first National Specialty was held in the Eastern Region; in 1969, the first in the Western Region. Since the 1970s, the National events have rotated among the three Regions, giving Golden folks in all corners of the country a chance to attend a National. And as the Golden population has grown, so has the National. From the first events, where the Field Trial was the main attraction, with a bench show held the evening before the trial, and an informal field dinner ("field dress requested") where awards were made for the trophy winners, the National has grown to an extravaganza of seven to ten days of showcasing all facets of Golden activity.

During this period, through the 1950s and the '60s, the Golden Retriever was still largely maintained as an all-round, versatile dog. At the Nationals, many dogs who showed on Friday night ran in the Field Trials on Saturday and Sunday. In 1957 the Best of Breed winner, Ch. Rusina's Mr. Chips**, earned a CM (Certificate of Merit) in the Qualifying Stake the next day.

By the late 1960s things were changing, not only in Goldens but in purebred dogs in general. The expansion of suburbia, increased leisure time and discretionary income, improved highways and the Interstate system, the commonality of the automobile—many factors contributed to the phenomenal growth of interest in purebred dogs and participation by one- and two-dog owners in all forms of organized dog activity. Training classes popped up all over, giving the dog-owner not only guidance in civilizing the household canine but opening to the novice a glimpse of worlds hitherto unknown. So many, many dog fanciers started the same way—taking the unruly beast to training class; getting drawn into showing in obedience, then conformation (which often led to the acquisition of another dog or dogs); and, in the natural course of events, breeding.

POPULARITY GROWS

Once an obscure minority breed, by 1974 the Golden was instantly identifiable. President Gerald Ford's "Liberty," a Golden Retriever in the White House, undoubtedly gave a solid push to the popularity of the breed, although the trend was already there. Soon increased registrations put the Golden in the "top ten" in numbers registered. Unfortunately, in 1974 the 20,933 Goldens registered in that year alone exceeded *all* Goldens registered in the twenty-five years from 1932 to 1957.

The increase of activity in all phases of the dog sport meant increased opportunities for the owners of Goldens, with their wide range of talents. The dogs who had been so carefully bred for a wonderful capacity to work for people were proving to excel in Obedience, shows and Tracking, as well as in Field Trials.

Ironically, as skills and level of competition increased in each area, the Golden gradually became less of a generalist and more of a specialist. Strikingly different types evolved for different purposes. The big winners in each area of competition were used in many breeding programs, often creating new styles and trends. Whether a show dog could retrieve was immaterial to some; whether the Obedience dog looked like a Golden mattered not; and the seeking of that upbeat, energetic, indefatigable ring competitor in many cases produced dogs who were not just "up" in the ring but were overactive "showing fools."

BREED CONCERNS

Another force that had great effect upon the breed was the awakened concern about genetic defects. First, *hip dysplasia* was recognized as a crippler of dogs. Some dogs worked successfully because their gallant hearts overcame faulty hips; others could not.

About 1956 the GRCA made the membership aware of this problem, largely through the efforts of the GRCA Secretary, Verneca Bower. With the advice and assistance of concerned veterinary radiologists, Mrs. Bower's committee worked with extraordinary diligence in establishing the GRCA's Advisory Council on Hip Dysplasia. Breeders, alerted to the problem, started having their dogs x-rayed and the X rays read by the Council's panel of three radiologists. Soon all responsible breeders routinely x-rayed all breeding stock.

By 1966 the Advisory Council had been absorbed into the newly formed Orthopedic Foundation for Animals, set up along the same lines for the interpretation of radiographs for all breeds. *Breeders of Golden Retrievers, along with those of Labrador Retrievers and German Shepherd Dogs, were the strongest supporters of the OFA as a tool in lessening the incidence of hip dysplasia.* Their diligence has definitely resulted in a general lessening of the severity of dysplasia; it is not nearly as common to see crippled dogs as was the case forty years ago. Old-timers can remember incidents such as the field champion who retrieved with speed and style but had to be carried back to the car and lifted into the crate, or six-month-old puppies who could not get to their feet without help. In the attempt to rid the breed of such unsoundness, a number of otherwise excellent dogs were eliminated from breeding and their genetic diversity lost.

Eye problems were less obvious a problem in Goldens; concern was based upon the ravages of hereditary eye diseases in other breeds such as Irish Setters and Cocker Spaniels, where early blindness due to different diseases was a widespread problem. Early attention and detection of juvenile cataracts and progressive retinal atrophy may well have prevented eye defects in Goldens from gaining as wide an occurrence as in some other breeds. Other hereditary or suspected-to-be hereditary problems were also discovered—there's a saying that "if you go looking for problems, you'll find them." Greater awareness and better means of detection and diagnosis have enabled breeders to add more to their list of concerns, making the breeders' work even more difficult.

The development of breed subtypes for specialized competition and the concern with hereditary defects widened the gap between the general population of Goldens and the quality dogs produced by breeders with a definite goal in mind. Even though the dogs produced by knowledgeable, responsible breeders increased, the numbers of Goldens produced by the uneducated, unconcerned general public increased five- to tenfold more. For each puppy kept by the responsible breeder, there were probably five to eight puppies owned by John or Jane Q. Public, who thought it would be nice to have a litter of cute puppies from their dear "Sandy" bred to "Prince" next door.

THE 1970S AND LATER

By 1974 registrations had passed the 20,000 mark (almost exactly ten times the number in 1954) and remained on an upward course that would continue for another twenty years. Along with registrations came a corresponding increase in activities in all areas: show, Obedience, Tracking and Field. The most rapidly increasing area was the "pet" sector—dogs whose owners did not participate in any organized activities at all. In this sector we find a large percentage of dogs from casual breeders, whose primary and perhaps only reason for breeding was that they had access to two dogs of the same breed.

As Goldens became popular and marketable, the commercial breeders jumped on the bandwagon and added Goldens to their unhappy collection of breeding animals. Most of these people were unfamiliar with such considerations as soundness and temperament; those qualities were far less important than the opportunity to make money. Commercial breeders could range from the "backyard breeder" with a couple of mediocre bitches bred to whatever neighborhood Golden was available, to the wholesale "puppy mills" who kept a resident stud dog to service as many as thirty or forty bitches, all kept at a minimum of expense, generally in deplorable conditions. One might also include as commercial breeders some who operated at a somewhat higher level

Am. Can. Bda. Ch. Cummings Gold-Rush Charlie, born 1970. Professionally handlled by Bill Trainor, Charlie set an unprecedented record for show wins by a Golden. Among his many champion offspring were the sisters Ch. Russo's Pepperhill Poppy, a Specialty winner, and Ch./OTCh. Russo's Gold-Rush Sensation, the first dog of any breed to hold both show and Obedience championship titles.

of expense (though often not of ethics), perhaps getting some show titles on dogs, yet still breeding many litters each year and selling large numbers of puppies at substantial prices, and sired by the latest and most in-demand stud dogs.

The '70s were dominated by three closely related dogs, Ch. Misty Morn's Sunset CD TD WC, Ch. Cummings Gold-Rush Charlie and Ch. Wochica's Okeechobee Jake. The first two were both sired by Ch. Sunset's Happy Duke, and Jake was a son of Misty Morn's Sunset.

"Sam" (Ch. Misty Morn's Sunset CD TD WC), owned by Peter Lewesky, was a real show dog and a prolific sire. Charlie, owned by Larry and Ann Johnson, set a record for Best in Show wins in the breed. Sam's son, Jake, was one of only two dogs to win the National Specialty three times ('72, '74 and '77); he was owned by Susan Taylor. Handled by skilled professionals, all three were dogs of great personality, flashy coat and movement, and the "ring presence" that caught the judges' eyes. They won, they impressed people, and many bitches were sent to them. The three produced some 266 champions or UD dogs, half of these by Sam. Charlie became the cornerstone of the Johnsons' **Gold-Rush** kennels, a large breeding/showing operation. Sam's son, Ch. Wochica's Okeechobee Jake, also accounted for a considerable number of champions. From these three dogs and their descendants developed a number of influential kennels and sublines that set the style for the Golden show dog for many years.

Unfortunately, generations of not very knowledgeable breeding for a superficial "look" and glamor led to exaggerations and extremes, quite literally changing the breed. In the late 1970s and into the 1980s, show types tended toward a large, very heavy-boned dog with a great deal of coat. Some winning dogs were openly advertised as ninety-five pounds in weight. While the Standard's size disqualification did manage to keep height generally under the twenty-five-inch limit, some of these dogs were so ponderous they were not suited for any practical use. Along with the heaviness came shorter bones and less angulation.

Eventually the big, coarse dogs had to give way to a new type in the '80s: the real glamor dogs, with profuse, flowing coats and extreme animation. Speed was more impressive than an effortless, correct gait. Extreme coats required a great deal of grooming, and techniques of extensive trimming and barbering were developed in order to take advantage of the soft, profuse coats with so much feathering. Too often, the dog with a proper, practical, easy-care coat was overlooked in favor of the "pretty" ones. Correct, functional structure became less valued than "attitude" and showmanship. A few lines of correct types still carried on, fortunately, in some areas of the country, though often not getting the recognition they deserved.

In the field, changes were also taking place. In order to be in consideration with the Labradors, whose intense style had set the pace at Trials, Goldens had to be selected for speed and style as well. To have any chance of success in Trials, Goldens were trained intensely and arduously; new training techniques speeded up training and could develop amazing performers.

FORM AND FUNCTION COMBINED

Field

Several Golden breeders went at the task of creating Goldens specifically for success at Field Trials. Mrs. George H. Flinn, far better known as "Torch," has been a familiar face at Field Trials since before many present-day triallers were born. From her first successful litter, which produced show champions who placed in Trials, Torch has bred, bought and owned a series of Field Trial winners and champions of exceeding distinction. The providential breeding of Tigathoe's Chickasaw*** to FC-AFC Bonnie Brooks Elmer in 1971 produced the breed's last U.S. Dual Champion (and three other FC-AFCs).

Jackie Mertens (**Topbrass**) started in Obedience, then founded a successful Field line starting with show-titled bitches of show and field breeding, bred to proven Field winners. She made good use of AFC Holway Barty as a sire, producing among others the first Golden to win the National Amateur

Two of the "famous four" by FC-AFC Bonnie Brooks Elmer x Tigathoe's Chickasaw***, born in 1970. Left, FC-AFC Tigathoe's Kiowa II (Pat Sadler); right, FC-AFCh Tigathoe's Tonga (Ray Ernest). They and their siblings FC-AFC Tigathoe's Magic Marker and FC-AFC Tigathoe's Funky Farquar (later Dual Ch) all qualified for the National Amateur Retriever Trial.

Championship, NAFC Topbrass Cotton. The Topbrass name is also found on many successful Obedience Trial competitors.

FC-AFC Misty's Sungold Lad CDX, trained by young Val (Fisher) Walker and always amateur handled, set records in Field Trials and brought new blood to Field lines from his sire, (the imported) Sherrydan Tag. AFC Holway Barty and other Holway imports gave great style and trainability when bred with bitches of established American Field lines. Barty produced an exceptional number of Field titlists and qualified Field Trial dogs, and outstanding Obedience winners as well.

Obedience

The qualities that made a great Field worker also were useful in the Obedience performer, particularly the ability to absorb concentrated, often rigorous, training; and many top Obedience dogs came from Field-bred stock. When the Obedience Trial Championship was created in 1977, there was renewed emphasis on the competitive Obedience dog. Ironically, the Obedience hotshots so eager to be the first OTCh all had to step aside for a sweet, ladylike Golden Retriever named OTCh Moreland's Golden Tonka, show-bred (by Ch. Misty Morn's Sunset CD TD WC), owned, trained and handled by the seventy-something Russ Klipple. Although new to most of the then current exhibitors, Russ was certainly no stranger to the Obedience ring, as twenty years earlier he had trained and campaigned several of Betty Strawbridge's Ruanme Goldens to UDs and HSDIT awards. Some of the Obedience zealots criticized Tonka because she was not their idea of the energetic, "hard-driving" Obedience competitor, but Tonka was assured and businesslike; she simply didn't make many mistakes.

The Obedience rings were ruled by Goldens. Goldens in a number of years accounted for a quarter of all Highest Scoring Dog in Trial awards in all-breed competition. Some Goldens set truly phenomenal records, such as Tonka's more than 200 HSDT awards, and OTCh Tanbark's Bristol Creme, winner of more than 5,000 OTCh points (enough for fifty titles). Earlier (1957–1967), Al and Edi Munneke's Am. Can. Ch. Sun Dance's Rusticana UDT, WC, Can. UD) had an Obedience career spanning more than nine years, with dozens of HSDT wins and some 284 first places throughout the country. Goldens dominated the Obedience Champion lists from the time that title was established in 1977 and also consistently take many high placements at the various Obedience "tournaments" that have become popular.

All over the country, and especially in the Midwest, where Goldens and Obedience were so long synonymous, the fast-moving, "hard-driving," energetic Golden was premier. Some came from Field lines (which requires many of the same qualities); some were bred specifically for Obedience competition. In the 1980s, the Golden's place as "the" Obedience breed was challenged by the Border Collie, whose quickness, intelligence and agility makes it quite capable of the highest degree of speed and precision, but Goldens continue to be favorites for this work.

NEW TITLES, NEW OPPORTUNITIES

Expanding interest in all areas, but especially in performance events, led to the development of some new competitions and titles.

Field Trials had developed dog training into an art form. Tests became longer, harder and more complicated, with great emphasis on the dog who not only ran with style and speed but who could hold a line (go in a straight line regardless of hazards and distractions) and handle (obey the handler's whistle and arm signals at any distance). The use of the electronic collar or remote training device gave the field trainer a new and extremely powerful tool—and the opportunity to misuse its power and cause severe stress and pain to the dog. To achieve success in American Field Trials requires a very high commitment in time and finances. The services of a professional trainer will be required at some stage of training; even for the owner-trainer who has the time and resources (birds, training grounds, varied water and terrain), problem-solving with a good professional is invaluable.

After many years of sporting dog people talking about a more realistic alternative to Field Trials, something that the ordinary hunting-dog person could use to demonstrate the capabilities of the useful Field dog, the **Hunting Test** program was created in the early 1980s. The first organized tests were developed by the North American Hunting Retriever Association (NAHRA) and soon adopted by the AKC. NAHRA, having some differences of opinion about the program, moved away from the AKC and established its own separate tests and titles. Both have been very successful, along with the UKC's version as well. At Hunting Tests, the dogs participate noncompetitively; scores are used to determine only whether the dog passes.

There are three levels of testing, with **Junior** being the lowest, then **Senior**, and **Master** as the title for the ultimate hunting retriever. Junior is primarily to show that the dog has the basic aptitudes to do the work, which is more important than the degree of training the dog may have had. Senior level requires considerably more experience and training, as the dog must be steady, do double retrieves and honor. Master is for the dog who can work as a skillful, competent retriever under any conditions. Goldens have done very well in the Hunting Test program, including dogs with no Field Trial experience whatever, and trial dogs seeking other avenues to demonstrate their skills.

There are no placements in Hunting Tests; like Tracking, it is either pass or fail. A requisite number of qualifications earns titles, and it is quite possible for any number of dogs at a test to qualify. (This is sometimes difficult to get across to Field Trial judges, who are so accustomed to having to weed out competitors in order to get placements.)

Tracking tests saw the advent of the **TDX** title for **Advanced Tracking** tests. For this difficult and rewarding achievement, TDX trainers must be a dedicated lot who devote long hours to working with their dogs, often in the worst of weather. The track is longer, older, harder; there are more articles to be found, and more ways to fail. And as if that weren't difficult enough, the AKC (1995) now offers a **Variable Surface Tracking** Test (**VST**), which may make use of urban areas and presents new challenges to trainers and dogs.

In 1994, the AKC instituted a new Obedience title, the **UDX**. The dog must qualify in both Utility and Open class at ten Trials in order to earn this title; it is a means of recognizing and rewarding the dog who is a consistent performer, rather than just the few who score high for the OTCh points or class placements.

Another new area of recognized competition (1994) is **Agility**. Rather like some of the jumping competitions for horses, the dogs follow a course over (and through) various obstacles, with points off for jumping faults and time faults. Again, there are three levels of titles. Goldens who participate in Agility must be well coordinated and athletic, as well as be under excellent control by voice and signal. It is also great fun for all and has great spectator appeal.

In all these areas, the Golden is participating with distinction. There are some signs that at least a small percentage of the people having chosen

Am. Can. Ch. Gayhaven Lldiel, Am. Can. CDX, Am. WC, born 1960. Linebred to the English import Ch. Gilder of Elsiville, Diel was a well-balanced, typey dog who sired 8 U.S. and 17 Canadian champions in a very few litters. He earned his Working Certificate "the old-fashioned way," by completing the requisite tests at a sanctioned field trial.

the Golden as their breed in the 1990s are truly interested in maintaining the multiple capabilities of the breed, not as a group of divergent specialist lines but as a population of useful, sound, good-looking dogs with the capabilities of working well in multiple areas. The advent of new areas of endeavor, as have been mentioned in this chapter, opens a wider field for these versatile dogs and their people, particularly those who want to work their dogs afield but cannot undertake the enormous commitment of money and effort required by Field Trials. Many "show" dogs now participate with distinction in WC/WCX tests and in Hunting Tests, and many who thought themselves strictly practical hunters have been drawn into a wider range of activity.

The **GRCA's** establishment of the **Versatility Certificate** and **Versatility Certificate Excellent** awards was specifically to recognize and encourage Golden Retrievers who demonstrate a broad range of capability in the long-time tradition of the breed. More power to them.

In 1984 the American Kennel Club held an all-breed dog show to celebrate the 100th anniversary of the AKC. Best of Breed and winner of the Sporting Group was Ch. Libra Malagold Coriander, a 4-year-old male owned and handled by Connie Gerstner and bred by Cheryl Blair. Four years later, from the Veterans' Class, Corey won Best of Breed at the National Specialty celebrating the Golden Retriever Club of America's 50th year.

chapter 6

The Breed Standard— with Comments

When Golden Retrievers were first recognized by The Kennel Club in England as a distinct variety, a Descriptive Standard for judges, exhibitors and breeders was decided upon by the Committee of the Golden Retriever Club. This brief document gave the points distinguishing the Golden from other retrievers. It was taken for granted that readers had a working knowledge of dogs' basic structure and functions; therefore, much of what we now consider to be a useful description of structure and movement was simply not thought necessary then.

The Descriptive Standard of the Golden Retriever (Great Britain) before 1936:

Head. Broad in skull, well set on a clean, muscular neck; muzzle powerful and wide, not weak jawed. Good stop. Eyes dark, set well apart, very kindly in expression, with dark rims. Teeth, even, neither under nor overshot. 20

Colour. Rich golden, must not be as dark as the Irish Setter, nor cream coloured. The presence of a few white hairs on chest or toes permissible (white collar or blaze to be penalized). 20

Coat. Flat or wavy. Good undercoat. Dense and water-resisting. 5

Ears. Small and well set-on. 5

Feet. Round and catlike, must not open or splay. 10

Forelegs. Straight, with good bone. 10

Hind Legs. Strong and muscular, well-bent stifle. Hocks well let-down, not cow-hocked. 10

Nose. Should be black, but a light-coloured nose should not debar a dog—
good in other respects—from honours.   5

Tail. Should be straight, not curled at the tip, nor carried over the back.   5

Body. Well balanced, short coupled, deep through the heart. Loins strong;
back ribs must be deep and strong; good second thighs. Shoulders well laid
back and long in the blade.   25

General appearance should be of a symmetrical, active, powerful dog, a good
level mover, sound and well put together, with a kindly expression, not clumsy
nor long in the leg.

The preceding description differentiates the Golden from the other retrievers quite well. The scale of points was primarily to indicate the relative
importance of the various features, not for any type of quantitative scoring
in judging.

We see that great importance was placed on the body, the head, and the
coat and color as the qualities that defined the Golden from other retrievers
and made it unique. We today may feel that this leaves too small an amount
for running gear, and movement has no points allotted to it at all, but in the
period that this description was written, it was taken for granted that the dog
must move properly (as described in the last paragraph of the Standard).
Furthermore, *at that time* the emphasis was on establishing a breed type of
some consistency, and the qualities relating to that goal were of primary
importance.

Goldens as a whole varied considerably in overall build. There were many
who were racy, tucked-up, light-bodied; some with slack toplines, long and
soft in coupling, and with weak rears. Therefore, the stress given to proper
body qualities and the "symmetrical, active, powerful dog, a good level mover,
sound, and well put together, with a kindly expression, not clumsy nor long
in the leg." Head type varied just as much, and it was difficult to keep desired head qualities; the flat-coat influence tended to produce narrow heads
that lacked stop; some were houndy, with drooping flews and lowset ears.
Color varied as well; while some of the early dogs were a bright gold that
would be considered quite correct today, there were also very dark dogs (as
some of the Ingestre dogs, noted as "very red" or "too dark"). And there
were some who entirely lacked black skin pigmentation, having amber eyes
and brown nose.

During the 1920s and into the 1930s, the darker dogs were much more
popular than the light gold ones. The lighter dogs, however, gained acceptance and were acknowledged by the admission of "cream" in the British
Standard about 1936. But my impression is that the "cream" as used then
referred mostly to the admissibility of the pale shadings on gold-colored dogs,
and not to the nearly white dogs we now think of as "cream" colored. The

exact wording was "**Colour**—Any shade of gold or cream, but neither red nor mahogany. The presence of a few white hairs on chest permissible. White collar, feet, toes, or blaze should be penalised."

The aforementioned Standard (prior to the admission of "cream") was also used in the United States until a revision in the 1950s. The GRCA did add a Note (which appeared with the Breed Standard in the 1947 GRCA Yearbook) that "The ideal weights for adult dogs and bitches in good hard condition should be: Dogs, 65–68 lbs.; Bitches, 55–60 lbs., and heights at shoulder: Dogs, 23–24 inches; Bitches, 20½–22 inches." Also, the "General Appearance" paragraph became the first statement in the Standard.

The darker, redder shades fell from favor in Britain but remained popular in the United States for some time longer, through the 1950s and into the 1960s. However, the extremely pale dogs known as "cream" have never gained a large following in the U.S., although many have done quite well in shows in Great Britain and in Canada.

By the early 1950s in the U.S., it was felt that their Standard (identical to the original quoted at the beginning of this chapter) was lacking in many respects. A lively discussion ensued in the GRCA's official newsletter, led by Henry Norton and Bart Foster. Many suggestions were made, and the question of size even initiated a survey of winning Goldens in various parts of the country. There was real concern about the number of very tall dogs being shown, and winning extensively; the oversize dog was recognized by those who worked their Goldens as being absolutely contrary to working efficiency and breed type, yet they were eye-catching and stylish in the show ring, and the trend was seen as a real threat to the breed's best interests.

After considerable effort was expended, a completely new Standard was adopted and became effective in December of 1954. For the first time, the judge was to completely disqualify from competition any Golden Retriever who was over- or undersize, had overshot or undershot jaws, or had the eye problem commonly known as trichiasis, which was intended to include entropion as well. Monorchids and cryptorchids were to be disqualified as well, although an AKC rule applying to all breeds made that provision redundant. It was felt that these conditions were so major a threat to the soundness and usefulness of the Golden that dogs with these traits must be eliminated from any possibility of recognition in the conformation ring.

One of the major contributors to the new Standard was Rachel Page Elliott, later to be known worldwide for her slow-motion moving-picture studies of the structure and gait of all breeds of dogs, and her lecture program that evolved into the books and videos known as *Dogsteps*.

The 1954 Standard was again reviewed years later, by a committee appointed by the GRCA, and proceeded slowly for some years, albeit with

Ch. Ciadar Tactician CD shows a high degree of masculinity and power without any trace of coarseness. His forequarters and reach of neck are excellent as are topline and ribcage. Brandy was owned by Bev and Bill Severson, and trained and handled to his CD by 11-year-old Ellie Severson.

considerable useful discussion. About 1979 the chairmanship went to Betty (Helen W.) Gay, a breeder and exhibitor since 1950 (and now a well-known judge of Goldens). The intent of the committee was never to change the ideal Golden Retriever who was so well described in the 1954 Standard, but only to clarify and expand where necessary, the wording describing that same ideal appearing with the Breed Standard in the 1947 GRCA Yearbook. By 1981 the revision was completed and sent to the GRCA membership for their approval, and approved by the AKC in October 1981.

In the late 1980s the AKC felt a need to get all breed Standards—more than 120 at the time—into a more uniform format. Standards varied wildly and differed considerably in how they presented the information; some were a half-page in length, others six or seven pages. "Feet" might be under "Forequarters" in one breed, and under "Gait" in another. At the AKC's request, the Golden Retriever Standard was reformatted to conform with the AKC's suggested format in 1990. It was essentially a "cut and paste" job, with as little wording changed as possible. Again, no change to the ideal Golden was intended. This Standard, which is the one currently in effect in the U.S., follows:

BREED STANDARD FOR THE GOLDEN RETRIEVER (AMERICAN KENNEL CLUB)

General Appearance:

A symmetrical, powerful, active dog, sound and well put together, not clumsy nor long in the leg, displaying a kindly expression and possessing a personality that is eager, alert and self-confident. Primarily a hunting dog, he should be shown in hard working condition. Overall appearance, balance, gait and purpose to be given more emphasis than any of his component parts.

Faults: Any departure from the described ideal shall be considered faulty to the degree to which it interferes with the breed's purpose or is contrary to breed character.

Size, Proportion, Substance:

Males 23–24 inches in height at withers; females 21^1/$_2$–22^1/$_2$ inches. Dogs up to one inch above or below standard size should be proportionately penalized. Deviation in height of more than one inch from the standard shall disqualify. Length from breastbone to point of buttocks slightly greater than height at withers in ratio of 12:11. Weight for dogs 65–75 pounds; bitches, 55–65 pounds.

Head

Broad in skull, slightly arched laterally and longitudinally without prominence of frontal bones (forehead) or occipital bones. Stop well defined but not abrupt. Foreface deep and wide, nearly as long as skull. Muzzle straight in profile, blending smoothly and strongly into skull; when viewed in profile or from above, slightly deeper and wider at stop than at tip. No heaviness in flews. Removal of whiskers is permitted but not preferred.

Eyes friendly and intelligent in expression, medium large with dark, close fitting rims, set well apart and reasonably deep in sockets. Color preferably dark brown; medium brown acceptable. Slant eyes and narrow, triangular eyes detract from correct expression and are to be faulted. No white or haw visible when looking straight ahead. Dogs showing evidence of functional abnormality of eyelids or eyelashes (such as, but not limited to, trichiasis, entropion, ectropion, or distichiasis) are to be excused from the ring.

Ears rather short with front edge attached well behind and just above the eye and falling close to cheek. When pulled forward, tip of ear should just cover the eye. Low, hound-like ear set to be faulted.

Nose black or brownish black, though fading to a lighter shade in cold weather not serious. Pink nose or one seriously lacking in pigmentation to be faulted.

Teeth scissors bite, in which the outer side of the lower incisors touches the inner side of the upper incisors. Undershot or overshot bite is a disqualification. Misalignment of teeth (irregular placement of incisors) or a level bite (incisors meet each other edge to edge) is undesirable, but not to be confused with undershot or overshot. Full dentition. Obvious gaps are serious faults.

Neck, Topline, Body

Neck medium long, merging gradually into well laid back shoulders, giving sturdy, muscular appearance. No throatiness.

Back line strong and level from withers to slightly sloping croup, whether standing or moving. Sloping back line, roach or sway back, flat or steep croup to be faulted.

Body well balanced, short coupled, deep through the chest. Chest between forelegs at least as wide as a man's closed hand including thumb, with well developed forechest. Brisket extends to elbow. Ribs long and well sprung but not barrel shaped, extending well towards hindquarters. Loin short, muscular, wide and deep, with very little tuck-up. Slab-sidedness, narrow chest, lack of depth in brisket, excessive tuck-up to be faulted.

Tail

Tail well set on, thick and muscular at the base, following the natural line of the croup. Tail bones extend to, but not below, the point of hock. Carried with merry action, level or with some moderate upward curve; never curled over back nor between legs.

Forequarters

Muscular, well coordinated with hindquarters and capable of free movement. Shoulder blades long and well laid back with upper tips fairly close together at withers. Upper arms appear about the same length as the blades, setting the elbows back beneath the upper tip of the blades, close to the ribs without looseness. Legs, viewed from the front, straight with good bone, but not to the point of coarseness. Pasterns short and strong, sloping slightly with no suggestion of weakness. Dewclaws on forelegs may be removed, but are normally left on.

   Feet medium size, round, compact, and well knuckled, with thick pads. Excess hair may be trimmed to show natural size and contour. Splayed or hare feet to be faulted.

Hindquarters

Broad and strongly muscled. Profile of croup slopes slightly; the pelvic bone slopes at a slightly greater angle (approximately 30 degrees from horizontal). In a natural stance, the femur joins the pelvis at approximately a 90 degree angle; stifles well bent; hocks well let down with short, strong rear pasterns. Feet as in front. Legs straight when viewed from rear. Cow hocks, spread hocks, and sickle hocks to be faulted.

Coat

Dense and water-repellent with good undercoat. Outer coat firm and resilient, neither coarse nor silky, lying close to body; may be straight or wavy. Untrimmed natural ruff; moderate feathering on back of forelegs and on underbody; heavier feathering on front of neck, back of thighs and underside of tail. Coat on head, paws, and front of legs is short and even. Excessive length, open coats, and limp, soft coats are very undesirable. Feet may be trimmed and stray hairs neatened, but the natural appearance of coat or outline should not be altered by cutting or clipping.

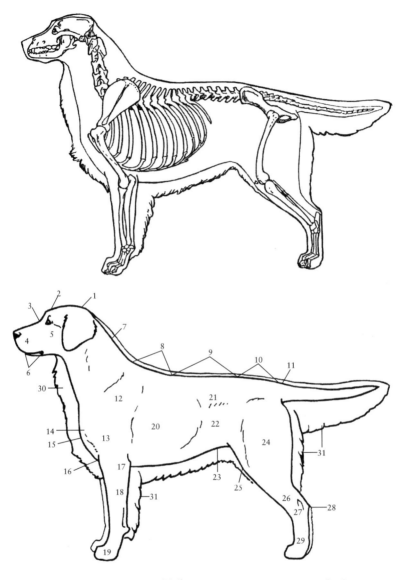

1 Occiput	11 Tailset	22 Flank
2 Frontal bones	12 Shoulder	23 Tuckup
3 Stop	13 Upper arm	24 Thigh
4 Muzzle	14 Point of shoulder	25 Stifle
5 Cheek	15 Forechest	26 Second thigh
6 Flews	16 Brisket	27 Hock joint
7 Crest of neck	17 Elbow	28 Point of hock
8 Withers	18 Forearm	29 Rear pastern
9 Back	19 Front pastern	30 Ruff
10 Croup	20 Ribs	31 Feathering
	21 Loin	

Good Heads

Good profile   Faulty profiles

Ear too large   Lowset, heavy   Too high

Good topline   Short neck   Good neck   Weak, upright neck

Faulty: "lumpy" topline   Incorrect sloping topline

Very good topline and tail carriage   Acceptable   Faulty

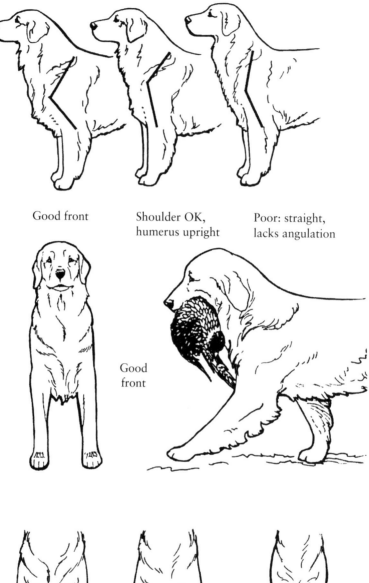

Good front

Shoulder OK, humerus upright

Poor: straight, lacks angulation

Good front

Bowed front

"Fiddle front"

Narrow, toes out

Balance and proportion contribute to athleticism and the capability of performance as well as success in the show ring. This is Can. Ch. Butterblac Some Fools Dream, Am. UD, WCX, JH, Can. UD, WCX; bred in Canada by Doug Windsor, trained and owned by Christine Zink, DVM. Bannor also earned a considerable number of OTCh points.

Color

Rich, lustrous golden of various shades. Feathering may be lighter than rest of coat. With the exception of graying or whitening of face or body due to age, any white marking, other than a few white hairs on the chest, should be penalized according to its extent. Allowable light shadings are not to be confused with white markings. Predominant body color which is either extremely pale or extremely dark is undesirable. Some latitude should be given to the light puppy whose coloring shows promise of deepening with maturity. Any noticeable area of black or other off-color hair is a serious fault.

Gait

When trotting, gait is free, smooth, powerful and well coordinated, showing good reach. Viewed from any position, legs turn neither in nor out, nor do feet cross or interfere with each other. As speed increases, feet tend to converge toward center line of balance. It is recommended that dogs be shown on a loose lead to reflect true gait.

Temperament

Friendly, reliable, and trustworthy. Quarrelsomeness or hostility toward other dogs or people in normal situations, or an unwarranted show of timidity or nervousness, is not in keeping with Golden Retriever character. Such actions should be penalized according to their significance.

Disqualifications

1. Deviation in height of more than one inch from Standard either way.
2. Undershot or overshot bite.

Good rear   Too straight   Over-angulated

Hindquarters produce
power!

Good

Toes out   Cowhocked   Bowlegged

— — — — all faulty — — — —

Good: balanced, coordinated trot

Loose, bouncing topline

Over-reaching; over-extended; not correct

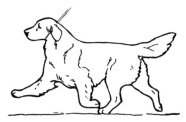

Tight lead; padding; not coordinated

Good front,   Too wide   base-wide   Good rear,   Cowhocked
moving   at elbows   moving

COMMENTS ON THE BREED STANDARD

The following comments are meant only to further explain and clarify the wording of the Standard, and in no way replace any part of it.

GENERAL APPEARANCE: This paragraph retains some of the original wording of the very first (1911) Standard, and is unchanged since 1954. Every committee charged with reviewing the Standard since that date has found no way to improve upon it. This initial paragraph is a capsule definition of an ideal retriever. In reformatting, the sentence pertaining to "Faults" was moved to this section.

SIZE, PROPORTION, SUBSTANCE: A retriever must be large enough and strong enough to perform effectively, and small enough to be practical in boat or blind, and easily transportable. Moderation in build contributes to endurance for long hours of work. The Standard allows a range adequate for all intended uses and functions of the breed. Cloddiness and massiveness detract from the agility and suppleness needed, as well as from endurance, and are just as undesirable as is over-refinement or weediness.

The overall proportions are of a normal canine, slightly longer than tall. While the Standard specifically warns against legginess and clumsiness (which in early years were major worries), currently we must be equally on guard against a trend toward short-legged types, who may look very well in the show ring and move very true, but who may also indicate a creeping in of a type of dwarfism or achondroplasia.

Keep in mind that while the Standard allows a variation of one inch from the ideal size, dogs and bitches outside the ideal are to be faulted even if "measuring in"; and the degree of fault in judging is to accord with the amount of departure from the ideal; hence a dog measuring in by a hair must be considered extremely faulty.

The Head

The head, as all other areas of the dog, is within normal canine limits and without exaggeration of any sort. Because there are no extreme characteristics (such as the length and narrowness of the Borzoi, the flat face of the Bulldog or Pug, or the massiveness of the Newfoundland) the qualities that make a Golden's head outstanding are more subtle. It must be clean-cut, strongly made but without coarseness, reflecting the sturdiness, balance and

A very beautiful, expressive male Golden Retriever head with the natural, untrimmed ruff called for in the breed Standard. This is Can. Ch. JoNoRe's Courthill Timothy, Am.Can. UD, WCX, owned and trained by Cindi Olson.

Full face views of two very nice males. Note the breadth between the eyes; the broad, slightly arched skull; and the muzzle that is broad on top, full and deep, without lippiness or loose flews. Pigmentation is very good. Expressions vary from inquisitive to calmly confident. Ears are good.

workmanlike qualities typical of the ideal Golden, and also the intelligent, kindly, responsive nature that is so important.

As the carrying of game is a prime function of the retriever, proper construction of muzzle and skull is imperative, and also the musculature of the neck and head. For ease in scenting and breathing, breadth, length and depth of foreface and skull, and large open nostrils allow free passage of air. Clean lips without pendant flews are less likely to collect feathers, and allow for a more efficient pick-up. Even if not retrieving, a wet slobbery mouth with hanging flews is quite undesirable, from both the aesthetic and practical viewpoints.

EYES

Retrievers need to mark the flight and the fall of game, and also to be observant of their surroundings and their handler, often at considerable distances. This requires eyes set for both frontal and peripheral vision, and without any defects affecting vision. Close-fitting eyelids are less likely to collect field debris, and offer the best protection for the eyes. Round, prominent eyes such as in the show-type Cocker are more subject to injury, as well as giving an improper expression. Too small or deeply set eyes are also undesirable, giving a foreign expression and also being inclined toward the development of entropion. Darkly pigmented eye rims protect the exposed skin from damage from the sun, as well as contributing to the proper expression.

While the eye color is preferably dark brown, a medium brown that does not detract from the desired expression is quite acceptable. This refers to the color of the iris, of course; the pupil is always black. Lighter eyes verging on yellow are much less acceptable, and the rarely seen very light eye gives a hard, fierce expression completely foreign to the Golden. Also rarely seen is the too-dark eye sometimes called "black," which also harms expression, as these dogs often look blank or vacuous. Eye color is in part related to skin pigmentation, as may be seen in liver-pigmented dogs (chocolate Labrador, liver Flat-Coat, Chesapeake Bay), where eye color ranges from hazel through amber to yellow, but yellow eyes may also occur in dogs with black skin pigmentation.

Dogs showing any noticeable tearing or irritation, or any sign of any functional abnormality of the eyelids or eyelashes, are to be excused from the show ring by the judge, in the same manner that lameness is treated. Thus, if the condition proves temporary, the dog may be shown again. The Standard lists several possible abnormalities, which may have a hereditary component and which should be guarded against in selecting working and breeding animals, not just in the show ring.

The shape of the eye opening is difficult to describe; it is neither exactly round nor exactly triangular but something of a rounded triangle. Shapes may vary somewhat from one dog to another. An exact terminology is unnecessary; if the eye accords with the description given in the Standard, and "looks right" for that dog, it is acceptable.

EARS

The retriever needs the ear canals protected from water, wind, and field debris by a fairly short ear flap that covers the ear canal, is cleanly set and somewhat mobile in order to focus hearing on the handler's commands when at a distance. A low-set ear more easily admits water when the dog is swimming and tends to obscure the ear canal. Properly set and carried ears contribute greatly to the Golden's look of quality and the expression, but it is not necessary for the dog in the show ring to "show ears" more than very briefly in order to determine whether the ears are properly carried at attention. Large, houndy ears are objectionable, as are "fly-away" ears that stick out awkwardly. Ears that are held folded tightly back may be indicative of failings in temperament. Be aware, however, that the most lovely ears may assume comical positions with certain dogs when they are in a silly mood!

The lower part of the ear should be well furred with naturally short, soft hair. Slightly longer hair is normally found at the attachment. While it is acceptable to tidy stray hairs for the show ring, evidence of cutting or scissoring on the ear flap may be taken as prima facie evidence of incorrect coat that requires trimming in order to approximate the correct coat pattern. It is

Some contrasting head studies of excellent bitches.

"English type"; deeper and squarer in muzzle, mostly an effect due to more lip. Excellent top profile of muzzle and skull. Stop and length of muzzle are appropriate. Ear size and placement are good. A very strong, but not coarse or masculine, head for a female.

Very nice overall, clean-cut, well-made head. This photo also shows a clean, strong neck without throatiness, and very good ears held in a relaxed position. Goldens do not need to have "ears up" at all times, nor should they be strung up with the collar.

allowable to shorten hair under the ear flap around the ear canal for neatness, and to ensure ventilation and cleanliness of the ear canal.

NOSE

The nose should be large, with well-opened nostrils for easy air passage. The color should indicate basically black skin pigment, even if faded, as often happens in the winter. Liver is undesirable, though rarely seen. Pink or light brown indicates a lack of pigmentation and means that the nose is subject to damage from sunlight, as well as being aesthetically unattractive. A "snow nose" is a dark nose that has faded, often looking smudgy, but still retains dark pigment around the edges. The eye rims and the lip edges should remain dark.

A well-constructed Golden should demonstrate a well-coordinated gait with good reach and strong impulsion. This dog is exceptional in maintaining a perfect topline, foot-timing and coordination at a fast trot—and at 13 years of age! Am. Can. Ch. Trowsnest Whirlwind, UD WC, Can. CDX.

TEETH

The scissors bite as described in the Standard is the ideal. The illustration shows correct dentition. An even bite, with the incisors meeting edge to edge, is allowable but is less desirable because it will be much more subject to wear and to injury. It may also be indicating nearness to an undershot jaw relationship; the relationships of the side teeth should be examined very carefully if the incisors are even.

A retriever's mouth is essential to the dog's function and purpose. Normal, well-developed, sound dentition is highly desired. Minor irregularities, or a level bite, must be judged individually; if proper function and soundness are not compromised, they may be considered conditionally acceptable. Teeth broken or damaged from field use should not be held against the dog. While a single missing first premolar is of little consequence (compared to some other faults), missing teeth that leave obvious gaps, particularly the large premolars and molars, do detract from optimum ability to pick up, hold and carry. As missing teeth are often a hereditary fault, they should be considered quite seriously. Overshot and undershot bites are disqualifications. Malocclusions resulting from improper jaw relationships often have a hereditary basis and can be very difficult to breed out.

A minor misalignment of incisors due to teeth being out of line with their neighbors in the same jaw is an imperfection, but each dog must be judged individually. Extreme misalignment, sometimes seen as "dropped" central incisors, must be considered faulty as the teeth will wear abnormally and simply are not normal, desirable dentition.

Extra teeth are occasionally seen, usually as an extra first or second premolar. If the relationships and positions of the teeth appear normal, it is probably not of great consequence. If the teeth appear crowded or wrongly positioned, or cause any interference with occlusion, the condition would warrant penalty.

Body

NECK, TOPLINE, BODY

The neck is medium in length, long enough for ease of movement and picking up, short enough for strength and stability, and quite muscular for carrying ability and power. It runs well back and smoothly into the withers and shoulders, indicating good mechanical support. A long, upright neck is *not* correct, no matter how "elegant"; a weak ewe-neck (usually accompanying short upright shoulders) is a severe fault. A heavy ruff left natural may give the appearance of a short neck, so careful examination is necessary. Conversely, careful sculpting of the coat on the neck and shoulders may make a faulty neck appear correct.

The Standard's demands for essential body characteristics are explicit, although far too often overlooked in favor of superficial qualities. The backline is to be level and strong, whether standing or moving. Any roaching (upward arching) or sagging is wrong, as is a sloping backline, often indicating lack of balance fore and aft. The running gear (front and rear quarters) is based and attached to the spine and ribs, and therefore the correct configuration of the spine and ribs is very important. If the spine and ribs are wrongly made, the rest of the dog cannot be right.

The rib cage (including the back ribs) is deep, long and capacious, as suits a swimming dog needing buoyancy as well as heart and lung room. The ribs spring out from the spine to help form a broad, well-muscled back, then curve downward in a somewhat oval fashion. The foremost ribs, under the front leg assembly, will be flatter than the middle and back ribs in order for the forelegs to move efficiently alongside the rib cage. The back ribs are well sprung—that is, outwardly arched—and also long enough to give proper depth to the dog's body, well carried back—there should never be a "wasp waisted" look to a retriever, and the tuckup is not pronounced.

The shape of the rib cage and placement of foreleg assembly produces a definite forechest. A hand on the prosternum (breastbone) that is run down the front of the chest between the forelegs should find a wellfilled front not unlike the bow of a boat—but not a sharp prow (think a tubby rowboat, not a clipper ship!). Dense coat and heavy ruff can disguise various faults here, so hands-on examination is essential.

The loin should be wide when viewed from the top, and deep, seen from the side, with very strong, heavy musculature. The dog will give the impression of being short in the loin due to the relative length of rib cage, but being extremely short-coupled will limit the dog's suppleness and agility in working. As long as the loin area is well made and strong, that is more important than measurement of length.

Faults of the body such as slabsidedness, narrowness, lack of depth and long weak coupling must be considered seriously as they are all both contrary to retriever type and detrimental to efficient fulfillment of the breed's purpose.

Tail and Running Gear

THE TAIL

The tail is a continuation of the spine and is an essential part of the retriever, not just an ornamentation. It is useful to the retriever as an aid for balancing in movement and in swimming, and also in expression of the dog's "body language." Its carriage can indicate emotion and temperament. Its substance and muscularity are indicative of the same qualities elsewhere, and also enable the tail to be actively used; it is not a passive appendage. A proper tail is essential to complete the picture of a sound, typical Golden.

When the dog is moving at a trot, the tail may be carried level with the back (parallel with the ground) or somewhat higher, when it will generally have a slight upward curve. The tail should never come off the croup in an upright position as in a hound, and the tail that is carried curved right over the back is quite wrong. Be aware, however, that dogs under certain circumstances, especially males when "displaying" to other males, may carry the tail much higher than ordinarily. Tails with a ring at the end, or that extend notably beyond the point of the hock, are atypical and not desirable.

Occasionally we see a Golden whose tail seems to be paralyzed, hangs limply or moves only with effort. In most cases this condition, called "water tail" or "cold in the tail," is temporary. It seems to be a transient neuralgia that is a result of swimming or bathing and usually clears up in a few days. Often it seems to happen just before an important show, when the dog has been bathed and confined, to dry and stay clean! A daily dose of enteric coated aspirin, perhaps with a little steroid *as advised by the veterinarian*, may help get things back to normal.

FOREQUARTERS AND HINDQUARTERS

Ease and efficiency in all movement, not just at a show-ring trot, are achieved by proper coordination, harmonious relationship of parts, and the muscling of the skeletal structure. "Balance" refers to much more than just matching angulation front and rear. As the visual appearance of angulation is affected by the coat pattern and feathering, one must look (and feel) beneath the coat, and observe the dog critically both in movement and in natural stance. The dog's appearance when carefully arranged in stance by the handler does not always accurately represent structure.

The Standard is very clear about proper structure of the running gear. While it is fairly easy to achieve angulation in the hindquarters, getting well-constructed forequarters seems to be much more difficult. We may often see dogs who are much straighter in front than in the rear, and overangulation of the rear is not uncommon. Overangulation leads to instability of the joints,

A very attractive young bitch showing a well-made front with properly straight legs. Her head and expression are very pleasant. Her breadth of chest is good, and depth is adequate. Coat is quite sufficient and appropriate for a young female.

as the musculature is not adequate to support extreme angles and long bones, especially in a dog of the Golden's weight.

It is not possible to achieve proper forequarter structure without a correctly made foundation of rib cage and spine upon which to place the foreassembly. There is a very intricate relationship of the scapula and humerus with the associated muscles, the neck, the thoracic spine [vertebrae], the rib cage and the lower leg. Well-developed, firm musculature is *always* desired, especially in the neck, back and hindquarters, which are so important in galloping, jumping and carrying. The retriever, as a swimming dog, also needs good musculature in the chest and shoulders and the long flat muscles over the ribs.

Good hindquarters, broad and well muscled. Straight from hip to heel, with strong hocks turning neither in nor out. The dog stands well up on his toes. Coat is proper.

THE FEET

The feet are essential to the working retriever. They must be large enough and strong for traction and weight-bearing, showing sturdy toes closely held together; durable, thick pads, and useful nails that can help grip the terrain. Retrievers work on all sorts of surfaces; they may need to haul themselves up a slippery river bank or clamber over fallen trees and stone walls. Tiny feet with poorly developed side toes; or thin, flat feet or weak, soft, splayed feet, are extremely undesirable. While clever trimming may improve the appearance of poor feet, the judge is well advised to examine with more than a glance. While it is permissible to trim the hair neatly to show the foot's natural size and contour, sculpting into an exaggerated shape is to be avoided. The practice for show purposes of cutting back toenails so far that they are useless is to be deplored.

Coat and Color

In the matter of coat, practical, serviceable qualities are a first consideration. This includes resistance to cold and moisture, and protection from

A very handsome dog showing desired natural coat pattern without any barbering or stylization. This is Ch. Tangleburr's Classic Note CD. "Ripper" was owned by Marilyn Schmeising and Mary Jean Smith and was handled by Jim Schmeising at the Badger GRC Specialty in 1981.

field hazards, without interfering with motion and without carrying excess water, mud, burrs and debris. Proper texture and weather-resistant qualities also mean a coat that is largely self-cleaning and easily maintained; and these are extremely valuable qualities not only for the field dog but for the retriever working at any job. A coat that requires extensive care in order to remain presentable is simply out of the question for guide dogs and service dogs, who may have owners with no sight or with limited use of their hands.

- The proper topcoat is firm in texture, neither silky nor wiry, lying so as to follow the contours of the body surface, and never groomed to stand off from the body or legs. The coat is longer and thicker where it protects the chest, neck, tail and underbody from harsh vegetation, ice and other hazards. The feathering serves as a sort of "drip edge" to channel water away from the body after swimming or when the dog is working in wet conditions, but must not be so profuse and long as to retain an undue amount of moisture and field debris.

- The topcoat may be straight or wavy without preference. A coat of proper texture, lying in flat waves, is absolutely not to be penalized. Some "break" on the shoulders or hips is typical and acceptable. Texture is far more important than whether a coat is straight or wavy. The dead-straight coat is more likely to be undesirably soft; a wavy coat is often of good texture, with the "spring" that allows it to lie properly.

- The undercoat is dense, with excellent insulating qualities. The undercoat "fills out" the top coat, creating insulating airspace, and the tips of the longer hairs of the topcoat do not stand off but lie so as to follow the general contours of the body and present a weather-resistant surface rather in the same way as a bird's feathers do.

- Fluffy, soft, absorbent coats; limp, silky coats; open coats lacking undercoat; hair that stands off from the body or legs as occurs in a Chow Chow (whether naturally or by grooming) and excessive length of feathering—all are very faulty and extremely undesirable, no matter how eye catching or glamorous they might be.

- Normal shedding and seasonal cycles are not faulty in an otherwise correct coat, so some consideration must be given, and judges should be familiar with these variations. For instance, a proper coat that is short and new, just coming in after a seasonal shed, is always to be preferred over a glamorous but incorrect coat.

Color

Color is essential in defining the breed as the "Golden." The Standard includes as acceptable a range from pale gold through deep reddish gold as the predominant body color, and it may or may not have lighter shadings. "Golden" requires a brilliance of color that is definitely yellow or reddish-yellow, not a dull tan or flat cream. Lighter shadings extending upward from the underbody in varying degrees are quite typical and acceptable; the novice must not confuse these pale shadings with white markings.

- White markings will typically be found on the head as a face blaze or mark on the forehead, on the toes, as a patch on the chest or strip on the throat. Such markings are still occasionally seen in Field or working lines, less often in "show" lines. While not desirable, white markings are much less important than structural and temperament characteristics. The "few white hairs" on the chest may be interpreted to mean anything that is not immediately apparent to the eye; a patch less than two inches in longest dimension is so minor as to be disregarded in most cases.

- The gray or white hairs that come with advancing age are not to be penalized. These usually start on the muzzle or around the eyes and may progress in extreme age throughout the entire body coat. Very old dogs may have a completely white face, feet and tail tip, with white hairs mixed throughout the body coat. Some lines gray much later than others; and many dark dogs, oddly enough, gray very little. The amount of graying has absolutely nothing to do with the dog's health or longevity, and is unimportant.

- Dogs whose color is predominantly cream or off-white, or a dark red approaching the color of the Irish Setter, are not truly "golden" and should be judged accordingly. The breeder has more latitude than the show-ring judge in this area, as it is easy to modify color by judicious breeding. Both breeders and judges, however, must be careful not to select (consciously or unconsciously) for too narrow a range of color; there is a range and variety of coat coloring in Goldens that is historically and absolutely acceptable.

- The light-coated puppy who shows proper color on the ears, and often in a narrow area down the back as the adult coat comes in, will generally be an acceptable shade at maturity, and may be given some latitude during judging. Black shadings or spots, or areas of other off-color such as sable (black-tipped) hair, may have no effect on function or performance but must be considered a serious fault in the show ring if of such an extent as to be noticeable. The random black spots due to a somatic mutation are not heritable (see the chapter on genetic problems), but a line must be drawn to guard against atypical coloring gaining any recognition or show awards.

Gait

As with other qualities, extremes in gait are not desired. The Golden should demonstrate a balanced, even trot on a loose lead, maintaining a strong, level "working back," freedom and ease of movement, with good coordination and foot timing. Extreme or exaggerated "reach and drive" are *not* called for. The Golden is not a specialist trotting breed; the retriever's working gaits include canter and gallop as well as the trot, and must include the ability to cover all sorts of terrain. True gait must have no interference from a tight lead in the show ring, nor is it demonstrated properly at racing speed (techniques more often used to disguise than to reveal).

"Good reach" does not mean extreme. It does not mean a high-flung front foot, or an over-extending, kicking-up rear. Remember that the leg does no work when it is not contacting the ground; *only when the foot is on the ground can it propel the dog.* The length of step by front and rear legs should appear equal, with a nice, easy-reaching stride that appears effortless. The dog who appears "hard driving" is expending undue effort, which will hamper endurance. The foot-timing should show no interference; the backline remains level, with only a slight flexing to indicate suppleness. Backlines that bounce, roll or whip indicate problems in foot timing or in lack of coordination.

Viewed from front or rear, the legs remain straight, with increasing convergence toward the center line as speed increases. Pasterns and hocks that twist or give as they take weight, elbows that flap like wings, feet that flail in the air—all indicate structural faults that reduce the dog's efficiency and soundness.

Temperament

Proper temperament is absolutely essential, and one of the hallmarks of the breed. Of course Goldens are individuals and will vary to a degree, but the Golden must demonstrate qualities such as calm awareness, acceptance, readiness to comply with the handler's wishes and compatibility with and tolerance of other dogs. Expression should be indicative of intelligence, adaptability, quiet alertness and a certain nobility. While puppies and novices may be somewhat unsure in an unfamiliar situation, qualities of excitability, nervousness, fearfulness, aggressiveness in the sense of hostility, or senseless hyperactivity are all most undesirable. The judge must be encouraged to not place, or to excuse from the ring, Goldens who by their actions demonstrate serious temperament faults. Even more important, *breeders and exhibitors must exercise extreme care regarding temperament in animals to be bred or exhibited for titles.*

Disqualifications

The breed Standard specifies two disqualifications; AKC regulations specify others. Among the AKC's, which apply to all dogs shown, are male dogs who do not have two apparently normal testicles normally located in the scrotum; and dogs who attack any person in the ring. Dogs who are blind (lacking any useful vision) or deaf (lacking useful hearing) are to be disqualified. Spayed bitches and neutered males may be shown only in certain nonregular classes such as Veterans, Stud Dog and Brood Bitch. Specific to the Golden Retriever are disqualifications of height and overshot or undershot bite.

HEIGHT

The Standard states an ideal range for height and, in addition, a range of variation (up to one inch outside the ideal) that is allowed; outside this range, dogs must be disqualified from showing. If in doubt, judges are obligated to measure following AKC procedures. Just because a dog "measures in," however, does not mean the dog is fault free. A Golden outside the ideal height range (23–24 inches for males, 21^1/$_2$–22^1/$_2$ inches for bitches) should be considered faulty both according to the degree of variation and the degree to which this variation would interfere with usefulness as a working retriever.

The height requirements are very specific and are intended expressly to keep the Golden a dog of moderate size, useful yet practical. While the show judge has little choice but to abide by the requirements of the Standard and the AKC regulations, the breeder does have more flexibility of choice. There may be valid reasons to breed a Golden who is outside the desired height range, but the breeder *must* be very aware of exactly what those reasons are and select from the offspring with extreme care.

BITE

Interestingly, the Standard approved in 1954 stated that overshot and undershot *jaws* were to be disqualified. In 1957 the AKC altered this to read overshot and undershot *bite*—that is, the relationship of the upper and lower incisors and canines to each other.

Overshot: For show-ring purposes, a dog could be deemed overshot if none of the upper incisors contacted the outer surface of the lower incisors.

For practical purposes, an overshot bite of more than one-sixteenth of an inch, generally with some interference between upper and lower canines, would warrant disqualification.

Undershot: If all the upper incisors are behind the back surface of the lower incisors, the dog must be considered undershot. Four or more lower incisors in that relationship would also warrant that decision, especially if the premolar relationships indicate that the lower jaw is farther forward than the upper jaw.

Again, the breeder has more flexibility than the judge, but one must be aware that improper bite occlusions are often strongly genetic, and while one may think that such problems have been eliminated, they have a nasty way of popping up when least expected. Those oriented toward working and performance dogs may feel that such problems are negligible, but remember that allowing "just a little" can lead to a shift toward or tolerance of greater variations. Then one day the realization dawns that there is a very well-established problem at hand, and one is really "up the creek without a paddle."

Some Other Considerations

GROOMING AND PRESENTATION

The Standard implies in several places that the Golden is to be a dog of natural appearance, never barbered nor stylized. The ruff is to be an "untrimmed *natural* ruff." Feet "may be trimmed to show *natural* size and contour." "The *natural* appearance of coat or outline should not be altered by cutting or clipping." "Removal of whiskers is permitted but not preferred." The GRCA has on three occasions since 1981 sent letters to all AKC judges stressing correct coat and grooming in an effort to counteract "fads" of grooming and trimming.

The Golden is not to have the coat extensively trimmed or sculpted. While it is permissible to "neaten stray hairs," this can by no stretch of the imagination be taken as outlining the ears with scissors, removing the ruff, scissoring the base of the tail or using clippers *anywhere* on the dog. There is no express prohibition against judicious use of thinning shears or a grooming knife to even out bunchy areas of coat, or tidy up tail feathering, but the scissoring to make a harsh "cookie cutter" outline, or shaping the coat to create misleading illusion, is quite wrong.

The practice of back-brushing the coat—often with the addition of sprays, gel or lacquer—is also wrong, and the addition of these "foreign" substances is against AKC rules. The coat should not stand off like a Collie's. The coat on the legs should lie flat, not be brushed and stiffened to stand out like a bottle brush. If the judge detects any foreign substances in the coat, such as stiffeners, oily residue or anything else that changes the natural texture of coat, the judge should not place that dog and, indeed, is empowered to dismiss the dog from the ring if the judge wishes.

As for changing the dog's coat color in any way with coloring agents or bleach, or altering the color of the dog's nose by chemical means, these practices are absolutely against the rules *and* blatantly unethical.

The use of cleaning agents, including powder, is legitimate (though it should be used only when really necessary), as long as *all traces* of the material are *removed before* the dog enters the ring. A thorough, deep brushing, and then letting the dog move around briskly and shake, should eliminate the powder. One should never see a puff of powder arising from a dog the judge has just patted!

It seems that handlers and exhibitors are too often anxious to do everything possible to ensure that their dog will be noticed by the judge. Many seem to feel a need to "improve" every dog by extensive trimming and grooming, when in many cases they should leave well enough alone. A dog with a correct coat in prime condition needs very little trimming and usually looks best with ample, regular brushing and a minimum of fussing. No matter how skillful the "presentation," no Golden should be placed over an inherently better dog simply on the basis of grooming and handling. Admittedly, this is a hard thing to get across to those who put the emphasis more on the "show" than on the "dog" at our dog shows, and conservative exhibitors are likely to encounter undeserved losses to the more glamorous and fashionable exhibits.

Judges, exhibitors and breeders each must be aware of the requirements of the Standard, and the *reasons* behind them. The Golden must never be allowed to deteriorate into a mere fancy piece for show purposes. Exaggeration and concentration on superficial features will destroy the breed.

Beyond the Standard: Color, Coat, Temperament

COLOR

The expected genetics of the Golden Retriever do not allow for any hair color other than the "extension yellow" series, which can produce color ranging from a very pale cream that appears almost white, to the deepest red. There will not be any black or liver pigment in the hair (with one exception, to be noted later). Examples of the whole range from deepest red to palest cream, as well as truly golden, may be found throughout the Golden's history. A wide part of this range of color is acceptable for show purposes, but dogs appearing either extremely dark or pale are less desirable in this country. Whatever the depth of color, it should always have a brilliance that is definitely golden (yellow or yellow-orange). In sunlight, the topcoat should reflect a glint as the metal gold does.

The allowable lighter shadings may vary a great deal. All are acceptable as long as the predominant body color is truly golden. The ears, back and body will be the darkest areas; the underpart, "pants" and tail plume will be the lightest. Subtle shadings on the face are quite acceptable and often add to the dog's expression; dogs who are all one continuous shade of color often have a somewhat blank look, and dogs with very dark faces without shading, or with dark "frown lines," may give an impression of harshness, neither of which accords with the desired expression.

Pigmentation of the hair does not necessarily relate to the pigmentation of the skin. Body skin can range from pink-white to nearly black on the abdomen. The exposed eye rims, nose, edges of lips and footpads are (ideally) black. Some dogs have very intense black pigment; others, brownish-black. Both are acceptable. In cold weather, some dogs' noses will fade to a smudgy "snow nose"; this is acceptable (these dogs will retain fairly dark lip edges and eye rims), but pink or flesh-colored ("dudley") nose and

147

Ch. Timberee Tenatious Token UDT WCX, followed the example of his talented parents in qualifying for the VCX (Versatility Certificate Excellent), a High in Trial winner and an outstanding producer. Bred, owned and handled by Sandra Fisher, he is by Ch. Trowsnest Whirlwind UD WC out of Ch. Beaumaris Timberee Tessa Ann UDT WC. Token carries a practical coat of good color with attractive light shadings.

light eye rims lacking pigment are faulty. Early in the history of the breed, dogs with true brown skin pigmentation and amber eyes were not uncommon (as in the Nova Scotia Duck Tolling Retriever, or the Brittany), but this has for the most part been bred out as being not aesthetically attractive. Unpigmented nose and eye rims may be susceptible to damage from sunlight, a condition that is definitely detrimental in a dog that's supposed to work outdoors.

The hairs that comprise the Golden's coat are usually lighter at the base and darkest at the tip. Some dogs have banded hairs, or hairs where the lighter base extends far up the hairshaft; these dogs may have a "pepper and salt" appearance. This is acceptable and in early years was more commonly seen (and showed up more in dogs with darker coat coloring) than at present, when a clear light gold dog is so popular. Interestingly, most of these "wild"-colored dogs had good coat texture and quality.

Goldens are a red/yellow dog due to the influence of the "extension yellow" gene. Goldens are all homozygous for the recessive e gene, which prevents the formation of black or brown (liver) pigment in the hair, even though the dog does carry B, a different gene at a different locus (place) on the chromosome. B is the dominant gene that produces black pigment in the skin, the nose, lips, eye rims and footpads. If E (as either EE or Ee) were present, B could also produce black pigment in the hair, but ee prevents that. B's allele is b; in the homozygous condition (bb), brown pigment is formed. If the dog carries one gene for each (Bb), the dominant wins and the pigment is black, as is also the case with BB, of course. If ee is present, the *skin* may be black (Bb or BB) or brown (bb), but the *hair* will not be because ee has the effect of oxidizing or "bleaching" the pigment in the hair into yellow. Dogs with both bb and ee will be yellow-coated with brown skin pigment, uncommon in Goldens but occasionally seen in Labradors and in Chesapeakes.

C affects depth of color in yellow dogs. Dominant C produces full depth of color, as opposed to its alleles c and c^{ch}, which can produce (at the extreme end of the range) pale cream or essentially "white" dogs; they may have a slight shading of cream on the ears or down the back. Many of these very pale dogs also have intense black skin.

S is the "solid or spotting" series. SS produces solid-colored dogs with no white marking, or very small amounts of white on tips of the extremities or the midline of head, chest or throat. The next gene in this series, s^i, allows more white; $s^i s^i$ dogs have the typical pattern of white collar, blaze, legs and tail tip, as seen in Collies. There are also "plus" and "minus" modifiers, which affect the extent of the white markings, so there is a great deal of overlap. SS dogs (which includes all retrievers) occasionally have small amounts of white, sometimes due to minus modifiers or for other reasons. Sensibly, the Golden Retriever breed Standard allows for that small area of white on the chest, that stubbornly resists elimination (and is a very minor point compared to everything else). Some early Goldens had rather noticeable white markings.

In short, our typical Golden is a solid-colored, yellow-coated dog, with black skin pigment and modifiers affecting shading and depth of color. There are several other factors for color patterns that may be present in the Golden's genotype, but they are not expressed because ee prevents formation of any dark (black or brown) coat pigment.

THE BLACK SPOT PHENOMENON

The "black spot" phenomenon consists of a limited and clearly defined area of black hair anywhere on the body. It may be as small as three or four black hairs, or extend to a large splotch of solid black or black-tipped (sable) hair. This also occurs in other breeds with the same color genotype as the Golden (yellow Labrador Retrievers, buff Cocker Spaniels, and so on). It is a random somatic mutation and is *not genetic* in nature. What happens is that at

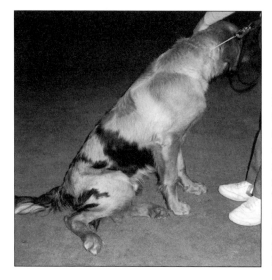

Black spot phenomenon in a Golden Retriever. This young dog has several large splotches of black but is otherwise of normal Golden coloration. The left side of the dog has no black at all. The spots are due to a somatic mutation that takes place in the body cells, and does not affect the dog's genotype. It is not hereditary.

some stage in the development of the puppy before birth, a body cell mutates from the recessive ee to the dominant E. Then, all cells that develop from that cell during the growth of the fetus will carry the formula for E, and this allows black pigment in the hair. Sometimes there are multiple areas of black, forming almost a mosaic effect. This may be because of the way the developing layers of cells form and are distributed.

According to the breed Standard, "any area of black or other off-color hair" is to be faulted. While puppies born with such odd markings are quite likely to be completely normal in all other respects, and in all likelihood will not produce similarly marked offspring, most breeders who have black-marked puppies turn up are uncertain what to do, and may destroy them. That is up to the breeder, but as otherwise quite normal dogs, they could be useful as working dogs or pets. They could be sold on a Limited Registration, which prevents them from being either shown in conformation or bred.

Pups who are born *solid* black, sable or any unusual coloring other than the random black spot discussed previously, in 99.9 percent of cases are due to breeding with a dog of a different breed. "But she was never with another dog!" Oh? What about the times she was out in the backyard alone? How about the Labrador from the next block who can clear a six-foot fence with ease? It's only a matter of minutes for the deed to be done and the visitor gone without a trace. What about the twenty minutes she disappeared when you took her out for a walk in the woods the week after she was bred? Who was lurking in those woods?

If a really off-color pup is born in your litter, and especially if there is more than one, you should not register *any* of the puppies. It is not possible to be sure about the parentage in mixed litters (and a *litter* can have multiple sires, although each *puppy* has only one). Some breeders destroy them all, but then the poor mother is desolated without her babies. Some think it more humane to leave her one or two and put down the rest. Usually a good home can be found for the little crossbreeds (who are often charming). Be sure that the owner of the sire is notified about this, as they need to know the litter is not registerable. If the misalliance was not their fault, there is no obligation to refund your stud fee.

Golden Retriever puppies are born lighter in color than they will be at maturity. They are very often born with pink noses and footpads, but these will quickly start to darken and by a few days of age should be black. In some lines, puppies may be born with pigment already developed. Small areas of pink on the pads are of little concern, although large areas may indicate some white markings on the toes. A small "tick" of white on the top of the head will generally disappear and is of no consequence. By seven or eight weeks of age, a puppy will give a fairly good indication of adult coloring by the color of the ears. Even very pale puppies, if they have rich gold on the ears, should darken to a satisfactory shade of gold by maturity. Puppies born dark may not darken as much proportionately as the lighter ones. Much depends on the lines you are working with.

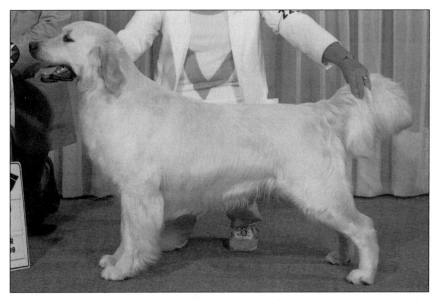

An influential stud dog in Canada in the 1980s and into the 1990s, this is the Norwegian import, Can. Ch. Mjaeromhogda's Kyon Flying Surprise CDX. Owned by Karin Klouman and Wally Barr of Kyon Kennels, Ontario. "Shea" achieved high honors at shows and proved a prolific sire of Canadian champions. His pedigree is effectively British, and he is of the "cream" coloration, a very pale tint of golden, which is popular in Great Britain and Scandinavia.

Because such a wide range of coloring is acceptable in Goldens, as long as the dog is within this range, judges should show no marked preference. "Gold" is always correct, and it can be light gold with pale shadings or a deep rich red-gold with little shading; within this range all are equal. Dogs who are a faded tan or a dull flat color are less attractive. Dogs whose entire body is a colorless cream or ivory, and dogs whose predominant color is so dark as to approach Irish Setter red, are outside the correct range and subject to penalty, although color must not overshadow features of basic soundness and structure.

THE COAT

The Golden's coat is distinctive among the Sporting breeds. It is a double coat, meaning that there are both a topcoat and a shorter, woolly undercoat, which insulates and gives protection against wetness. While the Labrador and the Chesapeake Bay Retriever also have double coats, the Golden's differs from these in length and feathering. This longer hair forms a ruff on the neck and chest, fringes on the back of the forelegs and the underbody, and the distinctive "pants" or breeches as well as the tail plume.

The Golden's topcoat is of a texture and firmness that makes it maintain its position; that is, if it is ruffled with the hand, the body coat will spring back into position.

The topcoat forms a weather-resistant jacket that lies along the lines of the body; it does not stand off like the coat of a Chow Chow or Samoyed. The topcoat is never to be soft and silky, although a prime coat has a pleasant, "polished" feel when stroked with the lie of the hair. The soft, silky, "flowing" coat will not stand up to work in the field and does not offer the degree of protection from burrs and other hazards that is necessary. Nor is it properly water resistant.

The undercoat is made up of shorter, finer hairs that are somewhat wavy. The slight waviness, the density (number of hairs per inch) and the natural mild oiliness of this undercoat give it the insulating quality and the resistance to water that protect the working dog. The topcoat is longer, enough to cover the undercoat. It also has a natural oil that is sufficient to give a degree of water repellency, but is not pronounced enough to be obvious or objectionable in any way. Too often dogs prepared for show have this natural protection removed by frequent bathing, making the coat softer than it should be.

A good Golden coat has a self-cleaning quality that makes it very easy to care for. Dried mud literally falls out of the coat, and a good brushing quickly removes loose dirt. Burrs and other field debris can be removed without damage to the coat if not neglected. The perfect Golden coat is a real "wash and wear" coat that dries quickly; most of the moisture is removed when the dog shakes after swimming, and little more than toweling and brushing is needed after a bath.

The wavy coat is equally as acceptable as the straight coat. The type of coat shown here, with a wave that lies close to the body, is almost always of good texture and weather-resistant quality. This is a very well-built young dog overall, with a particularly attractive head.

Proper coat is important to the working dog. It must be of a density and texture that repels moisture and not so profuse or absorbent that it handicaps the dog when working. Carrying quarts of water in the coat will slow down the dog considerably. This picture shows how the coat leads water away from the body, and the undercoat is merely damp, not soaked. Length of feather is adequate, but not hindering the dog searching for the game hidden in the swampgrass. *Credit: GRCA archives.*

The straight coat and the wavy coat are *equally* acceptable. The correct wavy coat lies to the body, with perhaps some "break" at the shoulders and hips. Frequent wetting and lack of grooming will promote a rough coat. A coat that curls away from the body or is formed into ringlets is incorrect. It is unusual to find really curly coats in Goldens, but they do occur occasionally.

The puppy coat may be softer, thicker and even rather woolly compared to the adult coat. Goldens may carry a puppy coat past a year of age, depending on what time of year they were born, and the climate. The first shed, when the puppy coat is discarded, can be very drastic, with the coat

Ch. Lorelei's Golden Rip** (born 1946). Keystone of Reinhard Bischoff's Lorelei line, Rip shows the intensity and style of the dedicated working retriever. In his day, there was no division between "show" and "field" lines. *Credit: GRCA archives.*

coming out in clumps and chunks. Usually the new coat coming in will appear noticeably darker than the old coat, and the puppy may develop a face mask or a stripe of darker coat down the back. These are temporary.

Dogs living in warmer climates will not develop the same type of coats as dogs living where the winters are cold and damp. While Goldens can acclimate to a great degree, they are more suited to cold weather than to hot, and Goldens in very warm, humid climates need some special consideration as they are not really suited for hard work in heat. The judge in such areas should be aware that the local dogs will not carry the same type of coat as their relatives in the north, but as long as there is an indication of proper texture and quality, they should not be penalized unduly. Likewise, Goldens "out of coat" due to natural shedding cycles should not be deemed "wrong." Shedding is natural, and while these dogs may not be at their best, this is less important than the dog with a really incorrect coat that is silky or excessively long.

The Golden Retriever must always have naturally short, smooth hair on the face and head, and on all legs except for the leg fringes and the heavier, longer coat on the back of the thighs that forms the "pants." There is a ruff on the neck that becomes somewhat longer on the front of the neck and the chest and brisket; this natural ruff is *not* to be scissored or stripped away. The ruff will typically be more pronounced in males.

The tail is one of the Golden's features. The body coat continues down the tail on the upper surface, with dense feathering, often of lighter shading, from the lower surface. The maximum feathering may vary from a couple of inches to perhaps six inches in length, varying from dog to dog, and also according to climate and season of the year. The feathering is not a thin silky fringe as in Setters, but is dense and has an undercoat just as the Golden's body coat does. A beautiful tail adds much to the Golden's appearance, but again, extremes are not desirable.

The tail may be tidied discreetly with thinning shears or a knife, and many dogs look better balanced if the hair at the tip of the tail is shortened a bit. However, the practice of simply cutting off the hair in a straight line across the end is wrong, and gives an impression like the unfortunate child with a "soup bowl" haircut. Nor should the base of the tail be trimmed short or sculptured, as is commonly done with Setters. The Golden's tail should be quite heavy and muscular at the base, and the natural coat both accentuates this and gives a smoother transition as the eye travels down the dog's topline, croup, tailset and into the tail itself.

Looked at as a whole, the Golden's coat should fit like a well-tailored jacket, with a bit of elegance added by the ruff and moderate featherings. The dog should not be awash in swags of long silky draperies: No matter how eye-catching or spectacular, that sort of coat is atypical and completely incorrect. While excessive hair may be neatened, a dog who requires extensive work in order to present the proper coat pattern has, *ipso facto*, a less correct coat. The Golden's coat, combined with the characteristic coloring, makes the breed quite distinct from any other breed in this country and is one of the breed's best features. It must never be made less practical nor corrupted simply for show-ring faddishness and false glamor.

THE "UNWRITTEN STANDARD": CHARACTER, TEMPERAMENT, WORKING APTITUDES

While the breed Standard describes the physical structure of the dog, it touches only very briefly on the dog's character, temperament and working aptitudes, which qualities are of very great importance. Even if these mental characteristics cannot be judged in the show ring, they are no less important because of that.

The Golden's character, temperament and working abilities are primary features of the breed. They have contributed even more than outward appearance to the Golden's tremendous growth in popularity in the past couple of decades. Without them, we have just an ordinary dog.

Some Thoughts on Temperament

In discussing temperament in Goldens, we must always keep in mind that, first, we must have more than a superficial understanding of the normal canine psyche and its variations; secondly, we must understand the temperament called for in the breed.

We must also realize that the temperament suiting one person and an individual's perception of "desirable" will differ from what suits other people and their reasons for having Goldens. Some people want a mild, amiable dog that never reacts other than happily and acceptingly, no matter the circumstances. Certain Obedience competitors want a "hard-driving," fast-moving dog. Field people may ask for "style, drive, and desire," plus the capability

AFC Holway Barty has had a phenomenal impact upon American Field Trial lines; he also sired many Obedience Trial competitors and service dogs for the handicapped. He is a distillation of successful English Field Trial bloodlines. Barty had essential aptitude and trainability and also the conformation of a fast, enduring field worker, with good proportions excellent topline, neck and shoulders; and strong galloping hindquarters.

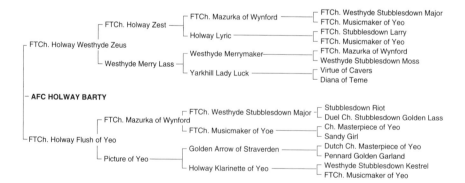

of accepting intense training. Show handlers like a dog that is always "up," that will "ask for it" by appearing alert, active, and untiring in the ring.

Can all these variances be reconciled? The Standard uses the words "*powerful, active* dog. . . a *kindly expression*. . . *eager, alert, and self-confident.* Primarily a hunting dog. . . *friendly and intelligent*. . . *friendly, reliable, and trustworthy.* Quarrelsomeness or hostility. . . timidity or nervousness, is not in keeping with Golden Retriever character." (The emphasis is added.)

The best type of Golden is an adaptable and sensible dog that responds suitably to any situation. When nothing much is happening, this dog is easygoing and rather "laid back," always willing to play whatever "games" the owner chooses, whether Show Ring, Obedience, Agility, or whatever. When games become a true vocation, as in field work or Tracking, this dog can really turn up the intensity level and become a supremely dedicated worker, having the basic stability of character *and* the proper experience and socialization to react appropriately if unusual situations arise.

Dogs do vary in their level of tolerance to stresses such as the crowded conditions at dog shows, and the occasional grumble or click of the teeth at an ill-mannered dog invading his space is not necessarily abnormal behavior, only the canine way of saying, "Don't bother me, you twerp." But this is very different from the dog that would rather attack than stand ground or retreat, the dog that *does not inhibit his bite* and causes, or intends to cause, real damage to another. This latter dog has no excuses. The ability to use the mouth with the highest degree of discrimination (bite inhibition; "soft mouth") is one of the unwritten essentials of the Golden Retriever.

Unfortunately, the quest for the high-powered, intense dog in various forms of competition can lead to selection toward dogs with these traits *without* the counterbalance of being sensible and easygoing in situations where they should be. Then we get dogs that are impossible to live with in the home; dogs so intensely possessive or dominant—with no inhibitions or safeguards on their behavior, lacking discrimination—that they become dangerous. For these dogs, the people who selected for that sort of extreme, or who failed to recognize it for what it is, must bear the blame. Competitors who want a dog high in energy and activity, a dog that will not fold up under intensive training, that is physically tough and can withstand what are sometimes severe corrections, are also responsible for the difficult task of maintaining balance with good temperament in their dogs. It is a credit to the breed, and to some skillful training, that so many dogs do remain in balance.

Within the requirements of the breed Standard for temperament and personality, there is enough range of variation that one can still find the dog that suits. If not, then it would be best to look to some other breed.

Characteristics for Work

The same qualities that help make the Golden an outstanding gun dog and retriever are the qualities that fit the dog for the wide variety of pursuits in

Can. Ch. and OTCh. Gayhaven Slightly Cinnamon, UDT WC VC, GRCA Outstanding Dam (Ch. Keeper of Willow Island CDX** x Am. Can. Ch. Gayhaven Cricket of Marjim, CD WC). Cinnamon had several Highest Scoring Dog in Trial awards. Placement in informal Field Trials included a first in Qualifying Stake; Hunting Tests were still far in the future when she was working. In her only litter she produced three champions with the Ciadar kennel name. Owned by Pam Ruddick.

which Goldens have excelled, and for changing roles well into the distant future.

Biddability Its basic meaning is that the dog is willing to do the bidding of the handler and do it without hesitation or questioning. Included are the qualities of willingness, responsiveness and forgivingness. The dog with these qualities is a joy to work with; while he may not fully understand what is asked, he will do his best to comply.

Honesty as used by trainers indicates a dog that doesn't shirk, but works to the fullest extent of his abilities. An honest dog doesn't sulk when corrected, but tries his best, time after time; reliability and steadiness are easily achieved by the honest dog.

Perseverance is the ability to focus on a goal; to maintain interest and action toward completion of action. That might be the finding and retrieving of a bird in difficult terrain, or the searching out of hidden con-traband, or the guide dog taking the blind person to a destination. Perseverance can be developed by wise training, but only if the basics are there to begin with.

More specific abilities include *retrieving, marking* and *nose*, all qualities that are essential to the retriever. The retrieving instinct is the basis

Can. Ch. Mossbank's Golden Honey Can. UDT** (1959–1971). Honey, owned and trained by Evelyn Smith of Torquay, BC, was the first Golden Retriever in Canada to achieve the Ch-UDT designation, completing the titles in 1964. Not only did Honey excel in Obedience with most scores in the high 190s (and one 200), she also placed in many informal Field Trials in Qualifying and Open stakes, and in her only licensed Field Trial won a Reserve Certificate of Merit (equivalent to today's JAM). Honey and her daughter Quamorly's Golden Sasha CDX TD were treasured by their owner not only as all purpose Goldens, but as loving and gentle family companions.

for many types of training; it is a variant of the "prey" instinct, the inborn urge to pursue and grasp prey plus the returning of the prey to the human partner. The desire to retrieve can be built upon to develop not only gun dogs, but also to develop the skills of tracking; search and rescue; detection of explosives, narcotics, or other substances; and in other areas of training.

"*Nose*" is a simple word for a talent, a sensory ability, that none of us humans can begin to really understand. The canine's ability to detect and to "read" scent is thousands-fold more than any human's, and Goldens as a breed have "nose" that is the equal of nearly any other breed. Scenting ability is essential to the fullest use of retrieving ability and can be utilized in a wide variety of work.

Marking ability is not only the keenness of vision necessary to detect the flight and fall of a shot bird, but the ability to "freeze" that picture or visualization in mind, and use that mental image in order to make an efficient retrieve. *Memory* in field parlance is the ability to store two or more of these visualizations in mind, even though differing in only minor respects. Marking and memory, obviously helpful in training for other purposes as well, can be highly developed by good training, but the basic ability must be there.

Soft mouth is the ability to hold and carry items tenderly without damage whether a shot pheasant destined to grace the dinner table or the baby's fuzzy toy. More than one Golden owner has been startled to find a live mouse (frog, bunny, baby bird) brought to them proudly and without harm, albeit a bit soggy. Allied with soft mouth is the ease of inhibition of bite as mentioned under temperament. A Golden can use his bite forcefully when necessary: Various Goldens have pruned shrubbery to the ground, pulled chain link from its posts and mauled attackers—but it is the ability to discriminate and to use the mouth appropriately that is so important.

A Golden is moderately sensitive to sound, that is, does not overreact to loud or sharp noises, but does pay attention to relevant sound such as commands and praise. Goldens have a rather high threshold for pain. This is definitely context dependent: A retriever may incur various minor injuries while working and not notice them, yet the same dog may be much more sensitive to having his toenails trimmed or his tail brushed.

The breed Standard does not include the *sense of humor,* playfulness, zest, and wonderful joy in living that endears so many Goldens to their owners. Most Goldens are willing to laugh along with us at their own actions; some seem to make a career out of being comedians—like the Golden who made three trips over the high jump with her dumbbell, just for the fun of it, while spectators and judge alike fell over laughing; and the young dog who grabbed his tail and turned somersaults behind his Obedience instructor owner's back. The instructor had no idea why the audience found his lecture so hilarious. Every Golden owner has stories of the wonderful funny things their dog has done, and a continually sober Golden is rather a rarity.

The character of the Golden consists of all these qualities and more. Goldens will vary of course, and there are many true individuals in the breed. Even with the best inborn qualities and potential, the dog must have proper socialization and bringing up in order to become the sort of dog we desire. We can never forget that they have a right to be dogs, not furry angels, not little people in fur coats nor cute stuffed teddy bears. They are real dogs, in all the complexity and glory and nobility of the canine species.

chapter 8

Activities for a Well-Rounded Dog

CHOOSING A PUPPY

Even before you actually acquire the lovable, furry little creature you are going to take home, there is much to be done. It helps a great deal if you have a clear idea in mind of what you want of the dog—not the superficial qualities of coat color, dark eyes or size, which so many new or first-time buyers mention, but the kind of dog you want to be with you for a lifetime. Do you want an easy-going, sweet friend for a family with small children, or an active, athletic companion to accompany you for hiking and camping in the mountains? Are you going to participate in formal Obedience Trial competition or try the fun of showing your own dog in conformation? Will this be a working gundog in hunting season and a participant in retriever Hunting Tests?

Do you really want a Golden? Goldens are not for everyone in spite of their great popularity. Goldens are good-sized, active dogs who demand daily attention and companionship. They do *not* do well isolated in a pen at the far end of the yard, with food tossed in once a day. They do shed—at times in great quantities. The coat requires care, nails must be trimmed, and teeth and ears have to be kept clean. Goldens love to swim, dig holes and play in the mud; and they will transport nearly any object they can get between their jaws. Although most will indicate with a woof or two when someone arrives at the front door, do not expect a Golden to offer "protection." Goldens are generally healthy dogs but are as mortal as any other canine; illnesses may occur. Routine vaccinations and checkups are required. No matter how careful the breeder has been in selecting the parents and raising the puppies, there is no foolproof means of predicting the appearance and development of most genetic problems. There is *always* a possibility of some problem such as hip dysplasia.

Ch. Elysian's Li'l Leica Reprint UDT MH WCX has won honors in many areas, including a Best in Show and Specialty Show wins. She is by Ch. Wingwatcher Reddi to Rally CDX WC out of Ch. Beaulieu's Akacia O'Darnley UDT; bred and owned by Jeannette von Barby of Colorado.

Does your life-style allow for a dog? While a *very* diligent and responsible owner can maintain a Golden in an apartment (although it is not recommended), a Golden needs far more exercise than a sedate walk around the block twice a day!! Responsible breeders will not sell a Golden unless the buyer has a safe area, usually a fenced yard, for the dog. Nothing infuriates responsible breeders more than having one of their dogs carelessly allowed to run loose.

Do you travel a lot? Will the dog go with you, or will you need to board the dog or arrange for a house sitter? Goldens often travel well by car, but the dog's needs must be considered. The dog must be taught to urinate or defecate while on-lead and to behave properly in unfamiliar surroundings such as at motels (not all of which accept dogs). Travel with a seventy-pound Golden is not the same as with a small dog! If you need to board the dog at times, are you prepared to pay the going rate for proper accommodations and care? House sitters will not be cheaper, although they may attend to things other than the dog.

Is there someone home during the day, or is the dog to be left alone for eight to twelve hours a day? If this is the case, some special arrangements will be required. You cannot simply shut the puppy in the basement or laundry room with papers on the floor (or worse yet, leave the puppy to roam freely around the house)—this guarantees problems in housetraining, to say nothing of socialization.

You must think about all these matters quite seriously before deciding whether you really need/want a dog in your life, whether that dog should be a Golden Retriever, and what you plan to do with that Golden for the next ten to sixteen years. Once you take on that furry critter, you are responsible for the entire life of the dog.

FINDING A KNOWLEDGEABLE AND RESPONSIBLE BREEDER

Let's face it, the only place you can go to get the right kind of Golden with a known background is the responsible, ethical, individual breeder. Pet shops and dealers are simply not to be considered, as dogs sold there are invariably of lesser-quality background, often poorly cared for and not socialized, and quite possibly not even the dogs their "papers" say they are. How about ads in the classified section of the newspaper? Perhaps—if the advertiser is the right kind of breeder—but you must be extremely careful as most often these are from casual or "backyard breeders" who unfortunately are the source of the vast majority of Goldens produced today. With this source, no real thought has gone into selecting dogs for breeding, no attention paid to temperament or soundness. Rarely will there be any information as to hip X rays, eye or heart examinations, allergies or other such problems. Nor will there be any known background for working aptitude, trainability and the other qualities you are looking for.

Responsible breeders usually don't need to advertise in newspapers, as their puppies are usually spoken for before whelping. You can find the right kind of breeder through inquiries with the American Kennel Club and the Golden Retriever Club of America, who will answer your inquiry through one of the many Information Officers or through referrals to any of the forty-five or more local Golden Retriever clubs. Your local telephone directory may have a listing for a local all-breed kennel club, which often has an information person or directory to guide you to a local breeder. Some local breed clubs may run an advertisement in the Sunday classifieds, giving a phone number for information and referrals. Your local veterinarian also may be able to refer you to a responsible breeder.

If you are not interested in any activities requiring a dog with a particular kind of background, you should consider contacting a Golden Retriever Rescue Service. These organizations salvage deserving Goldens, often from people who have abandoned them, and place them in new homes. The dogs are customarily screened for temperament and possible health problems before being placed. You may never know the dog's previous history, and

Mirror, mirror, on the wall, who's the fairest. . . ? Evaluating a puppy at six weeks of age. After all the homework has been done, picking a puppy is still a bit of a gamble. "Mother Nature" makes no guarantees, but choosing sound, proven bloodlines and a responsible, knowledgeable breeder does make the odds more favorable.

the dog will be neutered or spayed, but some lovely dogs have gained a new lease on life through a Rescue Service. The GRCA (see the Appendix) can provide you with contacts.

Similarly, Goldens sometimes are available at animal shelters and humane societies. Some of these organizations screen dogs before placing them; at others there may be no temperament or health checks. Again, the dog is probably of unknown background, and there are no guarantees whatever, so proceed with caution. If there is a problem, you may be on your own.

Choosing a Breeder

Armed with the names and phone numbers of three or four breeders, your next step is to contact each of them and determine whether they may have what you are looking for, or perhaps will have something in the future. Obviously, if you are looking for a show prospect, the breeder specializing in Field Trial dogs is not likely to have your "perfect" puppy. If your primary requirements are temperament and soundness, the breeder's main area of participation may be of less importance, as good Goldens can be found in all areas. One word of caution, however; if the litter is bred specifically for Field

Trials or for dedicated Obedience competition, the dogs may well be of an intensity and energy level exceeding what you require for "a nice family dog," unless you channel that intensity properly with serious training.

Be very open and honest with the breeder. If you want to try showing and Obedience, say so, but don't think this will necessarily get you a "first pick" puppy, as experienced breeders are a little wary of novices with grand aspirations. If you want just a family dog and companion, expect the breeder to require that you spay or neuter the dog, and/or accept a Limited Registration (which states that the dog's offspring cannot be registered until the *breeder* lifts the limitation).

Expect the breeder to ask you a great many questions—about your requirements, your life-style, the facilities you have for the dog, your plans for the dog, whether you will go to obedience class, and many more. Responsible breeders make every effort to place their treasured dogs in the best home possible, because the dog's welfare is of the highest importance.

In any case, you need to ask about such matters as the following:

- Does the breeder belong to a local Golden Retriever Club or the GRCA? To an all-breed or Obedience club? These are indications of a sincerely committed "dog person," and a person who continues to seek additional knowledge about the breed.

- What are the breeder's aims? If it is only to produce "nice pets," that's *not a high aim*. Remember that *all* well-bred Goldens *should* have the temperament and soundness to be good companions, although not all are suitable for all people.

- If the breeder tells you that they "don't sell pets," say good-bye graciously. Even the most aristocratically bred litter will have dogs who don't quite meet the rigorous standards required for the highest levels of competition. Also, there are just not enough "show homes" available for every puppy in every litter. Most responsible breeders are pleased to find really good homes with appreciative owners for puppies who are not the top choices; and these puppies have all the benefits of starting out as part of a well-cared-for litter from carefully selected parents.

- Does the breeder routinely x-ray for hip dysplasia, and have eye and heart examinations done on all stock? Actual reports should be available for you, with photocopies for your file if you do purchase a dog. They should answer openly all your questions about possible hereditary problems, health, temperament and longevity.

- Does the breeder supply a four- or five-generation pedigree and a complete health record on the puppies? The pups should have had at least one distemper-combination vaccination and been wormed at least once, probably twice, by seven weeks of age.

- Does the breeder give a well-written, comprehensive sales contract, with complete information? It must include the names and registration numbers of parents, the date of birth of litter and the names of breeder(s)/seller(s); and it should allow/request an examination by your veterinarian within no more than five days of the sale date, with a refund provided if the puppy is returned within that time. Avoid contracts *requiring* the new owner to show or breed the dog, or contracts with complex co-ownerships or "breeder's terms."

- The registration application, the "blue slip," may be available at the time of purchase, or sent as soon as possible (sometimes there are delays in processing). The breeder should indicate whether the dog is to have full registration or Limited Registration, which must be marked on the application. Under the Limited Registration, no future offspring of the dog will be registered, nor may the dog be entered at conformation shows. Some breeders will agree to lift the limitation if the dog proves to be of show or breeding quality when mature. Participation in Obedience and other activities by dogs with Limited Registration is allowed.

- If any "guarantees" are given for health or soundness, the contract should be *absolutely* explicit about all details and time limits. Who pays for veterinary bills? Who makes the decisions? Is the dog to be returned? Neutered? Destroyed? Writing a good contract is not easy. Don't expect an unconditional "lifetime" guarantee—given the nature of living creatures, that is unrealistic. However, if dogs prove to be unable to fill the function for which they were purchased due to some hereditary problem demonstrated within a certain time period (not more than two years), many ethical breeders will try to make some adjustment, perhaps a replacement. Some don't, feeling that they have done all they possibly could to help ensure soundness before the puppy was sold. These features are to be decided between you and the seller, and can vary according to what you both feel is appropriate. Again, *get it in writing*. Reputable breeders will be quite willing to answer your questions, and they will expect you to be honest and up-front with them as well.

- The next step is to make an appointment to go see the dogs. If a litter is under six weeks old, the breeder will probably be very cautious about having strangers visit; don't be offended. If you have been to a dog show, veterinarian's office or another kennel, even played with the neighbor's dog, don't even *think* about visiting until you have bathed and put on clean clothes and clean shoes. The risk of visitors carrying disease in to a litter makes breeders very nervous, believe me. Some breeders don't allow visitors at all until the puppies have at least had their first vaccinations, and this is not unreasonable.

When you arrive (and if you're going to be late, or can't make it, please be considerate enough to call and let them know), check out the facilities; they need not be fancy but should always be clean and in good repair. Runs should not have feces nor pans of old food lying around. The dogs should have proper shelter: snug and dry in winter, shady and cool in summer. Water buckets should be clean and filled. All dogs should appear well cared for—perhaps not trimmed to show standards but clean, well nourished and healthy. They may well bark at you (Hey! Visitors! Look at me!) but should not run away and try to hide, nor hackle up and snarl.

The puppy pen should be clean and large enough to allow the little ones ample space to play. If the pen is indoors, shredded paper or wood shavings should be available as a toilet area. Puppies should appear healthy, active and playful. If you arrive at nap time, they may be less active, but beware of any who don't want to move or who act as if they don't feel well. Some toys and perhaps other objects in the pen for stimulation and play experience indicate a thoughtful breeder.

Puppies' eyes should be clean, bright and sparkling. Ears should be clean inside, pink and with no objectionable smell. Open the mouth and check the gums; they should be pink and clean, with sharp little puppy teeth. Puppies have a distinctive scent, slightly "skunky" puppy breath and a coat that smells clean and healthy. Puppies should feel rather heavy for their size—firm and muscular when picked up. Pups should not mind being held for a few minutes in your arms, although they may well start to wriggle when they want to rejoin the group. The puppy should not appear pot-bellied nor scrawny. The coat may be rather short and smooth, or quite fluffy, depending on age and on family lines, but should be clean and invite being touched. Goldens with fuzzy soft puppy coats will not have much shine to them, and that is normal. Dull, flaky coats with dry skin or traces of flea dirt are not desirable. Puppies kept on newsprint may appear rather "tattle-tale gray" from the newspaper ink, but that is different from the dirt of neglect.

While sizes vary considerably depending on the rate of development of particular lines, at seven weeks of age a Golden puppy should weigh at least eight pounds, more likely about ten to twelve. While they should be plump

Can. Ch. Ambertrail's Honey Bee CDX***, one of the few show champions to reach Qualified status in Field Trials in Canada. By Am. Can. Ch. High Farms Jantze of Curacao CDX TD out of Can. Ch./OTCh Val's Dolly, bred by Mike and Val Ducross.

This future champion at 12 weeks of age shows exceptional quality, including excellent overall balance, angulation and topline.

and well fed, they need not be butterball-fat. Young puppies are rather helter-skelter and not terribly well-coordinated but by seven weeks should be able to trot quite nicely and gallop with abandon (although getting them to trot when you want them to is another question!). A puppy who shows a limp, or who "bunny-hops" rather than trotting or walking, has a potentially severe problem.

If you are selecting a puppy for a specific purpose, an experienced breeder should be able to steer you to the most appropriate candidate. After all, they have been observing these puppies for weeks and should be familiar with the developing personalities. Many breeders will already have utilized the popular "puppy aptitude tests" and have the information available for you. Don't expect to perform these tests yourself: Breeders, quite understandably, may not be happy to have a stranger subject their puppies to the novel experiences of these tests.

James Lamb Free, a noted retriever trainer and author of some years ago, said in one of his books that picking a puppy was simple—find the right litter from the right parents, and then simply grab a puppy. He's probably correct in that with a well-bred puppy the biggest factor for success is most often proper raising and training.

The best bet for most people is the "middle of the road" dog—neither markedly dominant nor overly submissive—a pup who submits to handling without strenuously objecting. When taken to an area away from other puppies and distractions, this kind of dog shows social attraction by readily following a person moving away and by also coming when called. The test that many trainers feel is of most importance is the "fetch test." A small ball or toy, even a wad of crumpled paper, is rolled a short distance away from the puppy as he watches. If the puppy follows the ball and picks it up, that's a plus; if he brings the ball back to the tester, that's a double-plus. The puppy is demonstrating not only the desire to retrieve but willingness to work with the handler.

Such testing is not of much use before six to seven weeks of age, at the earliest. Puppies are still developing their capabilities and are a long way from

Sometimes Goldens excel in spite of a far from perfect start in life. "Boo" was bought at 4 months of age to get him out of unfortunate circumstances. Betty Drobac started him in Obedience, and 12-year old daughter Connie showed Boo to his show titles. This willing, responsive dog became Am. Can. Ch. Shawn's Golden Boomerang, Am. Can. UDT WCX VCX, Can. TDX.

physical maturity. Any puppy can have an "off day" and may react quite differently at another time.

A Golden intended for *any type* of competition needs to be sound and well-balanced. The pup who appears to have overall balance, who moves freely and easily with a regular cadence, is always desirable. Head and tail should be carried happily and confidently. The legs should, when viewed from front and rear, appear to stand straight and to move in straight planes without cowhocks, winging out, or other deviations. Small puppies tend to stand and move rather widely (compared to the adult), as their legs are comparatively shorter. Some length of neck is desirable, although many six- to eight-week-old pups appear rather short in neck; it is part of the general babyishness of the young puppy. The body should be wide and deep, with some indication of good chest width and depth, and ribs going well back with a fairly short loin; the topline, from withers to tail level, with no roach or sag.

Heads will vary with the bloodlines. Not only the skull but also the muzzle should be wide and rather square, with the muzzle deep and full. In puppies who are six weeks of age, I like to see the suggestion of a wrinkle or fat

It's really teaching, although the puppy thinks it's all fun. The handler keeps the puppy attentive and happy; the lead behind her gently restrains puppy from wandering. A great start for later formal Obedience work.

pad on the top of a wide, blunt muzzle, indicating that the muzzle will be substantial. The eyes should be set far apart and have well-pigmented dark rims, and should be dark, but they may appear bluish at this young age. A greenish color of iris may indicate light eyes. Ears should be set rather far back on the skull, and reasonably high on the sides of the skull. The bite should be scissors or slightly overshot; a level bite at seven weeks may well be undershot later.

The age of seven weeks is the earliest that a puppy should leave the litter and go to a new home. It is important for proper socialization with other dogs that the puppy not be deprived of interaction with and companionship of littermates. Dogs who are taken from the litter too young often never learn to relate properly to other dogs, although they may well bond strongly (too strongly) to people. Conversely, puppies who remain with the littermates too long may fail to develop any attachment to humans. Pups who lack experience with people until after sixteen weeks of age will likely be extremely difficult to train; in extreme cases, this "kennel dog syndrome" results in a dog who is simply impossible to work with. Responsible breeders will be very careful to give puppies the needed experiences and socialization that will facilitate later learning and bonding.

Often it seems that the puppy is the one who picks the new owner. There is just something that "clicks" between the two. When a Golden puppy climbs into your lap and says "I'm yours"—well, sometimes the heart rules the head. Heck, if this is the right litter, this may be as good a way as any to choose.

Buying at a Distance

Sometimes the litter you have chosen is at a distance, and the pup will be shipped to you. In this case, you need to describe as clearly as possible what you are looking for, what you intend the puppy for, and so on. The breeder should be able to describe the individual puppies fairly well, both for structure and personality, and send photos. Many breeders now are making videotapes of the litter, each filmed individually, standing, moving, retrieving or being puppy-tested. Modern technology is wonderful!

Let the breeder know as quickly as possible of your selection, and make final arrangements. Airlines require dogs to be eight weeks of age or older for shipment, so don't be at all surprised if the breeder delays shipment until nine or ten weeks of age, when the puppy is better able to cope with the stress of shipment. Air cargo shipment is fast and efficient in most cases. A direct, nonstop, flight is by far the best, as every stop and every change of planes increases the opportunity for errors. If there is another airport within a couple of hours' driving time to which you can get a direct flight, it is certainly worth the extra drive in order to eliminate a change of planes. Sometimes it's feasible to travel yourself and return with the puppy as excess baggage. The American Dog Owners Association has a very good pamphlet available on air travel for dogs.

The shipper should give you complete information as to times and dates, airline, and so on. It is wise to call the airline's cargo facility at your end and get information as to their hours, their location in the airport and any other information. Often the air cargo facility is a long way from the passenger terminal (and usually has better parking, which is a bonus).

The buyer customarily pays shipping costs, so don't forget your checkbook or charge card. When you are safely home with the puppy, do give the breeder a call to say the puppy has arrived. We all worry!

THE PUPPY AT HOME

If at all possible, schedule the puppy's arrival for a weekend or a vacation time when you have more time available. Do try to set the routine to fit your regular schedule, and stick to it even on weekends. Puppies don't understand why Saturdays are different from workdays! Dr. Milani's book *The Weekend Dog* has many excellent suggestions for making the best use of your limited time and raising a dog well even though you aren't at home all day.

When you arrive home with the newcomer, try to keep excitement at a minimum; he has a lot to contend with already. Caution children in advance that the puppy needs a quiet homecoming and a chance to get acquainted. Confine the festivities to one room, and start the routine of housetraining right now. Preferably this will be the room where the puppy's crate will be located (probably the kitchen or family room), and close to the door to go outside for "business." Give puppy a chance to piddle outside before coming into the house, and allow the dog to run around and get acquainted with this new place without too much fussing. The dog can get a drink of water and, after a while, have dinner, go out again for a bathroom trip, and then be ready for a nap in the crate that you have set up with a blanket and a toy or two.

If you haven't already, schedule a trip to the veterinarian in the next day or two just for a general examination and checkup. This should be provided for in the sales agreement. It will also serve to introduce puppy to the veterinarian (and vice versa) without any urgency. Most veterinarians are happy to help out and make it a pleasant experience for the new pup; they appreciate being able to work with dogs who don't get uptight because of apprehension about being at the vet's office.

After a few days, you may want to send a note to the breeder that all is well (or make a phone call if you have questions). You and your new friend are on your way to a bright future.

SOME GENERALITIES FOR A VERSATILE DOG

There is a very old saying that applies to dogs as well as to many other beings: "As the twig is bent, so the tree shall incline." From the first day your Golden enters your life, you will be affecting very much of what the mature dog may become. It is your responsibility to be certain that your little twig grows to be a sturdy, useful Golden oak.

Puppies have no conception of "right" or "wrong"; what they do is natural canine behavior, and it is humans who find certain behaviors either desirable or undesirable. One of the ways of forestalling undesirable behaviors (wetting the rug, for instance) is to prevent them (take the puppy outside when necessary). This naturally teaches alternatives—that is, the place for urination is outside, on the grass. These are positive methods and far preferable than after-the-fact punitive methods (smack puppy with a newspaper, yell and scream, throw puppy out the back door), which only show the puppy that you are an unpredictable creature prone to unreasonable outbursts. This certainly does nothing to build rapport and instill confidence in the dog.

There are many very good books on basic training available. Authors (and practical dog people) such as Dr. Ian Dunbar, Jack and Wendy Volhard, Carol Lea Benjamin, Patricia Burnham, Milo Pearsall, Gail Fisher, Dr. Michael Fox, Peter Vollmar and others have written extensively on the subject. Some are

"Fargo" at 8 weeks is already retrieving like a pro. Puppy-sized training dummies and short, simple lessons enable the little fellows to start learning very early. Easily conquered obstacles like the windrows of hay not only are fun but expand the puppy's experiences and develop his confidence.

listed in the bibliography. Another excellent text is Karen Pryor's book *Don't Shoot the Dog*, not specifically a dog training book but a well written text on teaching and modifying behavior. More and more, contemporary dog trainers are finding very practical applications for the increased understanding of learning and behavior, and while techniques may vary, all the best trainers make use of sound principles.

This chapter is not a definitive training text, but it touches on some points of particular pertinence to the Golden as a dog who may perform in any or all of various areas of performance.

SOCIALIZATION

One reason Golden puppies are so appealing, it seems, is because they facilitate socialization. Few things in life elicit such pleasant feelings as interacting with a fluffy, wiggly, plump little Golden. Faced with a group of furry babies, even the most staid adult may be turned into mush being gnawed on by needle-teeth. Such interaction is good for the puppy, too. They need to be handled and held, to experience different voices, smells and touches. They also need to experience various types of surroundings—to go for walks in town, in fields and parks, to ride in the car, to go to other homes and to puppy class at the Obedience club, where they can meet other dogs under supervision.

Until the series of inoculations is complete (about four months of age), you should be very cautious about allowing your puppy to go out in public areas where there may be disease. Parvovirus and other infectious diseases can be deadly. While avoiding public parks, places where strays and random dogs may have been, and so forth, you can still provide plenty of socialization experiences for the puppy.

Just as children benefit from an enriched environment, so do puppies. Early experiences have a lasting effect on both. The puppy can have wooden boxes, platforms and ramps in the pen or play area to explore and conquer, giving the future Obedience or Agility prospect a headstart. Cardboard boxes will be thoroughly experienced (and destroyed). Balls and toys of all sorts stimulate play; three or four at a time is plenty. A simple eight-inch board barrier in the run gate or in a doorway in the house will have the puppy scrambling, then hopping, over it, learning to jump with no effort at all on your part.

A variety of small articles such as a leather glove, plastic soda bottles, lengths of wooden 2 × 2s or broomsticks, and clean tin cans (no sharp edges) for play will accustom the puppy to carrying items of various shapes and materials, preparing for later work with scent articles and wooden dumbbells—or, in the case of guide or assistance dogs, for carrying the various items that may be required.

TRAINING

Young puppies, even at seven weeks of age, are capable of learning a great deal. It is up to you to make sure that they learn the things you *want* in a finished adult dog. The old notion of not training a pup before six months of age was demolished a long time ago. Pups *will* learn, and they may learn things you'd rather they didn't if you're not careful!

Sensible *control and confinement* help prevent the puppy from doing things that aren't desirable. A puppy safe in a crate can't chew the furniture or soil the rug. A securely fenced yard or dog run means the dog won't be running off or chasing kids on bicycles. A puppy wearing a collar and lead won't be dashing into traffic, and can be prevented from leaping up on people.

Basic Training

Integration means simply that right from the first, what you want the dog to do is made a part of everyday living. When the puppy goes for rides in the car, he does so in a crate. Of course puppies start off having no idea of what the command "Kennel" means, but when the command is given each time they are picked up and placed gently in the crate, they begin to understand. A word of praise and a bit of a food treat make getting into the crate a pleasant experience, and if the car ride means something else very enjoyable is about to happen (such as going to the park for a run, or to the pond for swimming and retrieving), by the time they're big enough, they'll be very happy to leap into that crate when you open the door and say "Kennel."

You cannot just *tell* puppies to do something—they have no idea what that sound (your "command") means until you have taught it. You can *teach* this by developing an association between action and sound. You can achieve

The puppy's interest in birds can be stimulated by games with a duck or pheasant wing. Puppy always wins in the end, catching the elusive feathers and being praised.

this by using food (or a toy) along with visual (body and hand motion) and verbal cues (words), which will later become commands. Sometimes restraint and guidance (collar, leash) will be helpful. All this can be rewardingly integrated into everyday living. While the five- to fifteen-minute training session every day is useful, it can be just as effective (and easier) to teach in many thirty-second bits during the course of the day.

For instance, you can teach Puppy to "**sit**" for dinner. You hold the food dish, and of course the puppy's attention is on you completely. Hold a bit of food just over the pup's nose; then move the food back over the puppy's head. As the dog's nose follows the food, the rear goes down into a sit. As soon as that happens, you give the puppy the food. After several repetitions, when you see your dog about to sit, add the cue word, "Sit." Very quickly, a bright puppy learns to "ask" for the tidbit by sitting. Eventually, you give the food only when the puppy sits *on cue*. Sitting *without* the cue should get no response from you (if it does, your dog is training you to give a treat when *you* get a cue [your dog sitting]). Further on in the training, give the food only randomly, gradually less and less often, and give a praise word with the food reward. As you phase out the food, the praise word becomes the dog's reward or positive reinforcement.

You can teach other movements in a similar fashion, using food or a toy as lure and reinforcement. To teach "**Down,**" you move the food lure downward in front of the puppy to the floor. Hold the food in your hand so that the pup knows it's there, but don't give the treat until your dog's elbows are on the ground. "Good puppy!"

Basic puppy training is well covered in such texts as *How to Raise a Puppy You Can Live With*, by Clarice Rutherford and David Neil. For the retriever puppy, basic training should also include an introduction to game birds, water and gunfire. Puppies have successfully been introduced to Tracking as young as nine or ten weeks of age, and they can easily learn, in an informal way, the basics of the Obedience exercises such as the Sit, Down, Stand and Recall, and to move and stand as is required in the conformation ring. Puppies' curiosity and love of exploration will facilitate an introduction to jumping and the various obstacles that may be encountered in the Field or the Agility ring.

Of course, you do all this teaching, or pretraining, in an informal, happy, upbeat manner. *There are no corrections; the puppy is learning, not being tested.* You must be very careful to set up every experience so that the puppy is successful. If the puppy is not successful, then you immediately make changes so that "failure" is not possible. For example, if the puppy runs away with the toy you have tossed for a **retrieve,** then you go *to* the puppy for the toy. The next time, throw the toy down a narrow hallway where the only way to go is back toward you with it. *Of course,* you will give so much encouragement and praise that the dog will think this wonderful thing was all her own idea! Even if it is necessary to attach a light cord to the collar to prevent a dash into the bushes with the newly thrown treasure, there will be a big reward for a successful retrieve. Therefore, the dog soon will think that returning directly to you is the only course of action possible.

"**Come**" or "**Here**" is something all dogs should respond to immediately. Mealtime is a great time to practice this command—calling, walking away if necessary, carrying the food dish, calling the puppy's name and saying "Here." Devise games such as "round-robin recalls," with two or three people, or even more, in a circle, calling the puppy by name: "Harry, here!" The caller should kneel or squat, with arms opened wide, big smile, happy voice: "Wonderful puppy! Here's a tidbit for you." Then a person across the circle will call in the same fashion. The puppy will soon catch on to this fun game and will be barreling full tilt to whoever is calling. In the house, the game can be played from room to room; outside, it can develop into "hide and seek." More than just a game, it teaches a good Recall. The pup will learn to use both nose and ears to find the person who is out of sight. It can also prove useful in sending messages or transporting small articles. Using these sorts of games, you can build up to serious tracking and searching.

Retrieving and Field work—Puppy Basics

With a puppy, you can work on the **retrieve** by using a ball or glove or stuffed sock. Tease your dog a little by dragging the glove in a zig-zag fashion so that the pup focuses on it. Then toss it a few feet and let the dog go to it, without your saying anything. When the puppy picks up the article, turn on the praise and encouragement so that your dog will bring it to you, and make even more whoop-te-do about it all when it's mission accomplished. Don't snatch the article away but allow the puppy to hold it for a bit while you praise with voice *and* hands.

When simple retrieves are mastered, hidden retrieves can add interest. At first, let your Golden watch you hide the ball behind the sofa or under a

A well-built Golden is easily trained to stand on her own and display all her best qualities, without being posed by hand. This is Am. Can. Ch. Gosling Daystar's Dawn CDX WC at age 8, handled by her owner Zelia Bohsen.

bush; then send the dog to find it. Soon you can walk out of sight, into another room (have an assistant restrain your dog), and place the ball (at first, where it will be seen promptly), then return and send the dog for the ball.

On your walks in the fields, take along a ball or a small training dummy, and do a few retrieves with the ball—sometimes in the open, sometimes in light cover. Your Golden will start working almost automatically. You will soon be able to add small obstacles such as a fallen log, or use a narrow stream that the dog can splash through to get to the object. At first, let your dog dash after it quickly to help develop speed and interest. Eventually, you can hold the collar for a few seconds of restraint, letting the dog go while still focused on where the object landed ("the fall," in retriever parlance).

Never overdo these play retrieves. If the puppy begins to lose interest or finds other places to focus attention, remember that you should have quit one retrieve earlier. Two or three retrieves are plenty. Keep a Golden wanting more, believing that retrieving is a privilege and a reward rather than a duty. The "duty" part comes later, when dogs are mature enough to accept the responsibility of retrieving as work rather than merely fun.

In the same manner, introduce the puppy to water, boats, gunfire, Agility obstacles and whatever other items may be a part of the future. Little puppies can experience shallow water in a wading pool, or even in the bathtub in very cold weather, with some toys to play with (be sure there is a nonslip mat on the bottom). If possible, the breeder can take the whole litter to a pond or stream with a shallow area where the little ones can follow Mom and human companions into the water. Later, you can take the puppy to a shallow pond or stream, at first just walking and playing where the puppy can still have a solid bottom under his feet, later doing simple retrieves with a boat bumper. As the puppy's confidence develops, you can gradually toss the bumper into deeper water; at first the puppy may hesitate, or stretch to get it, but soon she'll find she can swim. Often the puppy will follow another dog into swimming water. Sometimes it's helpful to get out into the water yourself with waders or a swimsuit.

Gunfire, properly introduced, is rarely a problem for Goldens. You do *not* want to make the first experiences overwhelming. Even without a gun, you can accustom the puppy to sharp noises by occasionally dropping a couple of food pans, or using a child's cap gun at a distance, perhaps while the puppies are playing or eating. Even if startled, they will go back to their dinner. Again, don't overdo it. If they overreact by running and hiding, ignore it; any "comforting" or "reassurance" you might offer will only indicate that there is something to worry about. Later, when they have developed real interest in retrieving, a starter pistol will be used at a distance, as the bird or bumper is thrown. The association of the gunshot with the retrieve will quickly teach dogs that gunfire is a prelude to the great fun of retrieving. "Gunshyness" is usually the result of improper introduction to gunfire, so proper conditioning is essential.

Objects to be used for serious retrieving should not be the same objects that the puppies may consider their own to be chewed and mauled. A stuffed sock may be used for small puppies. Disposable paint rollers with fuzzy covering are lightweight and very appealing (but don't use them in water). Older puppies should have boat bumpers (retrieving dummies) of appropriate size. While puppies are shedding their baby teeth and getting second teeth, they may be unable to easily hold a *hard* canvas or plastic dummy. A soft one is more easily handled. Canvas dummies filled with granulated cork can be opened, some of the innards removed, and the canvas stitched up again.

You can introduce your puppy to feathers by means of a wing from a pheasant or duck, loose or tied to a training dummy. Let the puppy sniff it; then tease her with it, perhaps dragging it along the ground, talking to incite interest. Toss it out a few feet, and when she picks it up, go into overdrive with excited praise, kneel down and call her in. *Don't* take it from your puppy right way; let her hold it and bask in your sincere congratulations. Then take it gently (more praise) and perhaps do one or two more similar retrieves.

After the young dog is accustomed to retrieving the feathered dummy, you can use a cold (but not frozen) dead bird. Many Goldens meeting their first bird will take one sniff and grab it, with the attitude "It's *mine!*" Great— pile on the praise, but use the lead to keep your dog under control. You don't want a pup taking off for parts unknown to further examine and perhaps destroy this new treasure. Other puppies are more cautious and may need encouragement. *Don't* stuff the bird in a reluctant pup's mouth and force the hold. After all, you haven't yet taught your Golden to hold

A lovely young male: Ch. Daystar Tornado Warning at 20 months of age. Tory's show career continued into his 10th year with several Specialty wins from Veterans' Class. By Ch. Trowsnest Whirlwind UD WC out of Ch. Gosling's Daystar Dawn CDX WC; bred and owned by the Bohsens.

and carry, have you? Some puppies are slow to "turn on" to birds, but after experience retrieving dummies, they will develop interest in feathers, so be patient.

The first live bird should be a small pigeon or partridge. The wings and feet should be tied with cloth strips, or the bird slipped inside a sock with the toe cut out; some pups will be put off by a flapping, scratching bird; others will be overenthusiastic and perhaps maul it, which could lead to the undesirable habit of crunching live retrieves. The young puppy doesn't really need a great deal of work on birds, just enough to develop interest and learn that every now and then he gets to have the fun of the "real thing." Some dogs like birdwork so much that they lose interest in retrieving dummies, creating a problem you don't need at this point.

You can start using a whistle with the puppy—any of the several whistles made for retriever training. The "**come-in**" whistle is a short series of three or four peeps, "*pip-pip-pip*." Use it with "Here" to make the association for returning with a retrieve, or to call the puppy to you. The whistle for "**sit**" is one sharp *pip;* again, this can be started in basic yard-work right along with Heeling and Sitting. "*Pip*," "**Sit,**" "good dog!" Use the whistle before the verbal command so that your dog begins to anticipate the verbal "**Sit**" with the whistle-pip.

A dog who responds to the whistle is handy even if you never do field work. Rather than shouting and screaming when your pup has wandered out of sight on a walk or is overly interested in the children's play at the park, you can use the whistle to summon the dog with much less fuss. The sound of the whistle carries much better than does the voice, and takes less of your wind as well.

The puppy who is retrieving enthusiastically can begin to be restrained just long enough to watch the bumper hit the ground. Then release with a cue to retrieve, which could be the dog's name or the word "Back!" or "Fetch!" Field trainers often use the dog's name, as they may be working two or more dogs at once and if all left at the word "Back" there would be major chaos! Conversely, if you plan to do Obedience work, you probably won't want any movement on the name but will want the dog to wait for a definite command.

Eventually the young dog will learn to wait and to watch (mark) the fall, and will not move until sent. Your hand and arm aligned next to the dog's head will help indicate the line to the fall; you move your hand forward with the verbal command to send the dog. There might be two or three falls to be marked, and the dog must observe and remember them. A leaping, barking, unhinged dog will simply not be able to mark with any accuracy, and can be not only an annoyance but a real danger in the field. Steadiness and enthusiasm are both great virtues, with a nice balance to be maintained between the two.

The dog's return with the retrieve is also important: An enthusiastic return is not only stylish but efficient. Running away from the puppy, clapping your hands and giving lots of verbal encouragement, you can speed up a slowing dog. Let your Golden catch up to you, and pour on the praise as you accept the retrieve. When coming out of the water, the dog should deliver the retrieve without stopping to shake (in which the retrieve could be damaged or dropped). You should be right at the water's edge, backing up and enthusiastically encouraging the dog to bring the object right in to you. Take it, praising your wet and soggy dog to the skies!

Everyday Training

As Goldens are definitely oral types, you will find your Golden carrying almost anything that can be picked up. They'll retrieve shoes, gloves, boots, newspapers, towels, the kids' toys—you name it. Again, much damage can be prevented by keeping such items out of reach, in the closet behind closed doors, in a cabinet, toy chest or clothes hamper. It's been said that having a Golden Retriever is a good way to teach children to keep their belongings picked up! Always encourage Goldens to bring to you whatever they might be carrying, and praise them for doing so. Then you can take it away gently, if need be, and give them something more acceptable in return. Don't snatch the item out of a pup's mouth and scold. She certainly won't see any reason to bring anything to you the next time, but instead will take it behind the sofa to chomp on.

Additionally, dogs who are continually discouraged from carrying things will later be confused about retrieving, and may well prove very difficult to teach. If the puppy does damage some item, yelling and punishment will not improve matters one bit. The damage is done. The most you can do is to hold the puppy by the collar in one hand, hold the object in the other hand, and tell the puppy quietly and sadly that this is a forbidden item. Place the item on the floor and release it; if the puppy makes a move toward it, very sharply say, *"NO!!"* Then remove the object and end the lesson.

"No" means stop *instantly* and, quite possibly, never even think about doing it again without permission. *"No"* can range from a mild warning to absolute condemnation, depending upon how it is said.

"Leave it," on the other hand, means that interesting as whatever *it* is might be, including dead frogs and horse droppings, *it* is not to be touched. You can use food to teach "Leave it": Place a small bit of food on the floor, saying "Leave it"; if the puppy moves to take it, give a sharp little tug on the collar; after a few seconds, pick up the food and give it to your pup, saying, "OK, you can have it." The dog will learn quickly that the treat will be given for obeying the "Leave it."

Vocabulary

Even a young puppy can learn many of the basic command words. You can work many of them into everyday training, the "life experience." You can vary the words to suit yourself as long as you are consistent. Some may later become formal commands:

Sit—assume the sitting position. Obedience trainers want a proper, straight sit, not slouched over on one hip.

Down—assume the lying position. It does not mean "get off the couch" or "don't jump up."

Here—to move toward the caller whether at a distance or close by; used by Field trainers; less formal than "come" and easier to say forcefully.

Come—to move toward the caller and assume an attentive sitting position in front, as used in Obedience training. Formal Recall.

Stand—assume and maintain standing position.

Heel—to move or sit beside the handler at the handler's left side. In formal Obedience, "Heel position" has a very precise definition.

Stay—remain in that place and position until told otherwise.

Informal cues that work easily into everyday life without much formal training are these:

Wait—don't go forward (through the door, into the crate).

Move—get out of my way (I need to open the door, pick up the rug, run the vacuum). Gently bump the dog out of the way.

Off—get off the couch; get your feet off me; don't jump on Aunt Emmie.

Go lie down—anywhere; just go and get out of the way.

Go to bed; place—specifically, go to that place and remain there.

Up—put your feet up here (on the grooming table; to be lifted into a high place).

Leave it—don't touch; leave it alone.

No—stop! Don't do that! Stop what you're doing.

Enough—that's all for now; that will do.

Quiet—no barking, no noise.

Easy—don't pull on the leash; cool it; hold still while I trim your nails, please.

Hie on—go play, run, explore; fun time. Hunters use "hie on" (pronounced "high on") to mean to go looking for game. If you anticipate doing this, use "go play" or some other term for this release word.

Okay or *all-right*—release word meaning the previous command is ended. There are many variations on this one. Border Collie people say "That'll do." Nice.

Kennel—get into your kennel or crate, or into the car or other place indicated.

Get busy, or *Hurry up*—cue for urination/defecation.

Good!—All dogs need a praise word to let them know they did well. If "good dog" is too plebeian, how about "*Sehr Gut!*" (German for very good) or "*Yayyuh!*" (Southern for the same thing). Be creative. Your tone of voice and facial expression are as important as anything else.

It is very important that if the puppy doesn't respond promptly as desired, you enforce the command word. If your Golden doesn't move out of your way on "Move, please," you just bump or physically move the dog with the collar. For not coming when called, give a quick snap on the leash, as a reminder that there is no other option. Then when your dog complies, your praise says "Yes, this is the proper response" (even if assisted); it's not that you're angry, this is just the way the world is, kid.

When you get further into Field and Obedience training there are additional words to be learned, including:

Fetch—pick up, hold and carry an object. Obedience people may use "Take It" or "Get it." Many Field people use the dog's name as a command to retrieve, often because two or more dogs may be working at the same time. The dogs probably consider it permission to retrieve, not a command; the act of retrieving in itself is reward for these dogs.

Back—go away from the handler; take a specific line or direction.

Over—to take direction to the right or left, from a distance.

There are many other commands that may be used. If you plan to work your Golden in several areas of activity, sit down and plan your vocabulary before you get too far along. It can be very confusing for a dog who knows that "Over" is a command to jump an obstacle, to start Field work and hear "Over" in a completely different context. In Obedience, you could say "Hike," which has a more forceful sound to it anyway. Or you could say "Broccoli." Words mean only what the dog has learned; they have no intrinsic meaning. "Heel" to the Obedience dog is different from the much more casual heeling for the Field dog, where "By me" or "Walk" could be used just as well. Old-time Field trainers used the words "Hup" for sit (Spaniel trainers still do) and "Charge" to lie down (originally "Down charge," making the dog lie still while the hunter reloaded, or put a new "charge" in the gun). Think about what you say to the dog. What's a poor dog to do when the owner says "Sit down" anyway? If you say "Come," "Come here," "Get in here" and "Right now!" to mean the same action, the dog will have no idea what's going on— it's just that person making noise again.

SHOW TRAINING

Training for the conformation ring is simple compared to Field or Obedience work. The dog has to learn a few basics: to trot along on-lead in a straight line; stand still for examination; look alert and happy—that is "show," usually for a special tidbit. Dogs must also learn to stand and sit quietly on a grooming table, to accept being crated or confined in an exercise pen and to travel well. These are things useful for any dog and any owner.

Puppies think this is all a game and lots of fun, and showing should always be enjoyable for the dog: You simply cannot force a dog to be happy. The unhappy dog will certainly be at a disadvantage in the show ring.

Start with puppy on a lightweight lead, or no lead at all. Have an ample supply of tidbits, such as boiled/baked liver or microwaved hot-dog slices in your pocket. With a few in your right hand, hold the treats just at your dog's nose level, moving a step or two until she is standing squarely on all four feet. Reward with a *tiny* tidbit. Repeat a few times; then you can both relax. Gradually you can bend over and stroke your dog lightly along the back, letting her nibble on the tidbit as you praise lavishly. Don't worry about where the feet are, as long as the dog is standing. Use the word "Stand" (or whatever other word you may have chosen).

To get a puppy to move along at your side, in most cases all you need to do is start walking; the natural instinct for following will bring him along. Talk to him with any kind of quiet, encouraging chatter that will keep his attention and convey praise for moving along. With older puppies, use a lightweight show lead, a slip-on collar and lead combination. The puppy should be trotting along briskly but not too fast, head and tail up happily. Just going a few feet will be enough at first; then stop and praise, or bait the pup into a Stand again for a few seconds. *Don't try to give bait while moving*, as it creates awkward positions or forces the dog to turn sideways, looking for the goodies.

The Show Pose

You can teach the show pose, or "stacking," on the ground, or, with young or small puppies, on a table, which is certainly easier on the handler. Of course, you will *always* have at least one hand in contact so that the dog cannot fall and get hurt. Practice posing, lifting one leg at a time and placing it in a nice square stance. Keep one hand under the pup's head for steadiness and encouragement. Always add a little stroking and quiet words of praise.

Most Goldens really do look their best standing on their own, without interference from the handler. A really skillful handler can make the dog look stunning without seeming to do a thing while in reality using very subtle cues of body language, a tiny amount of prompting with the show lead, or just the suggestion of bait. Such a handler will let the dog walk into a good square stance, perhaps make one or two minor adjustments, and then fade into the background so that all one really sees is a beautiful dog. Well, most of us aren't *that* good as handlers, but it does give us something to aim for.

In most areas, there are show handling classes that teach the basics: how to pose the dog, the different patterns of gaiting (moving the dog), ring etiquette and so on. They can be worthwhile, especially for beginners and for starting young dogs. There are also some books on show ring training, although not nearly as many as are available on Obedience training. You can learn a great deal by attending shows without a dog and carefully observing the handlers—not only in Goldens, but in other breeds. Labrador Retriever handlers, for instance, are often very good at showing the dogs without excess posing and manipulation. Of course, there are great differences between breeds in how they are shown, but it is always useful to observe.

Thea and Gena were started in tracking at 10 weeks of age, and it became a lifetime love for both of them. Left, Anthea of Setherwood, Am. Can. UDTX was the first Golden to earn a TDX in Canada. Right, Kyrie Genever, Am. Can. UDTX, Am. Can. WC. Both earned their American TDX titles at 10½ years of age; they were owned and trained by Marallyn and Ed Wight.

The Golden should stand squarely, with front legs parallel and vertical, somewhat under the body. The back legs are placed so that the rear pasterns are vertical and a line dropped from the point of the buttocks falls just barely in front of the rear pasterns. The back should be level, the neck slightly extended. The tail, if it is held, should never be higher than the level of the back. If the dog will stand with a level, wagging tail, without the handler's assistance, so much the better. The practice of hauling the dog's head up with a stranglehold on the collar is not at all attractive, nor is a skyward-pointing tail.

When gaiting, a moderate trot is best, the dog moving in a straight line without pulling on the lead or hanging back. Goldens are not intended to be speed-demon trotters. A good working trot, of the sort that a dog could maintain for hours at a time, is much more appropriate. The dog should be taught to gait properly on a loose lead. Trying to make the dog look stylish by means of holding the head up with the lead only interferes with proper

Beautiful and talented as a Golden may be, an owner who will devote to the dog the necessary time, effort and understanding is also essential for success. This is Roseanne Carpenter's Ch. Wingwatcher Calypso Music, UDT WC VCX (1983–1994), by Ch. Trowsnest Whirlwind UD WC x Beaumaris Fair Victory CD. Calypso also earned a CDX under UKC rules.

movement, shortening stride and throwing the dog off balance. A proper lead is neither tight nor hanging sloppily; it can have some slight tension when necessary to guide or control the dog.

Fashions in showing do change. Years ago it was unheard of to bait a Sporting dog; the dogs were posed like statues with head and tail extended gracefully. Leads were removed and placed on the ground. Some dogs were so well trained they would remain motionless for minutes on end, until the lead was replaced. Now, baiting and the desire for a dog who "asks for it" is often so overdone that the dogs can get out of control, or stand still only when gnawing on a chunk of liver. Sometimes all the activity may be used to conceal something the handler doesn't want the judge to see.

THE BROADER PICTURE

Every dog needs a different approach to look best. What works for one dog may not be appropriate for yours. It is very helpful to have a friend observe your dog and give you some feedback. It's also useful to practice in front of a large mirror—you can even use a reflective shop window. Ask an experienced, successful handler (amateur or professional) whom you respect to give you some lessons. Offer to pay them appropriately; they might not accept the payment, but their time and helpfulness are worth it, and they can give you help with your individual dog that may not be available in all-breed handling classes.

With competition in Goldens as strong as it is today, and with large entries common in many areas of the country, completing a championship is not easy. Some owners don't feel competent presenting their dogs to best advantage, or can't manage the time and travel required. For this reason, there are professional handlers. Many are very expert indeed, and in many cases can finish a dog to championship much more quickly than the owner could. But you have to weigh what you want from showing. Do you want the fun of earning a title yourself—that is, you and your furry friend together? Or do you want to get that title as expeditiously as possible and then do other fun things, such as Obedience or Hunting Tests, Tracking or Agility?

USING A PROFESSIONAL HANDLER

If you decide to go with a professional handler, be cautious. Observe potential handlers. Do they show Goldens well? Are their crates and grooming areas clean and well organized? Are the dogs fed, watered and exercised efficiently? Do the handlers have a reasonable number of dogs, or are there so many that the assistants rather than the handler that we hired have to take dogs in the ring? The American Kennel Club does not regulate handlers, or agents as they are often called; it is up to you to find out how your dog will be cared for, both on the road and at the handler's kennels, if the dog stays there. There are professional organizations, such as the Professional Handlers' Association (PHA) and the Dog Handlers' Guild (DHG), and if the handler carries the designation CPH (Certified Professional Handler), certain standards will have been met regarding facilities and experience.

Good handlers will be clear about their fees and other requirements. They will provide references and offer a well-worded contract to cover all contingencies, as well as insurance covering your dog. They should bill regularly for their services, which will be clearly defined on the statements. They will let you know promptly of all wins, sending copies of catalog pages and all ribbons and trophies (by custom, handlers get to keep any money won). And if your dog is not of a quality to win honestly, they will tell you and not try to con you into continuing with a dog who has little chance of winning.

There are, however, many successful owner-handlers of Goldens. If you plan on learning as much as possible about Goldens and the wide range of activities in which you can participate, you should at least make a serious effort at doing it yourself, and that includes conformation showing. Whether or not you succeed in getting a title on the dog, you will have had a valuable learning experience.

FORMAL OBEDIENCE TRAINING

A wide range of methods and techniques will work, at least to some degree, with most Goldens. The Golden's willingness to work, and forgivingness of handler's blunders, make up for many failings on the part of the trainer. Many trainers, after acquiring more experience, find out just how forgiving their first dog really was!

Obedience training, like so much else, should start early in life. The puppy who is brought up knowing the basics of Sit, Down, Come and so forth, has a big start on training. This dog has "learned to learn," which is extremely important.

Puppy Kindergarten Training classes were first advanced by Milo and Margaret Pearsall more than thirty years ago, and developed further by others. Some Obedience clubs hold these useful classes. The emphasis is *not* on formal Obedience exercises but on such topics as socialization with other dogs, learning to accept being handled, gaining a variety of experiences and learning the meaning of simple commands in order to develop a solid foundation upon which further training can be done.

Positive, or motivational, techniques are the best way to *teach* the dog, to get that first basic understanding. *Training* is the later developmental stage, and some compulsive techniques may be needed: They can be used because the dog already has some understanding of what he is supposed to be doing. In teaching, food may be used as motivation—also, praise and play used as positive reinforcement. Eventually food must be phased out (or kept for only occasional use) and replaced by secondary reinforcers such as praise. As the dog gains in understanding, he learns that working with the handler is not only enjoyable and rewarding but also the way to avoid less pleasant consequences. As one clever trainer said, "The secret to dog training is to make the dog believe that it was all his own idea." Another phrased it this way: "The dog must be responsible for his own choices."

Behind these simple statements lie thousands of pages written on learning and behavioral theory, and hundreds of dog training books.

As an example, in developing the response to the word "Sit," the trainer first uses a bit of food to attract the dog's attention and lure the dog into a sitting position, upon which the dog immediately gets the tidbit and praise (positive reinforcement). When the trainer adds the verbal cue "Sit," the dog very soon learns that the action of sitting upon hearing the word "Sit" has a result the dog is willing to work for. This is the teaching phase.

In the training phase, a straighter Sit position can be developed ("shaped") by reinforcing (rewarding) only the best responses. Compulsion can be introduced. A properly timed short snap of the leash encourages a faster response if the dog learns to avoid the snap by acting more quickly. The lead can also be used to guide the dog or to restrain, or for corrections such as the quick snap on the collar.

While some trainers advocate purely "motivational" techniques, some degree of compulsion is necessary in training because there invariably comes a time when the dog would rather do something else. When a squirrel scampers across the sidewalk while you're working, your dog is not going to remember the cookies in your pocket! But the Golden who takes off after the squirrel and comes to a cartwheeling stop at the end of the lead learns the consequences of choosing to chase rather than "Heel."

There also comes a time in nearly every young dog's life when she seems to be "testing"—just like human teenagers, dogs test the limits. When the ten-month-old dog looks up at you upon hearing "Come" and says "Why?", you must have some means of enforcing the command. "Because I said so!" If Megan fails to come, you must attach the lead or long line and remind her just what "Come" means; otherwise, the pup learns that "Come" means "Come if you feel like it." Don't be upset when the teenage Golden (or even older dog) suddenly seems to have forgotten what she did so charmingly as a puppy; it's quite natural. When you "explain" clearly and uncompromisingly, with real praise for complying, understanding will return.

Most Goldens don't need harsh correction; when they understand what a correction is for, there is little problem. It's the confused dog who simply gives up and stops trying, and many sensitive Goldens are easily confused as the result of the trainer's inconsistent or contradictory actions.

QUESTIONS ABOUT THE VERSATILE PUPPY PROSPECT

Q. What personality traits are looked for in a puppy?

A. The traits most often considered important are self-confidence (does the puppy willingly explore a new place and check out new objects? is the puppy responsive?), alertness to voice and body movement, and a "come a'runnin'" attitude (is the general attitude alert and confident, but neither bullying nor overly submissive?). One of the most useful tests is the simple retrieve or "fetch test": Does the puppy not only follow and go to the object tossed a few feet but also return with it to the person? The pup who does so is usually a good prospect for work.

Q. Do most puppies have the potential for versatile achievement?

A. This depends on the dog, the handler and the goals. Most Goldens should have the basic qualifications for some level of work in some area; a CD or CDX and a WC or JH *should* be within the reach of most well-bred Goldens. Conformation showing depends on more subjective factors, and a smaller percentage of dogs will achieve a championship. If by versatile achievement one means a Ch-UDT-MH, then a very small number of dogs will reach this level, primarily because it requires an exceptional commitment of time and work by the owner. There are probably more dogs with the intrinsic capability than there are handlers, but a truly exceptional dog can often inspire the handler to go on to higher levels!

Q. Are there particular physical characteristics that are considered?

A. Most trainers do look for certain qualities in conformation, notably basic soundness and balance. Most agree that any disqualification or severe fault under the breed Standard is unacceptable. Very large size and coarseness; notable lack of angulation; extremely long, excessive coat and clumsy gait with poor coordination are also felt to be very undesirable.

Q. What about the pedigree?

A. Knowledge of the dogs in the pedigree can give some idea of the basic strengths and weakness that the dog may display. A pedigree containing many multititled dogs indicates that some degree of trainability and willingness to work should be present in the descendents. Although sometimes a lack of titles means only that the people who owned those dogs weren't interested, it may also indicate that any consideration of those aspects has been completely neglected. A pedigree alone is not enough; one must know the dogs.

Q. Does training begin in one particular area or in different areas concurrently?

A. Successful trainers like to start puppies with informal basics as part of the daily routine: Sit, Come, Stay, Off, Kennel and so forth. Retrieving is another basic that is started early with balls, birds, bumpers, toys. Basic grooming starts early as well. Several like to start tracking training with puppies; others wait, sometimes due to climate or lack of suitable areas. One trainer says "When a puppy begins to show a desire to learn more, is when I add new topics or begin more formal training."

Q. Is it preferable to concentrate on one area at a time or train for multiple titles at the same time?

A. While dogs may learn in different areas concurrently, some handlers prefer to separate the training—not doing both Field and Tracking the same day, for instance, or doing a little conformation practice in the morning and Obedience class in the evening. Some don't train formally for conformation at all, just lead training, grooming and a few fun match experiences. All agree that the dogs easily know the differences between Obedience and conformation by the differences in collars, handlers' body language, cues and commands, and that, sensibly handled, the dogs have little problem doing both.

Q. What daily or weekly time commitment is involved?

Am. Can. Ch. Amber-trail's Bargello Stitch, Am. Can, UD, TDX, WCX, Bda. CDX, TD; owned by Barbara Tinker. Another exceptional performer bred by Mike and Val Ducross from the combination of Am. Can. Ch. High Farms Jantze of Curacao CDX TDX Can.Ch./OTCh. Val's Dolly.

A. This varies a great deal. People who work full time will need to fit training into their schedule; some may do short sessions before and after work, with longer times on the weekends. Field training or advanced tracking may well take several hours to a full day, including travel time; those working with two or more dogs will need more time. Once a dog is trained to top level, however, often daily drillwork is not needed and a brush-up session once or twice a week is sufficient, plus whatever events may be scheduled for the weekends.

Q. Is there a conflict between Field and Obedience, or conformation and Obedience? Does Field work present a problem for the show dog's coat?

A. Using a definite separate vocabulary for each area is one of the best ways to prevent confusion. As mentioned previously, there are many factors that help a dog easily discriminate between show and Obedience work. Most agree that if the dog has a proper Golden coat—dense and weather-resistant, without excessive length and softness—there is no real problem with Field work. Some people use a spray such as Pam on the dog's legs and underside to help prevent snarls when working in areas with burrs, more for the dog's comfort than for "protecting" the coat.

Q. What role does the professional handler or trainer play?

A. Some feel that using a pro handler in showing is the quickest way to get the championship title; others feel that it's much more fun to do it themselves. The owner's expertise (or lack) is a factor, as is the area of the country. Owners in areas where shows are far apart or few in number may feel that a pro handler is worth the cost. Most owners training in Field work feel a need for some professional help sooner or later, particularly when encountering a problem or working on something with which they are not familiar. This may mean a few paid lessons with the pro, or sending the dog out for training for a month or more. Golden owners working in Obedience usually make good use of training clubs and classes, and sometimes take private lessons with an experienced trainer/competitor.

Q. Is it essential to participate in all these different areas?

A. No, there's no "law" that says you must do so—and perhaps you have no interest in tromping across muddy fields or handling dead birds or trotting around a show ring for a scrap of garishly colored ribbon. However, if you want to get a better idea of the full range of capabilities of the Golden Retriever in general, and your own furry friend in particular, you might like to at least try some of the activities mentioned. Your Golden will enjoy using his talents, and you just might like it, too. Capable Goldens have led many people into areas they had never dreamed of in years B.C. (Before Canines)!

Caring for Your Golden Retriever

HOUSING AND HOUSE TRAINING

It's possible to keep a happy, healthy Golden in many types of homes and circumstances, but there are essentials, including proper socialization and basic training. The dog needs a specific *sleeping area*, probably a dog crate for the puppy, perhaps a rug or mat for the adult dog. There should be a securely *fenced area* where the dog may exercise—that is, a fenced yard or kennel run, ideally both of which ensure the dog's safety. While daily walks may take care of the dog's elimination needs, they will not fulfill the need for real exercise and play. The dog *cannot* be left to run loose unsupervised, or the day invariably will come when your Golden is stolen or gets in a dogfight, is shot by a farmer for molesting livestock or is found under the wheels of a car.

Goldens do shed, very heavily at times, requiring grooming and housecleaning on your part. They will retrieve any items left within reach—shoes, laundry, throw rugs—but they can be taught to carry only the toys provided for them. They don't mind being wet and muddy (some seem to glory in it!) and will bring all the slop and slush in on their big paws and wet coats. A mud room or kitchen or laundry with an easily cleaned floor, where dogs can stay until dried, is a definite asset. They will be bumptious and clumsy when youngsters, and wagging tails can remove glasses from the coffee table with disastrous results. As puppies, they will nibble books or table legs without concern, until taught what's off limits.

Housetraining is far more than merely learning to use an outside toilet area. It is mostly a matter of having your "eagle eye" on the puppy every second so that you can forestall an accident or mishap and provide an alternative. This takes a great deal of diligence, so it is very useful to utilize a dog crate as a bedroom, playpen and holding area for the times when you aren't able to keep your attention on the puppy.

The breed's top winning show bitch is Ch. Brandymist QB Gal, bred by Pamela and James Cobble, owned by them and William and Marie Wingard. "Meg" collected some 22 Best in Show awards and more than a dozen Specialty Bests of Breed. She was handled by Michael Faulkner, who has shown Goldens very successfully since he was a teenager.

Ch. C-Vu's Brigantine CD JH WCX, another who shows that Goldens can hold their quality for many years. Brig is pictured winning a Best of Breed award at 7½ years of age. Owned by Nancy Corbin, Brig is a son of her Ch. Hye Tyme's Clipper, UD JH WCX VCX.

Can. Ch. Comstock's Carmel Nut UDTX SH WCX VCX, Can. UD WCX. A son of Bainin of Caernac CD***, "Jazz" had 10 points in the U.S. and a Group 1st. His 7 High in Trial awards in Canada placed him in the Golden Retriever Club of Canada's Obedience Hall of Fame. Bred, trained and owned by Kathy McCue, DVM.

Set up a schedule of regular times for feeding, play and nap time that will work *with* the puppy's natural schedule of such activities. Stay with the schedule, and this aspect of housetraining should go fairly smoothly. Once the puppy learns, it will be for life; a few weeks' effort now can make a well-adjusted companion for fourteen or sixteen years. Puppies will need to go out immediately after waking (every time, not just in the morning), after eating, and at intervals during playtime, and will not wait for you to shower and dress in the morning, at least not until they are mature. After these "outings," you have a short period of relative safety, so this is a good opportunity for housetime (with you watching, of course!). After active playtime, any youngster will need a nap, so there is your cue to pop your pup in the crate with a toy or a small biscuit. After a nap, the pup should go out again, or you'll find a puddle on the floor, guaranteed!

At night, make absolutely sure that your puppy has gone out immediately before bedtime. Keep the last meal at least two hours before bedtime, and provide very little or no water after that time either so that your pup is "emptied out" before going to bed. Your Golden may cry or complain at being alone, but if she needs to go out, then you must take her. Allow five minutes to perform at the toilet area, and if she does, give her lots of praise. Then everybody goes back to bed. If not, the pup goes back in the crate, and it's "lights out."

It is perfectly acceptable to put the crate in your bedroom, next to the bed, where you can put a finger in to let the pup know she is not abandoned. This has the advantage of helping develop the closeness and bonding we like to have with a dog. Also you will not have to stumble sleepily around the house to go out when necessary! If your dog fusses for no reason (sometimes they just feel like running races at 3 A.M.), a low, firm "Be quiet!" will show you are not in the mood for such frivolity.

Whether you want the pup to sleep on the bed is for you to decide. However, it's certainly best to teach the puppy to sleep in a crate, on the floor or on the dog bed *first*. It avoids setting up the potential for problems such as wet muddy feet on the bed, or possible dominance or territory problems. If traveling and staying in hotels or in other homes, the dog will be more welcome off the bed. After the pup is grown and has good house manners, it's entirely acceptable to allow bed privileges—by invitation only—as a special treat.

THE DOG CRATE

If you have more than one dog (and multiple Goldens seems to be the case more often than not), each should have a specific place. Crates are definitely useful here so that each can have an individual "room" in which to be safe and secure. Older dogs need a place to get away from the annoyance of heedless puppies (or children). A dog can be fed in the crate without being disturbed, and one who isn't feeling well or is just plain tired after a long walk or a training session can relax comfortably. When you are travelling, the crate can go in the car and in the motel room as a "home away from home."

For everyday use, the most popular types are the folding wire crate and the plastic "airline" crate. The most useful type of wire crates folds down into a suitcase-size package. Be sure that you get a quality crate; too many of the cheap ones can be a serious danger to the dog. Buy the sturdiest available, with solid welds and a secure latch. All spaces between the wires should be close enough that paws and nose cannot protrude. Wider spaces can lead to injury, because each wire receives more stress and will tend to break more easily. Check the edges where the end panels and the top and bottom panels meet; there should be a positive locking device or catch so that the panels cannot be pushed apart. Puppies have wedged their heads through and been strangled because they could not escape.

"Airline" crates are molded plastic in two sections that bolt together. They have a wire mesh door, and wire openings on at least two sides. They are by far the best for shipping by air. If the dog is wet or muddy, the solid floor and walls keep the wet off your upholstery. They are very easy to keep clean, are easily disinfected and are lighter in weight than the metal crates. Air circulation is not as good as in wire crates, so some caution must be used.

A blanket or bath towel, which can be easily laundered and replaced if necessary, can serve as bedding. Puppies may well tear up their bedding, so don't buy expensive items. The imitation sheepskin fabric is super; it gives good cushioning and is also easy to wash. Crate pads filled with foam rubber look nice, but most Goldens get a real bang out of rendering them into as many very small pieces as possible! Hunters and Field trainers often use marsh hay as bedding in dog boxes on their trucks.

The crate should be adult size, approximately twenty-four inches wide by thirty-six inches long and about twenty-six inches high. Because of their shape, the airline crates of this measurement have an actual floor area somewhat smaller, but most Goldens are still quite comfortable in a "400" size airline crate. A very large Golden might take a 500 size. The dog should be able to stand up, turn around and lie down comfortably. Too large a crate when travelling, whether by air or car, can allow the dog to be bounced around excessively.

The best sources for crates (and most other dog supplies) are the major mail-order dog supply houses. Experienced dog folk are very familiar with these sources. Often crates can be purchased second-hand at bargain prices, but be sure to check them out very thoroughly for soundness and safety. Make sure all the hardware is in good shape. A good-quality crate, well cared for, should outlast the dog.

OUTSIDE KENNELLING

Even with a fenced yard, it is very useful to have an outside kennel or pen for the dog. Goldens are hardy outside dogs and will usually be happier in a comfortable outside kennel than cooped up in the house all day. While the sleeping dog is fine in a crate overnight, crating for eight or ten hours during the day as well is unrealistic. The outside kennel will keep dogs safe and secure, and assure you that both the house and yard are safe from canine experimentation. When non-doggy people come to visit, when workers are in and out of the house, or when wet, muddy pawprints are not welcome in the house, he can be safe and happy in his kennel.

The ideal situation is to have a kennel pen inside a fenced yard, which gives the security of the kennel when needed and the freedom of the larger yard for play and training. The outdoor kennel should be located at a handy distance from the back door and where it can be readily observed. The area should be well drained so that there is never any standing water from rainfall or from hosing it down. The area for one dog should measure a minimum of six feet by twelve feet; for two dogs, eight by sixteen feet. By having the run or pen at least this wide, the dog has much more freedom of movement and is less likely to step in droppings. A wall or building on the north and/or west side of the kennel helps shelter the dog from wind and inclement weather.

A certain amount of direct sunlight will help enormously to keep the area dry and clean-smelling. For the dog's sake, there must also be some shade. Lacking a properly located tree, you can make shade with a tarpaulin rigged appropriately. The special "shade cloth" that has an open weave also works well and allows for some air circulation. In very warm climates, a tarpaulin with a special silvery reflective coating will help reduce the temperature in the shaded area.

Concrete is often used for flooring; it does not get muddy and can't be dug up, and it can be scrubbed, but it must be sloped so that it will drain properly. It can be very warm under direct sunlight, and it has no resilience. It has the disadvantage of absorbing odors if not sealed properly and can be very slippery when icy. Concrete stays damp in humid climates, and dogs lying continually on concrete will form pressure calluses on elbows and other areas. A simple wooden resting platform is useful.

Pea gravel or crushed limestone at least four inches deep drains very well and is good footing for the dogs. Picking up solid waste on this kind of surface is easy; even though a small amount of stone is lost with the picking-up, it is easy to replace; and it can be disinfected fairly well by wetting it down with bleach solution. Crushed limestone packs down and stays in place better than pea gravel. A curb or boarding around the perimeter will help keep the stone in place. Unless precautions are made, such as laying wire-mesh flat on the surface before the stone is put down, the dogs will dig—and create something resembling a battlefield.

Patio blocks or pavers also have been used successfully. The ground must be levelled, and the blocks laid with no more than a half-inch space between them. Spaces can be filled with clean sand. Pavers have all the advantages of poured concrete but will drain better because run-off can go right through the cracks between the blocks. "Seconds" bought directly from a local manufacturer will be much cheaper than those found at retail outlets.

Shelter

You can provide a doghouse in the outdoor kennel, or, if you have used the wall of a garage or outbuilding as one side of your pen, you can build an inside pen (at least double the size of the sleeping box) containing a covered sleeping box or doghouse. For one dog, a sleeping box with an inside area of about thirty by thirty-six inches is sufficient; for two dogs, about thirty-six by forty-eight inches. For an outside doghouse, add to these sizes an entryway about sixteen inches wide to shelter the inside from blowing wind and snow. You can choose from several types of pet doors; the flexible plastic ones are the quietest and won't damage a tail that gets caught. One kennel I visited had some very efficient aluminum or steel swinging doors, but every time the dogs went in or out, the doors slammed so loudly that it sounded like a volley of gunshots! Many kennels use no doors at all on the openings, particularly if the doors face south or east; the orientation avoids much of the weather.

Sleeping boxes or doghouses should have some absorbent bedding, preferably either pine shavings (not cedar) or marsh hay. Pine shavings are inexpensive when bought in paper-wrapped bales. Cedar shavings have a very strong scent that may interfere with a hunting or tracking dog's scenting abilities, and some dogs react to the oils in cedar. Never use hardwood shavings, as some, such as walnut, are toxic. All bedding must be changed often enough that it never remains damp. A good grade of straw may be acceptable, but straw sometimes contains mites than can cause itching and skin problems.

Doghouses and sleeping boxes should be of ⁵/₈" or ³/₄" plywood, and be painted inside and out with a good grade of exterior paint so that they can be easily cleaned and scrubbed. A roof that lifts up for cleaning is essential. The floor of the house should be raised above the ground to keep out dampness. Don't use shingles or shakes on the doghouse—they are far too tempting to chew.

Your dog would appreciate some sort of porch or resting bench; it can be as simple as a platform of boards nailed to 2 × 4s. This gives the dog a dry resting area up off the dampness or chill of the ground. DO NOT use lumber pressure-treated with a preservative, as this solution can be toxic to dogs who are in close contact or who chew on it. Resting platforms are also available commercially, made from a type of recycled plastic; these are fairly expensive, but very attractive, durable and easy to keep clean. Any dog enjoys having a raised resting area from which to survey his kingdom.

Water should always be available—indoors, a non-tippable crock or bowl; out of doors, a ten-quart metal bucket. Galvanized metal is quite adequate, although stainless steel will last much longer. Water containers need to be kept *clean,* which in summer may mean scrubbing them out every day. Water freezing in the metal bucket can ruin it quickly, so you may have to have to have two buckets; when one begins to freeze, replace it with the other with fresh water. The rubber buckets used for horses are also useful, and ice can be knocked out of them easily.

You'll need to secure the bucket with a clip to the fence, as most Goldens like to paddle in the buckets or dunk their faces in the water. If your dog is a male, you may need to put the bucket up on a small platform or base (a few bricks or a concrete block will do) so that if he lifts his leg on the bucket he won't contaminate the water.

The Electronic Fence: Chains and Tie-Outs

Some people use the "electronic fence" if they live in an area where regulations prohibit regular fencing. This is a buried wire around the perimeter of the area. The dogs wear collars with small radio receivers. When they get near the buried wire, dogs feel a brief stimulation warning not to cross the wire, and a stronger zap if they get too close.

Unfortunately, however, there is no deterrent to other dogs, cats or people, who, of course, aren't wearing the collar-receiver. Some tough dogs learn to accept the brief shock received when crossing the wire and continue on their way. It may be worthwhile to inquire whether the prohibition against fencing allows a well-made, discreetly located kennel run or pen. Clever landscaping and scrupulous maintenance can make it quite acceptable.

No Golden should be kept chained routinely. Leaving any dog tied up for hours is very detrimental to temperament; the dog is defenseless against invaders and, being very aware of this, becomes morose or aggressive. The collar and chain can injure the dog, and the dog develops bad habits such as barking and stereotypical pacing or circling. Do not plan on keeping your Golden in this fashion.

FEEDING THE GOLDEN

With the many excellent commercial diets available today, feeding a dog properly is certainly not a major chore. While a homemade diet made from meat, cereal grains and other ingredients can be successful, it must be made very carefully in order to ensure balanced nutrition. Most of us prefer the convenience of commercial foods that have been thoroughly proven in both the manufacturers' "test kennels" and in everyday practical use.

It is very true that *proper* nutrition is important to the growing dog, but there is strong evidence that overnutrition and unbalanced nutrition of young dogs can be very detrimental to their growth and health. Diets that are very high in protein and fat content can lead to problems in bone formation particularly, by stimulating very rapid growth in which the actual structure of the bone is not laid down properly. While these puppies may not always appear to be fat or overweight, their growth pattern can be disturbed, resulting in poor bone structure. This may result in a degree of hip dysplasia in dysplasia-susceptible animals that is more severe than it might have been otherwise, or in other orthopedic problems such as osteochondritis dissicans (OCD). A more moderate diet, and a more moderate growth rate, may help to produce a sounder dog at maturity.

With that caution in mind, many breeders quite successfully use a high-quality puppy ("growth") diet for very small puppies, gradually changing to a combination of puppy and adult (maintenance) food when they are three or four months of age, and by six or seven months of age the puppy is on the adult diet. There are many quality national brands that have been used very successfully—not necessarily the most expensive. Most Goldens are "good doers" and utilize their food quite well. One should avoid the cheapest brands, little-known local brands and the "generic" type dog foods, far too many of which are made of poor-quality ingredients.

Dry food in a pelleted or kibble form is the best main ration. It is more appealing to the dog, and better digested if moistened with warm water or perhaps leftover soup or broth. Canned food is useful for adding to the dry food as a special treat or just for added flavor appeal, but not as the primary diet (except perhaps in the rare case of the dog needing a specially formulated veterinary "prescription" diet). In feeding Goldens, one must keep in mind that the recommendations as to amount fed listed on the bag of food should not be regarded as accurate. Most Goldens will do very well on considerably less, possibly half as much as recommended, for sedentary house dogs.

If the food is a well-proven national brand, it is not advisable to upset the balance of nutrients by adding specific vitamins or minerals. If you feel your dog needs a supplement, it should be a complete product that has all the necessary micronutrients to maintain everything in balanced proportions. Consult your veterinarian for recommendations.

We've had good success starting a puppy out with a good commercial puppy diet, mixed with warm water and left to soak until of a soft crumbly texture. A small amount of canned-meat dog food adds extra flavor appeal. At eight weeks, the puppy gets three meals a day of this, about three-fourths cup per meal (this may vary considerably). We adjust the timing of the meals to our schedule, whatever it is, but the puppy is fed on a fairly regular schedule (puppies just don't understand about "sleeping in" on the weekend!). As the puppy grows, of course we adjust the amount and let the food soak for less time. By the time the puppy is five or six months of age, two meals a day will be sufficient. Some people feed a mature dog only once a day, but many people continue a twice-a-day schedule for the dog's lifetime. This may be more agreeable to the dog (Goldens generally love to eat!) and less likely to overload the stomach and GI tract.

Should you allow the dog "ad lib" feeding, by keeping food available at all times? *Definitely not.* Most Goldens are absolute pigs when it comes to food and will happily eat themselves into oblivion, given the chance. If you have more than one dog, this may result in arguments, or one dog hogging the food and the other going without. Feeding a measured amount of food at regular times enables the owner to know whether the dog is eating properly, and also facilitates a regular schedule of elimination.

If the dog does fail to finish a meal, don't leave it down. After ten minutes or so, pick it up. At the next meal, give a little less food, and again, if the pup's not interested, don't coax or wheedle or pile on the goodies to make it tempting. Just take it away without comment. A healthy dog can miss a few meals without any adverse effects. Of course, if the dog acts in any way ill, or wants to eat but is having difficulty, that is another matter entirely and may deserve veterinary attention.

It is always best to stick to routine as much as possible; dogs are very much creatures of habit and will be both healthier and more content. The dog's schedule will depend on yours, of course; any time can work, as long as the dog has the opportunity to go out after eating and is not expected to do strenuous activity or hard work for at least an hour after eating.

Fit and trim, in excellent muscular condition and ready for work. This is Midas Belvedere Houston MH***, bred in Canada from English and American Field lines, owned by Mercedes Hitchcock of Texas.

"People food" and leftovers are certainly not forbidden for a Golden, but in order to maintain a balanced diet, you should keep these to a reasonable amount, *never* more than one quarter of the total diet, usually much less. A boiled egg or a small amount of cottage cheese are healthy treats. Dogs who tend to become overweight, as many older Goldens do, may be happy with the addition of vegetables such as cooked green beans or carrots as "fillers." Some Goldens happily devour anything edible (and some things not even remotely edible!), while others are more discriminating.

Many Goldens love raw tomatoes, apples and pears. Golden owners have been known to put chain-link fencing around their gardens to discourage raids by veggie-munching Goldens.

Recently a neighbor to a household with several Goldens raked up a great many windfall apples from his tree and dumped them in a far corner of the yard. This particular corner abutted the Goldens' yard. The dogs were delighted to discover a treasure trove of fresh apples lying against the fence, but were frustrated because they could not pull apples through the fence wire. Eventually their pawing created a shallow hole under the fence, and a tug on the wire resulted in an apple or two from the pile rolling conveniently into the hole. The Goldens found that they could paw at the fence and be rewarded with a nice juicy apple from their very own apple dispenser, and they lined up like shoppers at the market for their treats. No doubt the neighbor wondered who was so interested in his discarded apples!

Feeding the canine athlete may mean some adjustment in diet. Goldens who work hard need higher levels of certain nutrients, usually protein and fat. Working in cold weather increases the demands even further. Dr. Chris Zink's book *Peak Performance* addresses not only feeding but many other aspects of maintaining the canine athlete. Goldens who are undergoing the stress of the show circuit often need an adjustment in their diet, and some who are not good eaters may even need hand-feeding in order to maintain show condition. There are several very good commercial diets, made by major manufacturers, that provide for these specialized needs.

The elderly Golden has special needs as well. Most Goldens do quite well on their normal adult food until at least middle age. This may be as young as six or seven years for some, or as late as eleven or twelve years or more, for others. At one time it was thought that older dogs should have a lower level of protein in their diet in order to lessen the workload on the kidneys, hence the development of lower-protein "senior" foods. Currently, however, it is recognized that the older dog needs:

1. High-quality protein that is easily assimilable.
2. Enough of this protein to repair stresses on the aging body, sometimes even higher levels than maintenance. If your older dog is thin or losing weight, it might help to go to a premium food with slightly higher levels of high-quality protein. Some owners have used a quality puppy food with very good results on the aged dog. Others find they need only to add high-quality food such as a boiled egg or a few tablespoons of cottage cheese on a regular basis.

TOYS AND THE GOLDEN RETRIEVER'S "ORAL FIXATION"

Goldens are retrievers; they *need* to carry things. If you don't provide some sort of toys for your Golden, he will retrieve shoes, boots, newspapers, laundry items and small rugs. When one is in a hurry to get ready for work, it is a bother to have to hunt for the shoe that Harry has removed, especially when it's found dropped in the dog's water bowl. One Golden who had the misfortune to live with a lady with no understanding of retrievers, resorted to pulling the spread off the bed and dragging it to the front door to greet her puzzled owner. Another Golden developed the habit of carrying around a compliant cat, who apparently enjoyed this reversion to kittenhood. If the children don't want the Golden to de-trieve their toys, teach the kids to use a toychest with a lid, and a closet with doors.

The best solution is to be sure that the dog has *acceptable* items to carry and play with. He can learn which are his and what items are off-limits.

Durable toys for Goldens include solid rubber balls and "kong" toys made of very heavy rubber, nylon composition chewtoys (Nylabone) made specifically for heavy-duty chewing, and treated natural bones that have been "petrified" and sterilized. These items in the larger sizes will last quite well even with a dedicated gnawer, as many Goldens are. They're available from dog suppliers, both mail-order and local.

Play toys to be used *under supervision* include stuffed items made of acrylic fleece (Goldens *love* fuzzy toys)—be sure they are well made and sturdy.

Deremar Ameche Liberator, born 1973, by Eng. Ch. Sansue Camrose Phoenix x Eng. Ch. Deremar Rosemary. "Toffee" was a dog of classic English type, as befitted the son of two of England's outstanding Goldens. He was Reserve Winners at the 1975 GRCA National Specialty and a GRCA Outstanding Sire. His head and expression are particularly excellent.

Squeak toys of latex rubber are a lot of fun, but some Goldens can shred them in an instant. Great toys can be made of odd socks tied in knots; these are particularly good for puppies. Tennis balls are great for play but not for serious chewing. Any toy or other item that is chewed into pieces and swallowed can cause serious trouble.

Items to avoid include those made of soft rubber or plastic, or sponge rubber; and anything small enough to be swallowed (no balls smaller than a tennis ball, please) or to get stuck in the throat. I know of several dogs who have died when a ball got stuck in their throat. I personally choose to avoid any "rawhide" items: Some are cured with questionable chemicals, and any that are swallowed can cause trouble with digestion or block the gastrointestinal tract. The same applies to cured pigs' ears and cow hooves, which smell abominably when chewed and can stain carpets and the dogs' coats. Toys of rope or fiber are doubtful at best, and absolutely dangerous if any part is swallowed.

Occasionally a Golden will adopt a particular toy and keep it for a long time, sometimes years. "Ghillie" had a squeaky in the shape of a chick in an eggshell; he had it for more than two years, carrying or gently squeaking it in his powerful jaws. One day another dog found it and tore it up. When given a new toy in the exact same shape, Ghillie refused to have anything to do with the imposter—it simply was not *his* chickie!

COLLARS AND LEADS

For everyday wear, the Golden needs a buckle collar to carry an I.D., license and rabies vaccination tags. This can be either nylon or leather, flat or rolled. The adjustable collars with the "instant" snap-lock buckles are very convenient. Puppies can wear inexpensive nylon buckle collars; they will be quickly outgrown, so check regularly to be sure that the collar has not become tight. Rolled collars are preferred as being less likely to leave a mark on the coat, as flat collars will.

Training collars include the ordinary slip ("choke") collar in either traditional chain style or nylon braid. They are *only* for training and are never to be left on an unattended dog. The danger is always that the ring can catch on things and choke the dog. Chain-slip collars should be of medium to medium-small links, with welded rings, smoothly made, preferably nickel-plated brass, which will not rust. As with most equipment, buying quality will be advantageous in the long run. Chain collars can cut the hair, and they do telegraph corrections by the sound of the links sliding through the ring. For training, avoid the very fine chains, as they can be very severe, like using a wire cable. You'll find this out the first time you get your fingers twisted in the chain!

Nylon slip collars are lightweight, strong, comfortable and silent. They are available in many colors and so can be matched to individual dogs. The medium to heavy, soft, braided nylon is best for Goldens. They are not expensive, so if yours becomes frayed, discard it and get another. The nylon collars have another advantage: If the dog happens to get caught on something, the collar can be cut with knife or scissors. Some years ago a friend had two young Goldens who were playing together after a training session; suddenly Ed noticed that they were acting very strangely, so he ran over and discovered that one dog's jaw had gotten under the nylon slip collar. When the other dog turned, the collar was twisted tightly, trapping the first dog's jaw and slowly strangling the one wearing the collar. It was impossible to untangle them, as both dogs were panic-stricken. Fortunately Ed carried a penknife and was able to use it to cut the nylon collar and release the dogs before any real damage occurred. Had the collar been of chain, the results might well have been tragic.

As for leads (leashes), for Obedience training, a four- to six-foot lead, either leather or the woven flat fabric called "web," is quite serviceable. Cotton web is soft and flexible, and easy on the hands, but may lose its strength with time and exposure to dampness. Good leather, especially the soft supple latigo, is strong, very flexible and easy to handle. Forget about chain leashes; they will shred your hands and are hopeless. Nylon leads vary; the soft ones can be good, particularly when you want something to stuff into a pocket; the stiff heavy ones are slippery and hard to handle.

For casual walking and exercising, the extendable-retractable leads (Flexi-lead) are useful. The eight-meter (twenty-six foot) ones for large dogs are best for Goldens. The cables and mechanism of the best-quality Flexis are extremely strong, although the bulky case and handle make them clumsy (especially for people with small hands). Walking two dogs on Flexis is a challenge—walking three is not to be contemplated, as they will weave a web of tangled lines you may never escape from.

BASIC GROOMING

The Golden is a relatively low-maintenance breed compared to many but still requires regular attention. Every dog should be brushed weekly, at a minimum; two or three times a week is better. Ears and teeth should be checked, and nails trimmed as needed. *Nipping off a little every week* is much easier than a major wrestling match with a dog whose nails have been neglected. While puppies don't need extensive grooming, putting the pup on the grooming table for a few minutes of brushing and gentle handling of the feet, ears and mouth (along with much praise for good behavior) will help teach that the grooming experience is pleasant—and result in an adult dog who enjoys it.

Basic grooming tools include:

- A good-quality pin brush (metal pins with blunt tips, in a flexible backing)
- A steel comb with both fine and coarse spaced teeth
- A slicker brush (fine wire with bent bristles, flexible backing)
- A rake (thick, stiff, blunt-tipped teeth in wooden, metal or plastic backing)
- Nail trimmers, either guillotine type or scissor (pliers) type
- Good-quality, straight haircutting shears, in a size comfortable for your hand

Optional, but useful (particularly for grooming for show purposes) are the following:

- A bristle brush—the "porcupine" brush with a combination of bristles is good.
- Fine-tooth thinning shears (single or double bladed, as preferred)
- A stripping knife or shaper blade
- A mat cutter or mat rake
- A nail file (or electric nail grinder, if preferred)
- A spray bottle or mister with plain water

You should keep grooming tools together in a kit bag, or a tack box; an inexpensive tool box from the hardware store can serve as well as a costly tack box.

The pin brush serves for the biggest part of coat brushing. In order to brush properly, one must get right down into the coat. Starting at the rear of the dog, or on the lower parts, use your left hand to part and hold back the coat so that you can get the brush into the coat, and brush out to the tip of the hair. On the next stroke, move your left hand back slightly to release the next bit of coat for the brush to work on. Working upward and forward, you cover the entire body. When doing the underside of the chest and body, you can have the dog lie down. With practice, you can brush the entire dog very quickly. If the coat is dry or has static, a faint misting with the sprayer, perhaps with a little conditioner added, will be helpful.

During shedding time, one must be more diligent, and a few minutes every day will be easier (and more effective) than one marathon session.

If a mat or snarl is encountered, many times it can be picked apart with the comb, using just one or two teeth at the end, then brushed out with the slicker or the pin brush. If the mat defies this treatment, then the straight shears are used to cut the mat into narrow strips, always cutting *with* the hair, never across the hair. The strips can then be brushed out, without leaving a glaring hole that would result from simply scissoring out the mat in one chunk.

Burrs and other bits of debris can be removed by using the comb to carefully pull the hair away from the burr, rather than trying to pull the burr out of the hair. A quick squirt of "tangle-free" spray may help. Dogs should always be checked for burrs after working in the field; if you don't remove them, the dog will do it, and you won't like the results when bunches of hair are removed along with the burrs. Foxtails and others have barbed seeds that can work into the dog's skin or ears and cause serious damage.

The steel-toothed comb is used to straighten the feathering and to comb out loose coat and tangles. Don't expect it to comb through the dense undercoat that is not shedding. The soft hair under the ears often forms small knots or mats and should be checked so that these may be removed before they become major. The areas under the forelegs and the groin should be checked as well.

While those grooming for show purposes may sneer at the lowly slicker brush, it is very useful when one needs to remove loose hair and shedding undercoat, and for removing bits of debris after working in the field. The bristle brush, which should have fairly stiff natural bristles not too closely spaced, will remove cleaning powder and dried mud, and when used vigorously on the topcoat, will bring up a good shine on a healthy coat.

The straight scissors are used for trimming the straggly hair from the feet. Even pet dogs look better with tidy paws, and less wet and mud will be tracked into the house. Trim closely around the edges of the pads and on the soles, and trim the hair that sticks out from between the pads. Don't cut in between the toes, but check for little mats or clumps of mud that can irritate, and comb them out carefully. On the top of the toes, the thinning shears can be used to shape the hair, if necessary.

For ordinary maintenance grooming, that may be all the trimming needed, particularly if the dog has a correct coat. For dogs who carry long furnishings (featherings) that collect leaves and other debris, it may be useful to shorten long featherings with thinning shears for a tidier look and easier

A nicely groomed Golden head, with natural ruff. The ears have been tidied but not over-trimmed, leaving a soft, natural look. Trimming of whiskers is optional; this dog retains them. This is "Bartlett," Ch. Classic Quote by Kyrie.

upkeep. It should not be necessary to use electric clippers on a Golden, except to trim around a skin lesion such as a hot spot or a wound, or for dogs with ear problems. Clipping short the hair under the ear flap, surrounding the ear canal, can help keep the ears clean and dry.

If you choose to utilize a professional groomer, for whatever reason, it is wise to make absolutely certain beforehand *exactly* what is to be done. Goldens are *never* to be trimmed like spaniels or setters—and please, no ribbons on the ears!

Yes, Goldens Shed—A Lot

Regular grooming will lessen the amount that accumulates as fuzzy "dust bunnies" under the furniture. Golden hair, fortunately, is easy to sweep up, as it doesn't work its way into carpets and upholstery fabric as the stiff hairs of short-coated dogs do.

The rake is a simple wooden handle with two rows of blunt, stiff, widely spaced teeth like comb teeth, used to remove loose coat when the dog is shedding. If you don't work at getting that loose coat out, the dog will look, as one owner phrased it, as if he were coming unstuffed, with clumps and clots of fuzz sticking out helter-skelter (and dropping all over the house). A shedding dog really appreciates a good grooming to get that dead hair out. Many of the "skin problems" that Goldens are blamed for are the result of lack of attention: A dead coat gets damp and itchy, the dog scratches, bacteria leap into the irritated area, and in a matter of hours the dog has a full-blown "hot spot," creating misery for dog and owner alike.

"Hot Spots" and Allergies

Regular and attentive grooming, along with proper diet, will forestall many of the coat/skin problems Goldens are said to have, as you can spot and treat potential problems long before they escalate. Wet dogs should be dried before being crated or kenneled. An active dog can withstand wet and cold, but a dog put away wet is not comfortable and may be subject to chills. Dogs who spend much time in the water need some extra attention, as do dogs in hot damp climates in which bacteria and fungus flourish.

Hot spots are unmistakable: The area is wet, irritated and inflamed, with sticky exudate. If you find a hot spot, best forget about trying to "save coat"— you need to respond quickly, and you *must* cut away hair so that you can remove all the wet, yucky, smelly stuff and the air can get to the area. Sometimes cleaning with a bactericidal cleanser such as Nolvasan scrub will be sufficient; often you will need to apply an antiobiotic spray or ointment such as Gentocin Topical Spray or Panalog. If one doesn't show results in a day or two, try another. Those containing a mild steroid will help control itching and pain. Do NOT apply anything containing peroxide or alcohol, as it will be extremely painful on the raw areas.

Some Goldens do have allergies. If you suspect an allergy, a veterinary dermatologist can test to determine exactly what substances are involved. If the offending substances cannot be removed from the dog's environment, in some cases the dog can be desensitized against them. Most allergies in dogs show up as skin reactions and itching rather than the respiratory symptoms so familiar in humans. Allergies can involve items as diverse as certain grasses and other plants, nylon carpeting or certain food substances such as wheat or beef or some additives in commercial foods. And of course, fleabite allergy is a major curse of all dogs, not just Goldens.

Dogs with fleabite allergy don't just itch—they can go into a frenzy of biting and scratching, resulting in self-mutilation, just from the bite of a single flea. They may rip out chunks of coat and create raw areas and hot spots. They are miserable, and so are their owners. Other dogs may harbor a zillion fleas and show very little response. The best preventive is still to keep fleas off the dog.

The simplest way to eliminate fleas from the dog is regular bathing with plain dog shampoo, or dipping with the mildest possible product. It may not have a lasting effect, but you can easily pick off the stunned fleas and send them down the drain. Don't bathe or dip your dog more than once a week. Flea powders and sprays are of limited usefulness on a heavy-coated dog (but could be useful if applied before going to a show or to areas where fleas may be encountered), and most flea collars are of use only, as one veterinarian said, if you can hold the flea down and beat it to death with the collar.

You should always avoid overdoing the use of pesticides. If you are going to use a spray on the dog, it should be the mildest possible (pyrethrins, for instance). *Never* double up using the same type substances, such as organic phosphate dip plus spray plus collar. Far better to err on the side of caution rather than subject your dog to toxic overdose. For puppies who are too young for dips or sprays, even nursing pups, you can *very carefully* immerse the puppy up to the neck in a tub of warm water at body temperature, ruffle the coat with your fingers, and as the drowning fleas come up for air, pick them off and dispose of them.

I prefer to avoid systemic flea-killers such as the pill (cythioate), which is given every three days or so; these kill fleas only when the flea actually bites the dog—which is what we want to prevent!

Nails, Teeth and Ears

Trimming nails is one of those things that every dog should be accustomed to from puppyhood. Little puppies learn to accept being held and cuddled while the sharp little nailtips are clipped off. Larger puppies can be held on your lap and gently restrained while sitting on the floor. You do not need to do all toes at one time; you can do the job in small increments. Gentle but firm insistence and praise for cooperation are essential. If the dog is on the grooming table, you can use the same technique. Handle the foot gently, trim a bit off one or two nails, and then go to something that the dog really likes, such as brisk brushing.

Teeth should be looked at during the regular grooming sessions, and it does help to scrub them, either with a regular soft toothbrush, or with a piece of gauze wrapped around your finger. This is an area often overlooked by otherwise diligent Golden owners, and a surprising number of show exhibitors as well. With the Golden's proclivity for carrying and chewing all sorts of objects, sometimes including rocks, regular observation of the teeth is recommended. Ordinary cleaning and examination may prevent the need for more complicated and expensive procedures. Your veterinarian or the technician can show you how.

Because the Golden has drop ears, often with heavy coat around the opening and often damp from swimming, ears should be checked regularly and cleaned as necessary with a suitable ear cleaner (consult your veterinarian), or baby oil on cotton gauze. In some cases a drying preparation may be advised for use after cleaning. If your dog's ears have an offensive odor or are red or swollen, or if the dog scratches or digs at her ears unduly, carries her head tilted, or rubs her ears on the ground or carpet, then you should have a veterinarian check her ears. If mites or an infection are present, medical treatment is definitely indicated.

GROOMING THE WORKING GOLDEN

The aforementioned basics apply to all Goldens. Working dogs who are often wet require being properly dried. Continual dampness can lead to chills, fungus infections and other skin and ear problems. Dogs working in the field, including Tracking dogs, should always be carefully inspected for burrs,

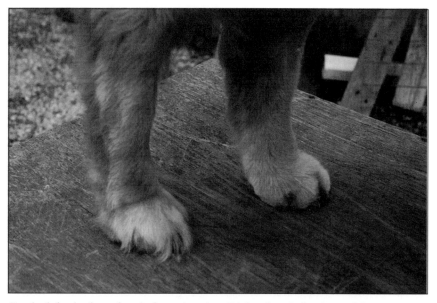

On the left, the front foot before trimming. Right, the nicely trimmed foot.

foxtails, grass awns, cactus spines and so on (depending on the area of the country). Ticks are a danger in many areas; an application of insect repellent before going afield may help, but you should always be alert for these pesky hitchhikers.

Dogs who are often wet may tend to develop a definite curl in the coat. Towel drying and brushing, or blow-drying and brushing, can help correct this. If blow-drying, use only warm or cool air, never hot; it is too easy to burn the skin or dry out the hair to the point of brittleness. The brushing is important as this both trains the hair and stimulates the natural oils and the circulation to the skin for a healthy coat.

Goldens with long feathering may benefit by being trimmed for field work. This merely means using the thinning shears to shorten the feathering on the underbody, the tail and perhaps the chest. Don't cut it down to the skin or use clippers, as there must be sufficient to serve as natural protection. Goldens with the sort of coat that was typical originally have a fairly short, dense feathering that is of a texture which repels water and dirt, and is easy to care for. Many field dogs carry this sort of coat.

The feet of the working dog need attention; thorns in the feet, or cut pads (an ever-present danger, unfortunately), need to be taken care of immediately. Nails should be kept trimmed to a proper length—long nails can get caught or broken, which is extremely painful. Some breeders routinely remove dew-claws from the front feet to avoid possible injury afield (Goldens do not have dewclaws on the back feet). A fungus infection of the feet, or interdigital cysts, demand veterinary attention.

GROOMING THE SHOW DOG

Here we enter upon a touchy area. "Purists" in the breed strongly advocate the natural appearance described by the breed Standard, with a minimum of trimming and special preparation. Indeed, a really correct Golden with a proper coat will need very little time spent to get ready for the show ring. "Show dog specialists" who prefer glamor and the current fashions in the show ring will do everything possible to make the dog conform to the "picture" they want, and which they think the judge wants.

Long before the entries are sent in, you will have attended to the dog's weight and condition through diet, parasite control and exercise, including plenty of free running and play. Regular basic grooming, including plenty of vigorous brushing, is essential. With those as "givens," we can get down to show preparation, which starts with more brushing. Before bathing the dog, you must brush the coat thoroughly, comb out all loose hair, and take care of mats or tangles, as wetting will make them even worse. If at all possible, bathe the dog two or three days before the show, and do it before trimming. Cutting a dirty coat dulls the scissors. Working with a clean coat is easier.

Bathing the Golden is easiest with a spray-head on a flexible bathtub hose so that you can reach all parts of the dog. Whatever means you use, you *must* rinse the dog thoroughly and remove every trace of shampoo. There are many excellent shampoos for dogs; experienced exhibitors will no doubt recommend their favorites. Shampoos for people are *not* the proper pH for dogs. Most dog shampoos work best if diluted before use.

After the bath, put the dog on the grooming table and start brushing, giving a quick once-over with the pin brush or the natural bristle brush, and lay a towel over her back. Then do concentrated brushing on a section at a time.

Use a small terry towel, or a chamois, to towel-dry an area, such as a leg or a part of one side of the dog. Then brush the area, alternating towelling and brushing until the area is almost dry. Then do another area.

When the dog is nearly dry, remove the covering towel and do a light all-over brushing. Depending on the type of coat your dog has, you might alternate brushing against the hair and with the hair, or primarily with the hair. Always finish up brushing with the natural lie of the coat. Brushing the wrong way will open up the undercoat and give a fuller look to the coat, but the topcoat should always lie naturally when you are finished. This last finishing off with the pin brush should be with a light touch. A light spray of water (perhaps with a little conditioner) will be helpful if the coat dries too quickly; brushing a dry coat can result in static and flyaway hair.

Dogs with good weatherproof coats dry quickly this way, and you may spend no more time (often less) on them than if you were using a blow-dryer. If using a blow-dryer, you simply use the blower instead of the towel while brushing. Dryers made especially for dogs are best, as they move more air and have more appropriate temperature control. They are fairly expensive.

Now the dog is clean and dry and ready for trimming. If you or the dog are ready for a break, take it. You don't have to trim immediately. Let her run around a bit and stretch her legs. Just try to keep the feet clean until they are trimmed. Then it's back up on the grooming table.

The areas that usually need attention are the feet, tail and ears. The basic foot trimming is covered under "Basic Grooming." When the foot is trimmed fairly well, let the dog stand on it and finish off the shaping with thinning shears to make the nice closely rounded look. Trim the back of the pastern to a tidy look, but not too closely, and never above the little "stopper pad" on the back of the wrist. The back of the pastern should parallel the front. The toenails should be short, but if someone tells you that nails must be cut back so far that they bleed, please consider that such cutting leaves an open wound through which bacteria can enter and cause infection, as well as producing pain and discomfort.

You do the hind feet the same way as the front. Comb the hair on the back of the rear pasterns up and back; then even it up with the thinning shears, approximately parallel with the front of the rear pastern. Tidy it, but don't cut it off short, as that thick fur is protection for the tendons on the back of the pastern.

The tail will probably benefit from some neatening. Brush it out completely, then let it hang naturally. Find the tip of the tailbone with your left hand; if the tailbone is longer than to the point of the hock, you want to trim the tip fairly short. If the tailbone is shorter than to the point of the hock, leave the tail hair a bit longer. Remember that you can always take off more, but you can't put it back on. Put your grip where you want the trim to start, then raise the tail to a level position and start trimming with the thinning shears, following a line that removes the straggly hairs and leaves an amount of feathering appropriate to the dog. If the dog has exremely profuse feathering, you may be removing quite a lot of hair. Too much hair on the tail can unbalance the appearance considerably. If you have a mirror in which to observe the dog, or a helper to pose the dog while you step back and look, that can be a great help.

When the balance of the tail is trimmed, be sure to shake it out, give it a bit of brushing, and look at it again. Be sure it doesn't appear chopped-off or squared, which looks very amateurish. It should look as if it naturally grew the way you trimmed it. Please do not cut away the hair at the base of the tail or around the anus, as is done with setters and spaniels. That is not appropriate for the Golden.

If the dog has a correct coat, the ears should need very little trimming. The convention of trimming and shaping the ear has become much misused. Yes, if the dog has long shaggy overhangs, they should be shortened and tidied. Never use the thinning shears across the hair, but always with the hair. Fluff up the shaggy parts with the comb or the pin brush; then use the thinning shears or a knife to shorten the shaggies. Be cautious: Always snip, then brush, and snip again if necessary. Lift the ear flap and shorten the hair around the opening to the ear. You can pull dead hairs by hand or with a knife.

Proper use of a stripping knife or shaper blade can give a more natural look to any trimming. The knife is held so that the hair to be shortened is positioned between the thumb and the blade; then you use the knife to pull the hair. The stripping knife will remove the hair, particularly if the hair is at the end of its cycle and is loose. A sharp blade will cut the hair, leaving a tapered end. You must work with just a few hairs at a time; the procedure is slower than using the thinning shears but gives a better look.

The practice of cutting around the edge of the ear flap with straight scissors gives a very artificial look that is not desirable. If the edges need to be evened up, use a knife as described above, or thinning shears. Trying to make a large ear look smaller by cutting off hair doesn't work; it only calls attention to the ear. Better to let the ear blend into the neck ruff somewhat.

Whiskers

The dog's whiskers, or vibrissae, are part of the sensory equipment. The breed Standard states that trimming of whiskers is optional—there is no preference one way or the other. Whisker trimming is best done with small scissors with blunt tips. When doing the muzzle, hold the dog's head steady, and position the scissors pointing toward the nose, not toward the eyes, so that if the dog moves, you will not cut or jab him. Frankly, it's much easier to leave the whiskers natural.

Other Trimming

Any other trimming should be kept to an absolute minimum. Our breed Standard specifies "untrimmed natural ruff," which plainly means that the neck and throat are not to be clipped short, nor is the hair on the sides of the neck to be removed, leaving a swag of hair hanging from the front of the neck and chest. The natural ruff is very important in giving the soft, kindly expression typical of the Golden.

It is permissible to tidy up ragged edges, such as the long hairs that sometimes hang from the underbody and inside the back legs. But by no means do we want a scissored outline or anything approaching a stylized look. The goal we are aiming for is a clean, tidy dog who looks as if he just grew that way.

EXERCISE

Every Golden needs sufficient exercise to maintain muscle tone, suppleness and general physical condition. What is sufficient for any particular dog can vary from a gentle stroll around the garden for a sedate old-timer, to an hour or more of intense field work and running for an athletic young dog in training. Generally speaking, puppies need plenty of opportunity for play and romping on natural footing—a large pen for little fellows, the backyard and short walks for older puppies. Two puppies will exercise each other very well, but they, or a single puppy, still need you for play and companionship.

While two pups of the same age and size usually will play together quite happily, it is not wise to let a youngster roughhouse with an older, larger dog. "Teenage" Goldens and adults can be quite rowdy, and the younger pup will be flattened in wrestling matches and may well suffer some hard knocks in games of chase and "dog tag." Pups can associate nicely with older dogs in controlled situations, where they will learn proper deference to their elders, you should use caution in any situation where the pup might incur any sort of injury.

Any type of *roadwork* or enforced movement on-lead should wait until the dog is reasonably mature. Long periods of trotting or running on pavement are never advisable, least of all for immature dogs. Making an immature dog exercise when tired overstresses muscles and may create real problems. By three or four months, the puppy can start with very short walks on-lead, perhaps just a block or two, and move up to longer walks very gradually. By a year of age, a sound young dog can be trotting/walking a mile or so daily; less on pavement, more in free running on natural footing, if you are fortunate enough to have that kind of area available.

Even in limited space, you can exercise a dog well with *retrieving games*. Use a tennis ball and racket, and work on your swing as well. Field work or Agility are also useful. Exercise should be regular; moderate daily or every-other-day work is far better than a marathon on the weekend!

Swimming is always excellent exercise for a Golden. For puppies, be sure the water is not too cold, and that they are well dried after swimming. And always watch out for hazards such as broken glass, hidden snags, junk or treacherous currents. One reason swimming is such great exercise is that there is no impact stress to joints, which makes it good for dogs who may have orthopedic problems such as hip dysplasia.

Some people like to exercise their dogs by having them run alongside a *bicycle*. This can be useful if done with care; continued work on unyielding pavement puts considerable stress on joints, ligaments and tendons. It might be wise to alternate days of this roadwork on-lead with days of free-running on turf or dirt, or swimming.

Some show exhibitors use a *treadmill* for exercising dogs, either one made expressly for dogs or one for humans that has been adapted. While this does have the advantage of being convenient, keeping the dog clean and allowing exercise in bad weather, it does not allow the dog to move in a really free, unrestricted manner. Many dogs whose major exercise is on a treadmill develop variations of gait such as moving wide, improper foot timing or restricted movement. If you use such a device, you must also give the dog adequate exercise moving freely on good footing.

GERIATRIC GOLDENS

If your Golden is one who enjoys a long life, you may have the special joys of the veteran. The annoyances and exasperations of puppyhood long gone, the elderly Golden has found the harmony of life and takes each day with what seems like a special awareness of its little happinesses.

By age seven or eight, *bitches should be spayed* (if not done earlier) in order to avoid pyometra and uterine malignancies. Yes, they may tend to gain weight if you do not adjust their diet and make sure they get ample exercise, but a little extra care will keep them trim and shapely. Spayed bitches often grow heavier, longer coats, so attention must be paid to grooming. Old bones will appreciate a softer bed, perhaps one of the foam-filled pads, or a folded blanket of acrylic sheepskin. Teeth and toenails need regular attention. The diet may need some adjustment—less food than when the dog was active, but food of high quality so that the aging body can make best use of it.

Keep an eye out for changes such as *lumps and growths.* Lipomas are benign fatty tumors, which usually don't need to be removed unless they are really disfiguring or in a place where they cause a problem. Old dogs often get little warty growths; again, unless they are a problem, they can be left alone. *Mammary tumors, testicular tumors* and any others that the vet feels may be potential problems should be removed promptly; it's much easier for *both the dog and surgeon to do it in the early stages.*

Hearing loss is common in old dogs. Don't think she's willfully disobeying when she can't hear. If you've used hand signals in training, that will be useful. Wake up the old dog gently; she may startle at your touch. Teach her to come to you in the dark by blinking a flashlight as a signal. If she's a little unsteady on her feet, or needs help getting up the steps, let her wear a harness that you can use as a handle to help her.

If you have younger dogs who take up your time with training, showing, hunting and other activities, still make time for the old ones. They don't ask a lot and will be so delighted to go out and fetch a few dummies in the field, or have the tracking harness buckled on once more, even if the track is only a few yards instead of a quarter-mile. The old show dog will still like to be groomed and go in the car even if only to the pet store to pick out a new squeaky toy. It won't take much of your time.

When the end comes near, as it will, be unselfish enough to let the old dog go, kindly and peacefully. When life becomes a burden and there is no longer much that's good in it, it's time. If there's chronic pain or incontinence or the inability to walk, it's time. Don't ever make the old love suffer because you selfishly won't make that decision. Euthanasia, the good death, is as simple as going to sleep and not waking up. It is the last good thing you can do for your friend.

chapter 10

Genetic Concerns in the Golden Retriever

Golden Retrievers are no different from most other comparable breeds in that they are associated with a number of problems with some known genetic basis. Whether an apparent increase in these types of problems is actual or is due to increased awareness and to better diagnostics, as well as to the great increase in numbers of dogs, is perhaps debatable.

HIP DYSPLASIA

Canine hip dysplasia was first recognized in the late 1930s and is also well known in humans. "Dysplasia" means incorrect development: The structure of the joint is apparently normal in very young puppies but later fails to develop properly, resulting in a joint that is abnormal in structure. Typically, the acetabulum (the hip socket cup into which the head of the femur from the thigh bone fits) is shallow with a poor fit of the femoral head into the acetabulum and joint looseness or laxity. The bone itself may be of poor quality; and this, together with the poor fit, creates abnormal wear on the joint surfaces and stress to surrounding tissues. Eventually there are changes as the bones remodel in response to the stresses, and osteoarthritis develops. These changes are considered degenerative joint disease. The dog may experience anything from mild discomfort to severe pain. The level of discomfort is not necessarily correlated to the structural changes seen on an X ray.

Hip dysplasia can appear in almost any breed of dog, but the larger and heavier the breed, the higher the likelihood of hip dysplasia. It is not uncommon in most of the retriever breeds.

Hip dysplasia in Goldens may range from a very mild degree, which never interferes with the dog's function at all, to a severe form that may incapacitate the dog. Fortunately, really severe hip dysplasia is not common in Golden

Am. Can. Ch. Ciadar Tintinnabulation UDT WC VCX; Can. UD; GRCA Outstand-ing Sire, born 1970. "Jingle" was Pam Ruddick's first home-bred champion and had several High in Trial awards, wins at informal Field Trials, and not only Group place-ments but a Best in Show from the classes in Canada. He was a wonderfully talented dog with a stable personality and great enthusiasm for living and working. By Ch. Gayhaven Kyrie Talisman CD TD x Gayhaven Slightly Cinnamon UDT WC.

Retrievers, and considerably less so now, as dedicated Golden breeders have conscientiously selected for better hips. It is also true that retrievers, who seem to have a high threshold for physical pain, often do not show pain or dis-comfort that other breeds would under the same conditions.

While hip dysplasia may sometimes be suspected by outward signs such as difficulty in getting up, weak rear, abnormal gait ("bunny hopping," with the rear legs used together), tiring quickly and stiffness after exercise, a ra-diograph (X ray) is required in order to make a proper diagnosis. The dog must be properly positioned for the radiograph, and the film should be read by an experienced veterinarian. While most veterinarians should be able to take an adequate radiograph, interpreting it may require one with special training in veterinary orthopedics or radiology.

The *Orthopedic Foundation for Animals* (OFA) was set up for the purpose of reading radiographs sent to it by veterinarians. A panel of three veterinary radiologists will read films of all dogs over twenty-four months of age, then issue an opinion. If the dog is, by consensus of the three readers, deemed to be free of hip dysplasia, an OFA number and a certificate

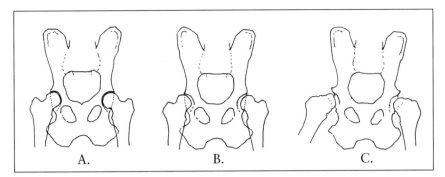

Variations in hip quality. Dog positioned in standard extended views. Keep in mind that the appearance of the hips does not necessarily correlate with how the dog feels; some dogs with hips similar to those shown in B or C function quite well, while others may show definite signs of discomfort or limitations in movement.

A. Good hips: deep acetabula (sockets) fitting closely around well-shaped femoral heads. No sign of wear or remodeling.

B. Hip dysplasia: acetabula shallow; femoral heads not deeply seated, and showing some flattening (remodeling). Femoral necks somewhat short and thick.

C. Severe hip dysplasia: shallow acetabula. Extensive remodeling and osteoarthritis, especially on rims of acetabula and on femoral necks and heads.

will be issued for that dog. The film will also be given a rating of fair, good or excellent; the OFA report does not, however, explain *why* a dog was rated fair or good rather than excellent. If the consensus opinion is that there is radiographic evidence of hip dysplasia, the report will show a rating of mild, moderate or severe hip dysplasia. No certificate or number will be issued. Experience in recent years seems to show that "mild" and "moderate" ratings in Goldens cover a fairly narrow range, with "severe" being used for everything beyond a certain point. Goldens rated "mild hip dysplasia" likely will be functionally sound, as may many with a "moderate" rating.

OFA will also read radiographs of animals under than twenty-four months of age and give a preliminary report, and a *temporary* number. These preliminary films are not necessarily read by the panel of three.

For OFA purposes, the dog must be positioned lying on her back, with the rear legs extended parallel to each other and to the table top. The femurs should be rotated so that the patellae (kneecaps) are centered over the stifle joint. OFA recommends that the dog be sedated for the radiographing, as the position is stressful, even uncomfortable, and a dog who resists can affect the positioning. Many veterinarians, however, achieve very satisfactory positioning without using sedation, particularly on dogs conditioned to accept such handling.

Radiographs may also be read by veterinary radiologists at most veterinary teaching schools; specialists will be board-certified by the American

College of Veterinary Radiologists. In Canada, the Ontario Veterinary College in Guelph will read and certify radiographs, similar to the OFA procedure.

The PennHIP program originated at the University of Pennsylvania also uses radiography to examine for hip dysplasia, but uses a somewhat different technique. The dog is radiographed under anesthesia in three views: the standard extended view and two variations, with the legs held perpendicular to the X ray cassette. In the first of these, the femurs are compressed or pushed inward to show them seated as deeply as possible in the acetabula. In the second, a "distraction device" is used that applies force to move the femoral heads outward. If the joint is loose—if joint laxity is present—this may then be measured by comparison of the two views. The difference, or Distraction Index, is expressed as a number relating to the radius of the femoral head: "0" would mean no difference between compression view and distraction view; 1.0 would mean extremely loose.

The Penn researchers found that dogs who x-rayed "normal" when positioned, radiographed and read according to conventional OFA requirements did not necessarily look that good when done by the PennHIP technique. A number of dogs whose hip joints appeared very tight on the standard extended view showed looseness in the distracted view. This was felt to be significant, and it was thought that the technique might be a more accurate means of detecting dogs who had mild hip dysplasia and would develop the signs of degenerative joint disease later in life.

In the breed used for the largest part of the study (German Shepherd Dogs), a Distraction Index of 0.3 was considered to be the dividing point: Dogs with a DI of less than 0.3 for the most part did not show, or develop, degenerative joint disease. Borzois, a breed in which hip dysplasia is extremely rare, all measured less than 0.3. Some other breeds were more variable; for example, some Rottweilers with a DI of more than 0.3 and obvious joint laxity never did develop degenerative joint disease. Breed differences certainly do exist, at least in part related to differing skeletal structure and musculature.

For this reason, the study of Golden Retrievers in the PennHIP study is ongoing, and one should not make premature conclusions at this point. There are indications that a good number of Goldens who have a DI exceeding 0.3 do not develop frank hip dysplasia or degenerative joint disease. Also, no long-range breeding studies have yet been carried out that merit conclusions based solely on a Golden Retriever's Distraction Index.

Concerned Golden Retriever breeders have made substantial progress in improving quality of hips over the years, using standard radiographs. While it was not uncommon in the 1960s and earlier to encounter Goldens (and other retrievers) who were very much affected by the stiffness and pain of hip dysplasia, it is far less common now. Unfortunately, Goldens have become so very much more popular that there are large numbers being produced by people who have no knowledge or concern about the problem, and this certainly hampers progress.

Readers desiring more information on either OFA or PennHIP may contact them at the addresses listed in the Appendix. The Golden Retriever Club of America recommends that breeders use dogs for breeding who have been determined to be free from hip dysplasia, and select for *better* hips whenever possible. In-depth knowledge of family background (ancestors, siblings and descendants) is recommended as well, as it gives a broader picture and more complete information.

A word of caution: The genetic transmission of hip dysplasia is still not clearly understood, and as environmental factors can definitely influence the expression of hip dysplasia, even breeding "normal" dogs from generations of "normals" cannot guarantee that all the offspring will be free of dysplasia. (Mother Nature just loves to throw a zinger into our best-laid plans!) Most researchers agree that it is a *polygenic* trait—that is, *several* inherited factors are involved. These specific factors have not yet been isolated, hence the inheritance pattern could be extremely intricate. Since the evidence of dysplasia can be affected by such factors as nutrition, growth rates, exercise and trauma, eliminating the disease by selection according to the radiograph (phenotype, or what is seen) is very difficult.

OTHER ORTHOPEDIC PROBLEMS

Goldens, like most other breeds, are subject to other orthopedic problems. One is osteochondrosis or osteochondritis dissecans (OCD). Typically, the **OCD** subject is a substantial, fast-growing young dog, more often male than female. The most commonly affected joint is the shoulder joint, but it can occur in other joints such as the stifle, elbow, hip or hock. OCD causes lameness, sometimes mild, sometimes acute and severe.

OCD is due to damage to the cartilage of the joint; there is a disturbance or variation in the proper maturation of the cartilage of the growth plates and covering the surfaces of the bones within the joints. Ossification does not procede normally, and the cartilage deteriorates. Then wear or trauma causes injury to these areas; there may be pitting, cracks, or worn areas, or a flap of cartilage may detach partially or completely. A loose bit of cartilage may form a "joint mouse," causing considerable pain and lameness. Radiography is necessary to confirm the suspicion of OCD, sometimes several X rays as the positioning must be exact.

If there is a **joint mouse**, the best course of action seems to be prompt surgery to remove it and allow the joint to heal. OCD may be due in part to genetic factors, but a high caloric intake and rapid growth rate are thought to be very much contributory.

The elbow joint may also be the site of developmental problems, sometimes called **elbow dysplasia.** Often these cannot be seen on X ray until the dog is seven or eight months of age. These problems are thought to be related to osteochondrosis, and some researchers feel that hip dysplasia may be as well.

Panosteitis, or "long-bone disease," is typically manifested as shifting lameness: The young dog is lame first on one leg, then a week or two later on a different leg. The disease is an inflammation of the bone marrow in the long leg bones, with no known cause. Dogs from five to twelve months of age are most commonly affected. *The disease is self-limiting and usually runs its course within two or three months;* by eighteen months of age, most dogs are normal clinically and on X ray. There is no relationship to hip dysplasia or osteochondrosis. Aspirin may help relieve pain.

EYE PROBLEMS

Responsible breeders will have their dogs examined annually by a board-certified veterinary opthalmologist. A number of eye conditions are of concern, and while eye problems in Goldens are not as widespread as hip dysplasia, it is only through diligent effort that we can continue to avoid major problems. As with many hereditary problems, there are some lines or families where problems are more common than in others.

Perhaps the chief concerns of Golden breeders are juvenile cataracts and **CPRA** (Central Progressive Retinal Atrophy). "Cataract" in veterinary terms indicates *any* opacity within the lens of the eye, whether it is hereditary, acquired or of unknown origin. This can be very confusing, as not all "cataracts" are of real concern, either from a pragmatic or breeding standpoint. Some definitely are, but not all.

Typical **juvenile cataracts** in Goldens are posterior, polar, triangular cataracts. This means they are centered on the back side of the lens and are triangularly shaped because they tend to follow the suture lines within the lens. In the majority of cases, these typical cataracts in Goldens do not seriously interfere with a dog's vision. In a few cases, they may. They are called "juvenile" because they occur early in life, usually before seven years of age, but occasionally they may appear later in life. For this reason, breeding stock should be examined regularly even after seven years of age—every two or three years, if not annually.

These cataracts should not be confused with the prominent Y-sutures sometimes observed in Goldens. These Y-shaped densities usually do not progress, nor do they interfere with vision. Yearly examinations generally prove them to be of little importance.

CPRA occurs in Goldens, but much more rarely than juvenile cataracts. It is a degeneration of light receptors beginning in the center of the retina, and is a different type of PRA from that found in the Irish Setter. CPRA is a progressive condition, as the name suggests, and most dogs who have it will probably go blind eventually. There is no pain, and in many cases the dogs learn to adjust to the gradual loss of vision. There are a number of other serious conditions that may be found in any breed of dog; glaucoma, retinal dysplasia and uveitis are some that would be of concern.

More information on eye problems can be obtained from **CERF** (Canine Eye Registration Foundation) or in current veterinary texts. CERF is an organization that compiles information from reports sent to it by veterinary opthalmologists and assigns registry numbers to dogs who are found free of significant hereditary problems. Certification is good for only one year; dogs must be reexamined annually. When you take your dog for examination by the opthalmologist, specify that it is for CERF, as a special form must be used.

The examiner will use both a direct ophthalmoscope and an indirect, also called biomicroscope or slit-lamp. The examiner will complete the proper areas of the CERF form and will give one copy of the three-part form to the dog owner. The examiner keeps one copy, and the third is sent to CERF for their information. All three parts have a unique number, and only the owner's copy carries information identifying the specific dog or owner. In order to register a dog with CERF and receive a certificate, the owners must submit their copy of the form (it will be returned on request), with a small fee. The CERF number may be used in advertising, but for complete information, a copy of the examination form may be more helpful.

CERF registration does not necessarily mean that the dog is free of eyelid problems, although those should be noted on the exam form. **Entropion** is an inturning of the eyelids, resulting in irritation of the cornea due to hair rubbing against it. It can be due to nonhereditary causes; any irritation of the eye, as from a scratch on the cornea or abrasion from sand or dust, may cause the dog to squint or the eyelids to go into spasm, initiating the inturning. Continued irritation from hairs compounds the problem. But in many cases entropion probably does have a direct or indirect hereditary cause; dogs with very deepset or very small eyes, or with considerable loose skin that causes the eyelids to not fit properly, may be more likely to develop entropion.

Other eyelid problems include **ectropion** (loose, outward-turning eyelids) and **trichiasis** and **distichiasis**, which involve abnormal position or location of eyelashes; these may also cause irritation of the eye and initiate an entropic condition. Trichiasis is an abnormal direction of the eyelashes. Distichiasis is extra eyelashes, ranging from a complete extra row of lashes to merely one or two soft hairs at an atypical location. The significance of each case may vary considerably.

HEART PROBLEMS

Like any other dogs (and people), Goldens may be subject to cardiac defects. Not many years ago, it became evident that some Goldens were affected with subvalvular aortic stenosis (**SAS**) and that it could be hereditary. Some dogs were only mildly affected, but others had severe defects. Some dogs appeared normal but died unexpectedly—and showed SAS on necropsy. In Newfoundlands, veterinarians and breeders have been aware of the prevalence of SAS

An unposed snapshot of Castle at about 2 years of age shows the well-balanced build that enabled her to work successfully in many different areas and earn a truly extraordinary array of titles and distinguished honors under AKC, CKC, UKC and NAHRA rules. Castle, born in 1977, earned her last title (the UKC UD) at age 12, with 3 first places. She is Betty Drobac's Am. Can. Ch. Heron Acres Sandcastle, Am. Can. UDTX*** WCX MH, UKC HRCH & UD, NAHRA MHR WR, GRCA Outstanding Dam.

for many years, and based on experience in that breed, it was assumed that the condition was probably genetic.

Detecting dogs with the more severe grades of SAS is not a problem, as there are obvious typical heart murmurs. Murmurs are graded on a scale of I to VI, with I being extremely mild, VI very severe. It can be *very* difficult to detect dogs who are only mildly affected, as the absence of a murmur is no guarantee. Even completely normal dogs can sometimes have a slight murmur. At present, the "first line of defense" is to have all breeding stock and all prospective breeding animals examined by auscultation. The veterinary cardiologist will listen to the dog's heart with a stethoscope, usually at first with the dog at rest, then after a brief period of brisk exercise. The dog's pulse and heart rate will also be checked. Many breeders will have their puppies screened at seven to eight weeks of age before being sold, but it is also advisable to reexamine dogs at maturity. Repeat examinations may be useful.

While *auscultation* (a study of the heart's sounds) by a veterinary cardiologist (board-certified specialist) is the first and most essential examination, it should not be considered a "clearance." The examiner may state that at the time of examination no indications of defect were evident, but all will acknowledge that something could turn up at another time. Dogs who are found to have mild to moderate murmurs should be further examined, preferably by ultrasound (echocardiogram), the color-flow Doppler machine being the best type at this time. Echocardiography is painless to the dog and does not require sedation or anesthesia, but some of the hair may be clipped off the chest. Accurate echocardiography requires not only expensive, technically sophisticated hardware but also a talented technician. Unfortunately, as good as these machines are, they still are not a 100 percent clearance.

Breeders and owners undoubtedly are confused and frustrated by ambiguous reports, but we must accept the fact that these ambiguities will not be resolved for some time. Meanwhile, it is recommended that dogs who are definitely diagnosed with SAS not be bred. Goldens with no signs other than a trivial (grade I–II) murmur, who are apparently normal by echocardiography, and whose other qualities merit use, could be bred cautiously—that is, only to a mate with no evidence of any heart problem—and as many of the progeny examined at maturity as possible. As with many other problems, selection toward a goal can result in improvement. The cautious and selective use of such dogs, as well as dogs who have no signs of SAS, could enable us to maintain the structure, breed type, temperament and working abilities that we've been working toward for so long, without entirely discarding all dogs with ambiguous examination reports.

A beautiful leap off the dock: Maggie Happydaugh UD*** at 9 years of age still has athleticism and power. By Martdaugh*** x Cayennes' Happy Thought**, owned by Jeff and Ann Strathern.

DIAGRAM OF THE HEART

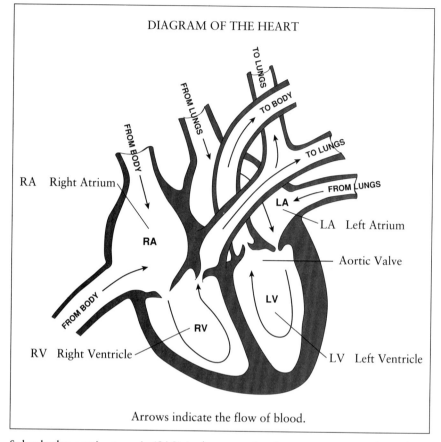

Arrows indicate the flow of blood.

Subvalvular aortic stenosis (SAS) is the anomaly of most concern in the Golden Retriever. A fibrous band or ring just below the aortic valve restricts the outflow of blood from the left ventricle to the body.

In addition, the practice of post-mortem examinations should be encouraged in order to provide the most definitive evidence possible, particularly for any dog who dies unexpectedly, and for breeding animals. Many people do not like to think about such things, but it is a way to really help further understanding of this problem in our breed.

SEIZURES AND EPILEPSY

Any dog of any breed, given certain circumstances, can go into seizure. But there are some dogs, and some lines of dogs, who have a tendency to seizures for reasons that we are not aware of. This tendency has been described as a low threshold for the stimuli (whatever they may be) that initiate the seizure. Apparently this low threshold may in some cases be the result of inherited factors.

Seizures may be the result of an accumulation of acquired or environmental factors that have the result of lowering the threshold. Such things as viral infections (distemper, for instance), high fevers, toxins of many sorts, deficiencies of trace elements or vitamins—all can contribute, as can disease or tumors in the brain, or trauma. Sometimes seizures may not start until weeks or months after an injury, such as a concussion from a fall or a blow to the head. In many cases we can never define the exact cause, nor can we always differentiate these outside factors from inherited ones. In some cases it could be a combination.

Typically, idiopathic (of unknown cause) epilepsy starts early in life, usually before three years of age. There is a pattern of recurring seizures, of typical *grand mal* or of other types. If the seizures are severe or frequent, the veterinarian will probably suggest medication to try to control them. If the seizures are infrequent (once a month or less) or mild, it may be better to accept and live with them, as medication can have undesirable side effects. Dogs who have recurrent seizures with no known cause (such as head injury and so on) should not be bred.

The dog who has one or two seizures late in life probably should not be of great concern. While a cause may not be pinpointed, the late onset and lack of pattern of recurrence indicates strongly that they are probably not due to inherited factors. Consultation with a veterinary neurologist would be a good idea but may still not be definitive. When in doubt, people must use their own best judgment.

One should also be cautious about misdiagnosing "seizures." Other conditions may give the appearance of a total or partial seizure: hypoglycemia, severe inner ear disturbance, spinal problems or others. One owner told the veterinarian that her old dog was having "seizures" when out in the yard, and the dog was put on Phenobarbital, which left her groggy and incapacitated. Further examination at the veterinary school showed that the dog's problem was a failing heart that caused her to collapse when exercising—it was not an epileptic seizure at all. Proper heart medication gave the old dog another year of happy life.

VON WILLEBRAND'S DISEASE

This is a blood disorder in which one of the clotting factors is lacking to some degree, and there is a test that measures the presence or absence of this factor, Factor VIII, and the presence of Factor VIII–related antigen. The resulting figures should indicate whether the tested dog is normal, affected or of "carrier" status—that is, apparently normal but possessing a gene for the vWD. This is not a widespread problem in Goldens; while numbers of dogs may test in the "carrier" range, it is not certain that all indeed have the vWD gene. Many things can affect the test result and give a lowered reading, particularly anything that affects the dog's immune system. Recent inoculations, a bitch in season or recently whelping, stress at time of drawing blood for the test or hypothyroidism—all can affect the results.

The test is done at only two or three laboratories; your veterinarian will have to obtain instructions, draw and prepare the blood properly and ship it to the proper laboratory. A pedigree will probably be requested as well, for the pedigree studies being done. All information is confidential.

Because actual bleeding problems in Golden Retrievers are rare, and because test results giving low numbers may or may not be particularly accurate, even many conscientious breeders do not routinely test for vWD anymore, even though they probably did when it was thought that vWD might be a widespread problem in the breed.

HYPOTHYROIDISM

A survey of a large sampling of healthy, clinically normal Golden Retrievers of various ages done by Michigan State University showed that as a breed, Goldens tended to test at the lower ranges of laboratory "normal" values. This does not mean that these Goldens were hypothyroid, only that the Golden Retriever breed may have a slightly *different range* of normals than that established by the laboratory, which is derived from a population composed of many breeds and mixed-breed dogs. MSU's recommendation is that a test result in the low to normal, or slightly below normal range, is not necessarily an indication that the dog needs to be supplemented with thyroid. If the dog is showing clinical signs of hypothyroidism, yes, certainly; but if the dog is otherwise healthy and normal, supplementation is probably not needed.

Yes, there are Goldens who require supplementation. Thin, wispy coats, thickened skin, excess weight and general lethargy, particularly in a dog less than six or seven years old, may be signs that should be investigated. Hypothyroidism *may* be inherited, but not necessarily. Older dogs may frequently have lower thyroid levels as their metabolism becomes less efficient.

Problems such as various tumors and immune-mediated diseases may also affect thyroid function. Remember that supplementation will probably depress normal thyroid function and the dog will thereafter be dependent upon supplementation. The practice of giving thyroid to normal, healthy dogs merely "to grow coat" or gain some theoretical advantage for competition is not only against the rules, it is to be condemned.

ALLERGIES AND SKIN PROBLEMS

Given the vast and confusing array of environmental substances with which our dogs come in contact every day, it is perhaps surprising that they don't develop more skin problems and allergic reactions than they do! After all, your dog is lolling around in the grass sprayed with pesticides, in the swamp where the polluted rivers dump their load, on the synthetic carpet treated with who-knows-what dyes and chemicals, and eating the mystery meal that comes from the store, and breathing the same noxious fog of cigarette smoke, industrial air pollution and automobile exhaust as we are. BUT, the poor dog can't change clothes every day or shower every day. Dogs who are not on the furniture much are often in direct contact with all these substances that are absorbed into the skin or licked up in efforts at self-grooming. Not to mention fleas. Is it any wonder that dogs itch?

The Golden's heavy coat and fondness for swimming also contribute to the tendency toward skin problems. Many of these can be forestalled by regular grooming and care, but some dogs will still have skin problems. If a cause can be found and removed, great. Food allergies or intolerances may necessitate a change in diet, but only under veterinary supervision. Poor-quality commercial food, especially the cheap "generic" types, can result in poor coat and skin. Even with quality food, some dogs simply do better on certain foods than on others. Keep your dogs off synthetic carpeting or cedar shavings, and don't kennel them in the garage or utility room where gasoline, paint thinners, cleaners, fertilizers, herbicides or pesticides may be stored. If there are fleas, get rid of them—but don't overdo it or the dog may suffer instead of the fleas. Use mild products with an IGR (insect growth regulator) which prevents fleas from developing but won't injure dogs or humans.

Dogs with true allergies (which are usually evidenced as skin problems) may pass them on to their offspring and therefore may not be good candidates for breeding. If other close relatives are similarly affected, this might be cause for concern.

LONGEVITY

For decades, the Golden Retriever was known as a hardy, active dog with a normal lifespan of twelve to fourteen years or more. Ch. Kyrie Jaen Cobi completed her UD title when just over eleven years of age (in 1973, when Goldens had to jump one and a half times their shoulder height); Ch. Heron Acres Sandcastle UDT MH WCX finished the last of her many titles at age twelve; and Lorelei's Golden Robber achieved his show championship at twelve years of age in 1959. Marc Owens' hunting companion Marc's Golden Buckshot was retrieving ducks on his seventeenth birthday, and lived past his nineteenth.

Unfortunately, many veterinarians now seem to feel that the average lifespan for Golden Retrievers is eight years or less because of the bloodlines they are seeing. Often these dogs are dying of immune system deficiencies or malignancies. Chief among the latter are lymphoma and related diseases, and osteosarcoma. One researcher at the University of Pennsylvania has attributed much of this increase as corresponding to an increase in the coefficient of inbreeding in the Goldens studied—that is, the greater the

Health and sound structure are essential for any dog to work well, and enable this dog to clear a 36" high jump. Wyzewood's Golden Rock UDT WC, Can. UD was both a winning obedience performer and a superb hunting dog. Owned by T.C. & Dolores Hoagland.

concentration of heredity from a limited number of specific ancestors, the greater the likelihood of lymphoma in the descendants. As the coefficient of inbreeding becomes greater (indicating closer inbreeding), the onset of the disease is seen earlier and the severity of the disease is greater.

Although we have eliminated many of the diseases, such as distemper and hepatitis, that used to kill dogs, other diseases will appear to increase. Also, in this modern age, our dogs are exposed to many more stresses and insults to their health than ever before, and that cannot be discounted entirely.

Whether buying or breeding a Golden Retriever, longevity is certainly a consideration. Losing a beloved canine friend at any age is sad, but there's a vast difference between death at the end of a long, productive life and the sudden death at age six or seven when the dog should be still in the prime of life.

TEETH

Since so much depends on the use of the mouth in the performance of the retriever's intended functions, tooth problems should be considered.

Missing teeth: Dogs who lack the second, third or fourth premolars, upper or lower, are of most concern. There may be from one to four or more teeth missing, and this tendency definitely is familial. The breed Standard says that dogs with obvious gaps caused by missing teeth are to be penalized in judging—and should also be so by the breeder. Absence of the very small first premolar does not seem to correlate with the lack of the second to fourth premolars that is a problem in Goldens.

Misalignment of teeth refers primarily to the incisors. Slight irregularities are usually a minor fault. Misalignments where the center two lower incisors are located completely ahead of all other incisors (this is called dropped incisors), or where the teeth are scrambled any old way, may warrant a more severe penalty.

Undershot bite is not uncommon in some lines, particularly some Field lines. Sometimes a young dog will progress from a level (edge to edge) bite to undershot by two years of age, as the lower jaw often continues to grow for a longer period of time than the upper. It can be very discouraging to see a nice young dog have the bite go "off" and ruin all hope of showing or breeding. Careful checking of tooth position may help predict mature bites. Normal jaws should have the third lower premolar positioned to point between the second and third upper premolars. If the lower third is pointing to, or ahead of, the upper second, that may indicate a problem.

WHAT DOES IT ALL MEAN?

Should every dog with any sort of defect be eliminated from breeding? Would this guarantee the elimination of defects or problems? Is it even possible to produce a dog free of all flaws?

The answers to the preceding questions are both simple and complex. First, if we were to eliminate from breeding all dogs with any sort of "defect," we would likely have no dogs left to use. The geneticists tell us that every living creature—dog, cat, human or codfish—carries a certain number of genes responsible for genetic problems, and it is neither possible nor practical to eliminate them all. What we can do is identify the major problems, those that most interfere with the animal's ability to live and function; these specific problems should be on the top of the list for elimination. Anomalies that have a lesser effect on the dog's function and quality of life would be of lesser consideration; and those that are only deemed faults because they do not conform to an arbitrary standard should be of least importance.

Would simply not breeding any dog showing evidence of a defect then guarantee no further defects in the offspring? No. This is the problem of the phenotype (what we can see) as opposed to the genotype (what is carried in the genes). As an example, simply breeding black Newfoundlands together for generations will not eliminate the gene that produces the occasional yellow or cream offspring. Yellow is a recessive, and one cannot tell by looking at a dog that she carries that recessive gene. If one parent is a yellow, then all black offspring will be "carriers," but otherwise, only by breeding carriers together will the yellow factor become evident.

Most researchers consider hip dysplasia to be *poly*genic, that a combination of genetic factors can initiate the development of dysplasia. This makes hip dysplasia a very complex item, genetically. Selection based on phenotype—that is, by choosing and using only the best of those animals available, and maintaining this selection through several generations—will tend to shift the resulting population toward the desired end of the curve, but it will *never* eliminate hip dysplasia in a large population of dogs. There will always be some percentage of the population that are at the other end of the range, and even some of the phenotypically best dogs will quite likely carry in their genotype some of the factors that contribute toward the development of hip dysplasia.

We should continue to eliminate as many of the worst examples as possible from breeding, and continue to select toward the ideal. Not only the parents should be examined but also as many siblings and as many direct ancestors as possible. This helps to select breeding individuals from better genetic backgrounds, who may be hoped to carry fewer of the undesired genetic factors. In this way at least, one can hope for fewer severely affected dogs, and the breed average can be shifted in a favorable direction. In England, a numerical hip-scoring scheme combined with pedigree study has identified parents called "improvers," which tend to produce better hips in their offspring.

It would certainly be helpful for all breeders to keep records on all dogs examined, and to cooperate with any researchers by providing dogs, examination reports and pedigrees for study. Only in this way will our knowledge and understanding increase.

Keep in mind that although some defects may remove the dog from a breeding program, the dog himself can remain functional and useful. So, even if a Golden with typical juvenile cataracts or mild hip dysplasia will not produce offspring, he may well never experience any discomfort or loss of function and can still be a very useful hunting, companion or service dog.

Every breeder and owner needs a list of priorities, including not only soundness but *all* aspects of the dog. You simply won't be able to "have it all"—that perfect dog—so figuring out what you do want and will accept is just common sense. Any items that are absolutely not acceptable would eliminate that dog from consideration. Everything else would be ranked in order, this varying somewhat from one person to the next. The Field Trialer would place high value on outstanding field aptitude and style, while another person might prefer a balance of basic ability to work as a personal gundog or participate in Hunting Tests, along with the quality to be shown in conformation with some success. These priorities may not be the same for everyone, but functional soundness and basic temperament, items without which any dog is of little value, must always receive serious consideration. *Breeding is only one of the Golden's many aspects, and not every dog should be a candidate for reproduction.*

PROMISE FOR THE FUTURE

Recent research aimed at exploring genetics on a molecular level is advancing knowledge of the canine genome. Within a few years, it may well be possible to have identifiable genetic "markers" indicating genes for many of the problems of such concern. Already, a study at the University of Michigan has found some 600 potential markers, as well as one specific for copper toxicosis in Bedlington Terriers. At Cornell University, a marker has been found for PRA in Irish Setters. This will enable identification of normal, affected and carrier dogs very early in life—and could mean elimination of these diseases within two or three generations. The prospect is encouraging, and we must all work to further these efforts.

Am. Can. Ch. Trowsnest Whirlwind, UD WC Can. CDX WC. Whirly was a personable dog who endeared himself to friends and fanciers, and passed on his many fine qualities to generations of Goldens. He sired not only champions, Utility Dogs and other titlists, but also at least 39 Guide Dogs for the Blind, plus Assistance and Therapy Dogs. He died in 1994, just a few days past his 16th birthday. Sired by Bainin of Caernac CD*** out of Ch. Valhalla's Trowsnest Folly UDT WCX; bred, owned and treasured by Marge Trowbridge.

chapter 11

Thinking About Breeding?

At one time or another every Golden owner thinks about breeding. The dog is so enjoyable, such a great companion—wonderful personality, good looking, all-in-all a terrific canine—that it seems only right that this excellence be perpetuated. And the puppies are so adorable, Goldens often have large litters, and are usually easy whelpers and good mothers; it will be such fun . . . and we can even make some money. . . .

Stop right there.

Golden Retrievers have reached such a level of popularity that an incredible increase in numbers has occurred. Goldens can be seen in ads for anything imaginable, in every city park with their owners, in pick-up trucks and in BMWs, in every veterinarian's office and Obedience training class, and as guide dogs.

They can also be found wandering as strays, waiting for death in animal shelters, serving a life of penal servitude in puppy mills, huddled in cages in pet stores, lying dead on roadsides, chained to ramshackle kennels in backyards. They also come to veterinary facilities with crippling skeletal defects or uncontrollable seizures or allergies, or to be destroyed due to temperament and behavior problems.

If you can't bear to think about things like this, you have no business even considering breeding, because unless you are *very careful*, and *very lucky*, any puppy you produce could be one of those unfortunates—or be the parent of some of them.

Why do you want to breed? Are you looking for a puppy "just like Sandy"? Or do you hope to produce dogs of a distinct type and quality? To start a strain of your own for competition and companionship? Because "it would be fun" or to "make a little money"? Going about the business of breeding *properly* is not "fun" (though it can be rewarding in some ways). It requires expenditure of much physical work and time, can be quite expensive, and can also be heartbreaking.

235

There are a number of very good books that cover the "mechanics" of breeding purebred dogs, which can give you excellent information on the actual breeding, whelping, raising of puppies and so forth. Some are listed in Appendix A. On the whole, Goldens are healthy, normal canines, but there are many things to be considered—some inherent problems and possible problems that can occur in any breed.

WHAT DO YOU NEED TO BE A GOOD BREEDER?

- Knowledge, determination, dedication, skills and responsibility

You must have certain knowledge and skills about dogs in general (about Goldens in particular), about bloodlines, structure, health, breeding, whelping, care of the dam and newborn puppies, their developmental stages, their physical and social needs and more. You must have the determination and dedication to learn (which is a never-ending process) and to carry through in doing it all. *Responsibility includes the understanding and acceptance of the fact that each dog you cause to be born is ultimately your responsibility.* Even if the dog goes to another home, at some point you may be called upon to help with advice or veterinary care, or even to take that dog back. If others fail that dog, you are his final recourse.

- A Golden Retriever of proven quality. Registration does not determine quality.

Just because she happens to be yours, and is a nice dog, doesn't mean she necessarily has any real contribution to make. She must be a very good to excellent example of the breed. She must be sound, free of major problems such as hip, eye or heart problems; immune deficiencies; seizures and so forth. She must have proper temperament and learning ability for the breed. Qualities such as severe shyness, timidity, stupidity, aggression or viciousness are *absolutely* unacceptable. She should have basic retrieving/working aptitude and be from a consistently strong, positive family background.

Whether a dog may have earned titles does not have *direct* bearing on the genetic factors that will be passed on, but accomplishment in formal competition, as evidenced by titles in the pedigree, may help to indicate whether those qualities exist in the pedigree and may contribute to the inherent aptitudes to be passed on.

- Physical facilities for proper care, whelping, housing and exercise

For the benefit of the dogs and your own sanity as well, proper facilities are essential. Not necessarily high-tech, but safe, comfortable and functional. This includes secure quarters for the bitch in season; quarters for the

The Stud Dog and Brood Bitch classes at Specialties are important and informative. Here, winning at the Mile-Hi GRC is Ann Bissette's Ch. Beaumaris Aspen Hill Tessa (left) with her daughters (center) Am. Can. Ch. Beaumaris Timberee Tessa Ann UDT WC VCX, Can. CDX (Sandra Fisher) and Ch. Beaumaris Autumn Sunset CD (Lori Bauman). Tessa Ann had the distinction of going both Best of Breed and High in Trial at Specialties. She and Autumn were sired by Ch. Beaulieu's Line Drive.

whelping that are warm, draft-free and easy to clean, with proper footing, size and lighting, away from noise, traffic and other dogs; an additional area for pups when they start to leave the nest, with both play and toilet areas in a pen or enclosure of proper size. This area must be secure and easy to clean, with proper footing, light, temperature and ventilation, and able to provide the puppies with the opportunity for socialization, play, exercise and learning.

- Time

You need time (in *addition* to your usual daily routine) for caring for the dogs; with a litter at four to eight weeks of age, this could easily be two to three hours a day for basic care. Illnesses or problems can add several more hours a day. There's the paperwork: record keeping, answering letters and phone calls, and making out pedigrees, advertisements and sales contracts. You will have to travel to the veterinarian and to pick up dog food and supplies and incidentals, all of which you usually will have to do at inopportune times. You also need time for visits by prospective buyers, showing them the dogs and being nice while answering the same idiotic question for the forty-seventh time. And it is essential to make time for the basic socialization and training of all puppies, while not neglecting the older dogs, your family, and your other responsibilities, not the last of which is your job!

- Financial resources

You need the financial resources for routine veterinary care and for special examinations such as X rays to detect hip dysplasia, eye and cardiac tests, and certifications. There are ovulation tests or vaginal smears to help determine optimum time of breeding and, possibly, artificial insemination and other veterinary costs. Stud fees ($400 to $600, depending on the dog's record and background, is not unreasonable) are payable at time of breeding, unless other arrangements are agreed upon. Shipping or transportation costs money, too: Air cargo for a Golden bitch can be $100 to several hundred dollars, each way, paid at time of shipping. If transporting by car, figure gas, time off work, motels and meals. Then there's the cost of buying/building suitable whelping areas, puppy pens, fencing, cleaning supplies, toys, bedding and shipping kennels. There will be extra dog food (premium brands can be very expensive), supplements, canned food, meat, eggs and so forth. Sales costs include advertising in dog magazines, photographs, copying pedigrees and incidental information on the litter, postage, stationery, business cards. There's possible emergency veterinary care: Caesarean-section delivery; care for sick puppies (parvo, corona, fading puppies, toxic milk syndrome); and veterinary costs for the litter (optional removal of dewclaws; fecal checks and deworming treatments; immunizations at six, nine and twelve weeks, and more for unsold puppies); presale veterinary examinations; and health certificates required for shipping.

- Your own emotional stability and resilience

Are you prepared to cope with all this? Are you willing to give up sports games or social events because the bitch has to go to the airport *today?* Will you stay home from work because she might whelp *today*—or tomorrow? What if the bitch becomes ill and aborts or resorbs the litter? What if she has trouble whelping and needs emergency veterinary attention, or a Caesarean section? You *will* be there with her to observe and assist with the whelping, no matter the hour or other social plans—won't you? What if she dies? Orphan puppies require an enormous amount of time and dedication. Can you face looking at and picking up (several times daily) the leavings of a mob of piddling, pooping baby dogs, who might be voiding live roundworms after medication and certainly will be wading through their food, sloshing in the water bowl, and tearing up papers and blankets? Are you willing to cull and destroy (have the vet euthanize) puppies with cleft palates, massive hernias, malformed limbs?

Are you prepared to cope with the strange and wondrous variety of people who will call about your puppies, and answer their questions (ranging from stunningly stupid to downright weird)? Are you willing to ask the right questions to determine whether these people are suitable for one of your cherished canines? And if these people are not suitable, are you willing to say, "No, I'm afraid there just isn't the right puppy for you in this litter (or any other!)" when they step out of the Jaguar with lizardskin checkbook in hand?

What will you do if, after investing two years and about $3,000, your bitch develops a pyometra after her first breeding and needs to be spayed?

Lying at right is Daphne Philpott's Strathcarron Seil of Standerwick, one of the few contemporary dams to produce both show Champion and Field Champion titlists. Her daughters are (left) Eng. Ch. Standerwick Thomasina, and (center) Eng. FTCh Standerwick Roberta of Abnalls. "Tommy" had 8 Field Trial awards, lacking only one win to make her a Dual Champion. She was sired by Eng. FTCh Holway Spinner. Roberta was sired by Belway Flick of Flightline. *Photo by Sally Ann Thompson.*

What will you do if your newly finished champion is diagnosed with hereditary cataract or PRA? What will you do if the "top show prospect" puppy you sold turns up with an undershot bite? What about the "terrific pet home" that turns into a messy divorce situation, and an angry phone call says, "Come get this dog before I take it to the pound"? What about the whispered rumors that one of your puppies has severely bitten a child . . . or is having seizures . . . or has been sold to a puppy mill?

What will you do if, when the litter is four months old, you still have five that are unsold? How will you react if the Rescue Service calls to say they have a puppy, or a litter, whose mother is a dog you sold two or three years ago? Will you still fulfill your obligation and responsibility in creating those dogs, as you so cheerfully assume the credit for the champions, the obedience titlists, the super companions and hunting dogs?

REALITY VS. FANTASY

Breeding dogs may conjure up pictures of fat, fuzzy puppies rollicking across green lawns, and proud owner/breeders accepting huge rosettes in amazing

Ch. Wingwatcher Reddi to Rally CDX WC (Ch. Trowsnest Whirlwind UD WC x Beaumaris Fair Victory). Rally, owned by Jan Owen, sired the remarkable litter of "over-achievers" that included Ch. Elysian Ski Hi Dub'l Exposure UD MH WCX**, Ch. Elysian Li'l Leica Reprint UD MH WCX, and Ch. Elysian Image of Oak Shadows TDX.

colors for the wins of their gorgeous Goldens or fat bank accounts from puppy sales and stud fees from the latest winner. Well, this may be what keeps you going, but before you get there. . . .

Reality is more like the instances described previously. The way to success as a breeder is through a great deal of plain hard work, very little of it glamorous. Can you cope?

- You need goals, and a plan, with priorities and flexibility.

You must decide where your priorities lie: To develop a consistent and distinctive family line of champions? To produce performance dogs for your own enjoyment in training and earning titles? To make Field Trial champions? To produce well-rounded versatile dogs who can make champion/ Obedience/Hunting/ Tracking titles? You can't do it all, so you must decide where best to direct your efforts.

You must also be realistic about what you have to work with, and your own resources. If you are limited as to number of dogs kept (as almost all of us are), will you place the nice dogs who are "not quite good enough" to get you another step closer to your goal? Or are you willing to rethink your goals and modify them to a more readily achievable level, or a different area more

The skilled breeder/owner/handler has always been essential to the Golden Retriever breed. Ellen Reiss and daughter Kathleen Lorentzen began when a very young Kathy trained her first Golden to a CDX. Several dog-generations later, Kathy showed her homebred 'Risto' (Ch Ocoee Sure Thing CD WC). (Beckwith's Echo of Loch Tay x Ch. Ocoee Lucky Streak). A GRCA Outstanding Sire, Risto's offspring include show and Obedience Trial winners, Hunting Test titlists and working guide dogs.

suitable to what you have or are capable of, and to get the most from the dogs you have?

One of the most common traps in dog breeding is keeping too many dogs. The old faithfuls you started with, the promising youngsters coming along, the one or two who are being campaigned right now, and of course the new litter that just might have that real world-beater in it. How many dogs can you really afford to support, with time—for each one—for socializing, training, grooming, show conditioning, Field work and so on? What arrangements will you make if you and all the family must be away for a few days or on vacation? What about an emergency? One breeder, after a flood invaded her home, decided that she would never have more dogs than she could get into her van in one load.

Oh yes, a litter of puppies would be such fun!

DO YOU REALLY NEED TO BE A BREEDER?

Keep in mind that you will not achieve your long-term goals in one generation—and possibly not in several. Are you willing to accept this and work slowly toward your goal? If not, perhaps breeding is not for you. If your primary interest in Goldens is in Obedience training, showing or competing, quite possibly you will find that you can make better use of your time and resources by acquiring your prospective competitor from an experienced breeder. Given the investment and the risks inherent in breeding, developing a good working relationship with an experienced breeder who produces the type of dog you like is probably the best and quickest way to success with dogs. Most breeders are absolutely delighted to sell or place a promising youngster with an experienced person who will develop and promote the dog; they have someone else to put in the time and effort in these specialized areas, and the buyer has the benefit of the breeder's years of experience and knowledge of those particular bloodlines.

IF YOU'D STILL LIKE TO BREED GOLDENS

If you think you "have what it takes," run through this checklist again:

1. Learn—and keep learning—about dogs; about Goldens; about behavior, structure, training, reproduction, daily care, handling, grooming and more.

2. Set your goals, short term and long term. How can you aim without a target?

3. Remember that you almost certainly will not achieve your goals in one generation, and quite likely not in three or four. Be patient. Be realistic.

4. Be flexible. Be prepared to modify your goals and the ways to them. Your views will undoubtedly change with experience and learning. Be open-minded.

5. Be prepared for disasters and setbacks. Have alternatives thought out in advance (the back-up stud dog; a financial cushion to cover the unexpected losses or veterinary expenses; a different bloodline if one doesn't pan out).

6. Be able to select and to cull (remove from breeding potential) ruthlessly. Don't fall into the "almost good enough" trap, which will compromise your standards, or the "too many dogs" trap, which will devour your resources.

7. Be sure your quest for success is true and honest, not based on falsehood. The most gorgeous "show dog" is spurious if she is not a sound, honest dog and a sound, authentic example of her breed.

The sacrifice of true basic quality in favor of fleeting wins should be abhorrent.

8. Don't compromise your standards. Yes, you will need to be flexible, and yes, you will need to accept less than perfection, but never deceive yourself. Set priorities, make them realistic and stay with them. Ignore the shortcuts and finagling (cheating) that other people may use in their pursuit of success.

9. Realize and accept that you need not be "number one" in order to be truly successful. True success, like happiness, lies within, and not in someone else's subjective opinion, nor on arbitrary parameters of rating systems, points or scores.

Evaluation

Any Golden being considered as a potential breeding animal must meet stringent requirements. There are many "nice dogs," most of whom won't be able to produce *better* dogs. All purebreds have been developed away from the canine norm in varying degrees. Random breeding, even within a breed, will tend to produce a drift back toward that basic canine, therefore in some degree away from the theoretically perfect dog of that breed. Without very careful selection of breeding stock, and equally careful selection of the resulting offspring that may be chosen to carry on, there is no hope of improvement.

No matter what area of achievement you may have in mind when breeding, there are some essential factors, not only in the sire and dam but *throughout the pedigree.*

Temperament must be sound and typical of the breed. This includes not only the disposition of the dog but such mental traits as intelligence, trainability, willingness, retrieving aptitude and more. A Golden who is nasty with people, and one who is devoid of retrieving instinct are equally atypical; although the nonretriever may still be a useful companion, the nasty dog is a detriment in any area. The working aptitude of the Golden Retriever is one of the breed's chief reasons for being. Without it, you have a nice golden-colored dog, maybe a sweet companion or a stunning showdog, but not a true Golden.

Soundness includes every aspect of the dog's health, all the physical aspects that enable the dog to function normally. In the Golden this includes basic normal canine structure throughout, as well as areas of concern such as hip dysplasia, eye problems, cardiac defects and so forth, as determined by a qualified veterinarian.

Conformation and Breed Type. While conformation includes general aspects of structure, "type" is made up of the qualities that distinguish this breed from any other. If the proposed sire or dam does not have these qualities in a very strong degree, there is little hope of producing offspring who do. To some degree one may be able to compensate for one parent's flaws by selecting a mate who is excellent in that characteristic, but trying to breed out several major faults at once is impossible.

Working aptitude was mentioned under temperament, but it is important enough to rate being categorized separately. This broad term includes all the factors that make the Golden Retriever a versatile dog. Each particular area such as Field work (hunting, Trials, Hunting Tests), Obedience Trials, Tracking, Agility, service dogs to assist the handicapped or any other field, requires specific qualities and aptitudes that must be considered.

One of the reasons breeding truly excellent Golden Retrievers is such a tough task is that there are so many facets that must be considered. Although it will be necessary to compromise in certain areas, there must also be a limit beyond which no compromise will be made. For instance, one would not breed to a dog with PRA (Progressive Retinal Atrophy) because it is certain that all the puppies would be either afflicted with or carriers of the condition; one might not necessarily strike off a dog because the eye examination report noted a very mild distichiasis (ingrown eyelash). A breeder with primary interests in Field work would be more tolerant of white marking on the chest than would someone concentrating on show competition, and the show person might not place as much emphasis on water entry. But the breeders dedicated to the all-around Golden have a real balancing act to perform: They must maintain a good level of quality in all areas without sacrificing any of the essentials.

How Do You Find Out Whether Your Golden Is Worth Breeding?

You've read the Breed Standard, and you've seen photographs of gorgeous Goldens—just like yours.

Some qualities are fairly easily determined; for example, the hip X ray and the eye and cardiac testing will rule out a dog who shows a serious genetically determined defect. With as many good-quality Goldens as there are, dogs with that kind of physical fault don't need to be bred. *Unless* you are a breeder of many years' experience *and* working with the advice of a competent canine geneticist, you are well advised to forego that gamble.

As for temperament and working qualities, the best means of determination is to actually train and work the dog. Lots of Goldens retrieve tennis balls for hours on end, but that doesn't tell you whether the dog will plunge into an icy lake for an angry, wounded Canada goose. Sweet as your Golden may be, if she takes a week just to learn "sit," you have a dog who will never get out of canine kindergarten. If earning a WC requires four months' training by a professional, the dog lacks a great deal in natural working qualities; the Working Certificate was originally designed as an aptitude test. This is one reason breeders seek to prove their dogs by *actual* achievements.

Small breeders can work together to develop a quality line of dogs. This gives them more resources than they would have individually. This is Gayhaven Ocoee Free and Easy (1979), bred by Ellen Reiss and Kathleen Lorentzen, and owned by Betty Gay. "Freebie" illustrates outstanding type and balance, with a perfect topline and superb front assembly.

As for conformation and structure, dog shows may be of some help, as a dog with major or disqualifying faults is unlikely to win much, if at all. But the dog show game has become so much of "show" rather than "dog" that it is not always a real help, nor can it tell you what you should be looking for in a mate to complement your dog. Your best bet is to find an experienced person to take a good look at your dog and give an opinion; preferably, this would be a breeder/exhibitor of Goldens with much experience and known to give a straightforward, honest opinion. If such a person is not available, perhaps a dog show judge known to be knowledgeable about the breed, or a professional handler specializing in Goldens, may be willing to give a private evaluation. The handler and the multiple-breed judge may not be conversant with the fine points of the breed, but at least should be able to comment on general structure and movement. Don't be hesitant about asking, and don't stop at one—a consensus of opinions is often helpful.

Bainin of Caernac CD*** bears the unique distinction of becoming an Outstanding Sire by having produced show Champions, a Field Champion and Utility Dog titlists. Bainin himself lacked only one Field placement of gaining his title. He was a dog of great personality and lived to be more than 17 years of age. Owned by Mimi Kearney, Caernac Kennels.

Once it has been proven that your Golden is of a quality worth breeding and has something to offer the breed—and you have formed a fairly solid idea of the sort of Golden you want to produce—then the search for a compatible mate begins. Potential stud dogs and their families must be evaluated as painstakingly as your own bitch. Granted, it is often difficult to gather all the information you want—sometimes it is just not available; sometimes stud owners don't want to divulge everything they might know. If you suspect the latter, it might be wise to ask elsewhere, such as other people who have bred to that same dog; what results did they get? OFA and CERF reports can be verified directly through those organizations; show, Obedience and Field Trial titles, through the AKC (addresses are in Appendix C). If you can't get the answers that satisfy you, then perhaps a different dog (or owner) would be better.

A proven stud dog should have progeny, so you may have some idea of what he will produce. Particular attention should be paid to his offspring from bitches of similar bloodlines to yours, if there are any. Investigation of the stud dog's close relatives (parents, siblings, grandparents and so on) will also be helpful. The owner should be open and honest about the dog, and answer your questions readily. If the owner states that the dog is perfection and has never produced *any* flaws, look elsewhere! Such a paragon does not exist except in our dreams!

It's helpful to keep a folder for each potential stud dog: pictures, pedigrees, examination reports, notes of telephone conversations and so forth. It's amazing how quickly all those little bits disappear, or comments are forgotten or confused with another dog ("Now, was it Rocky or his brother who had the light eyes . . . ?"). Perhaps in the future, you may be considering one of those other dogs.

OUTCROSSING OR LINEBREEDING?

One of those old questions that can't be answered dogmatically. It is true that linebreeding (breeding animals who are not closely related but may have one or more common ancestors), intelligently done, is a way to fix type and to concentrate the qualities of outstanding ancestors. It is also true that outcrossing (using *un*related animals) can be useful to bring in needed qualities and to maintain a needed range of possibilities in the gene pool available to you. You need to read books such as Dr. Willis's *Genetics of the Dog* or Dr. Hutt's *Genetics for Dog Breeders* and become familiar with the bloodlines and families behind your proposed breeding animals.

Inbreeding is best left only to very experienced breeders who have a comprehensive and generations-deep knowledge of what they are dealing with. Inbreeding is the breeding together of very closely related animals (parent to offspring, brother to sister, and so on). While it does offer an opportunity to fix qualities of those animals, it also is a means of revealing any undesirable or recessive traits that may be lurking unseen in the genotype. This can be useful, and it also can be a major headache. *Inbreeding does not create faults, but it does reveal and intensify them.*

Anyone breeding Goldens should also be aware that in many cases, the prominent winners of today are already closely linebred (have some of the same ancestors). While you may not see the common names in a three- or four-generation pedigree, an extended pedigree may well reveal that in the older generations the same names may appear many, many times. Remember that even as linebreeding (and inbreeding) can set desirable qualities in that line of dogs, it can quite equally set faults and intensify them.

MENTORS

For a beginner, one of the best ways to learn is to have an experienced breeder as a mentor. Often this will be the breeder from whom the novice obtained potential breeding stock, which may be an advantage in that the established breeder should have some knowledge and insight about dogs from that line and how they might best be utilized in breeding. A possible disadvantage is that the breeder may be more or less "kennel-blind"—that is, seeing only good things in his own stock. The best breeders are willing to give unprejudiced consideration to other bloodlines and animals, judging them on their merits and not dismissing them merely because they belong to persons who may be rivals.

Many breeders are willing to work as mentors with serious newcomers. However, one should not fall into the trap of becoming merely a follower. Unfortunately, some prominent breeders/exhibitors have their own "groupies" who seem to serve only as extensions of themselves. This is not what you are looking for, but someone who is sincerely interested in educating and helping you in your own efforts.

CO-OWNERSHIPS AND "BREEDERS' TERMS"

It often happens that after the novice has demonstrated some degree of commitment, the opportunity of co-owning a promising dog for show or breeding is offered. This is advantageous to the breeder because someone else is keeping the dog, working with him and paying the bills. It may also be advantageous to the newcomer, as a chance to acquire a dog of perhaps high potential, without a lot of cash outlay up front. It also offers the potential for major complications and headaches.

"Breeders' terms" is somewhat similar, in that the breeder places or sells a bitch of breeding potential, on some condition such as that the breeder will take the bitch back for a litter, or that the purchaser will give back to the seller the puppies from a litter. While this, like co-ownership, may appear to be advantageous to both parties, be aware that more times than not, the "deal" usually works only to the advantage of the person who has placed the dog with a gullible newcomer. Such a deal—that is, you put in all the time and effort and expenditure on raising, training and showing the bitch, and whelping the litter and raising it—and *all* the profit goes back to the other party. Almost without exception, any deal entailing "breeders' terms" should be avoided like the plague.

In every case, if there is *any* kind of special arrangement, every possible contingency must be spelled out in detail and clearly written, with a copy of the contract for each party signed by all concerned. *This is absolutely essential.* Even if the parties involved are two Supreme Court Justices, it is still essential that every single item be covered clearly. Who keeps the dog? When and under what circumstances may the other party take the dog? Who pays shipping? Stud fees? Veterinary expenses for the litter? Who gets how many puppies, and who gets to choose first? What if there is no litter? Or only one or two puppies? What if the bitch never passes her examinations for hip dysplasia, eye problems and so on? What if the bitch dies or is rendered nonbreedable? What if she simply is not good enough to contribute meaningfully in breeding? Who makes these decisions? These are some of the complications that can arise!

A few co-ownerships work out well—if both parties understand the agreement fully, have similar philosophies, are not too self-centered and *have it all in writing!*

SPAYING AND NEUTERING

For those who don't plan to breed, or to show in conformation, many potential problems may be forestalled by surgical neutering: spaying (ovariohysterectomy) of females and castration of males. Spayed bitches won't have twice-yearly disruptions by heat cycles, nor will they develop pyometra so common in older bitches. Neutered males are more mellow with other dogs, without the macho posturings that sometimes disturb a household with two entire males. They also won't be distracted from their work or be vaulting fences to follow the scent of a lovely lady drifting by.

Most veterinarians like to do this surgery sometime after a puppy is six months of age. Personally, I prefer to wait a bit longer, giving the dog time to develop the look of a reasonably mature animal. Males neutered too young never do develop masculinity; females done too young may develop incontinence later in life, requiring hormone supplementation. A healthy two- or three-year-old presents very little surgical risk.

ONE LAST NOTE

Breeding dogs properly takes a considerable investment in time, finances, hard work and emotion. It is not difficult to produce puppies. But it can be extremely difficult to produce *the right kind of dogs,* with the proper balance of temperament, health, breed type, working abilities, intelligence and soundness—and to do it honestly, ethically and responsibly.

Keep the balance. There is life outside of dogs, and it is important. Your home, your family, your job, the other components of your life must not be neglected or sacrificed. *Enjoy your dogs, respect them and appreciate them for all they are.*

The one and only Thistle. Ch-AFCh Riverview's Chickasaw Thistle UDT. No other single Golden has achieved these titles, nor is likely to do so. Thistle and her owner/ handler Sally Venerable had that special rapport which sometimes develops between dog and human, and which enables them to achieve the highest levels of accomplishment. Bred by Harry and Dawn Erickson, by Ch. High Farm's Band's Clarion out of Ch. Tansy of High Farms, Thistle was whelped in 1961.

chapter 12

The Golden Retriever Club of America

The Golden Retriever Club of America, Inc. (GRCA) is recognized by the American Kennel Club as the Parent (national) club dedicated to the advancement and protection of the Golden Retriever. Each of the nearly 140 breeds eligible for registration with the AKC is entitled to representation by a Parent club, but the size, structure and activity of such clubs varies greatly from breed to breed. The GRCA is one of the two or three largest and most active Parent breed clubs. This active, concerned organization has been working for the betterment of all Golden Retrievers and their owners for more than half a century.

One of the responsibilities of any Parent club is the preparation of the official breed Standard, the written description of the ideal breed specimen. This is used as a guide in judging. Any change to a breed Standard requires approval by the Parent Club membership. Parent Clubs are also entitled to elect a delegate to represent them at quarterly meetings at the AKC and to serve as a means of communication between their club and the AKC.

The GRCA was informally established about 1935, and formally incorporated in 1938 with some forty-three members. As Golden Retrievers became more popular, membership grew. Local clubs began forming in 1956, and these established the foundation for the GRCA's current network of some forty-five or more "GRCA Member Clubs" throughout the United States. GRCA membership in 1994 was more than 4,500, one of the largest AKC Parent clubs.

The GRCA Bylaws describe the objectives of the Club, the first of which is the following:

To encourage the members to perfect, by selective breeding, Golden Retrievers that possess the soundness, temperament, natural ability and

251

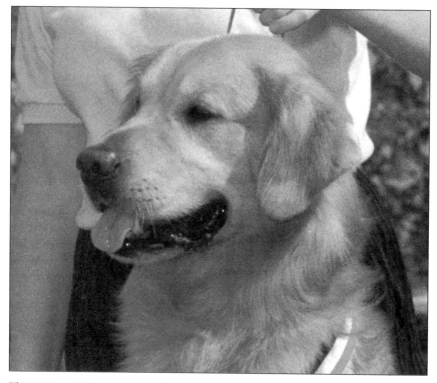

This is Ryan. His owner, Caroline McCormick, says: "Ryan exemplified the Golden temperament and trainability. He would do everything I asked, and more. He exceeded my wildest dreams, with everything he did, and lived to please me; and that he did in every way." American, Canadian, Mexican, Dominican, South American and International Ch. Beckwith's Main Event, Am. Can. UDT WCX, Dominican UD, Mex. PC, Am. JH, NAHRA Started; Ryan had 54 OTCH points and is pictured winning the Veterans' Class at the 1992 GRCA National Specialty at 10½ years of age.

personality that is reflected in the standard of the breed, and to do all possible to advance and promote the perfection of these qualities. All the remaining wording of the Bylaws is an expansion upon this theme, mentioning acceptance of the breed Standard, encouraging sporting competition in various areas of activity and describing how these objectives are to be carried out.

The organizational structure of the GRCA is similar to that of many national dog clubs. The day-to-day business of the club is run by a twelve-member Board of Directors: a president, secretary, treasurer, three vice-presidents and six directors. The secretary's office handles a great deal of correspondence from the general public, from the AKC and other organizations and from member clubs.

The GRCA has more than forty committee chairmanships and appointed positions. These report directly to the Board of Directors and, with the sole exception of the Nominating Committee, are subject to the final authority of the Board. These are a few: *General Education* develops educational material for the membership and the general public, and is responsible for regular columns and articles in the *Golden Retriever News. Breed Health and Genetics* is responsible for keeping the membership up to date on various matters such as genetic problems. *OFA/CERF Committee* acts as liaison with those organizations, and maintains the listings of OFA- and CERF- registered Goldens. *Judges' Education* develops and distributes material for use in furthering knowledge of the breed among conformation judges. The *Columnist for the AKC Gazette* is responsible for four yearly columns in the AKC's own monthly magazine. The *GRCA Archivist* maintains the Club's large collection of books, articles, photographs, scrapbooks and artwork, founded on the personal collection of Rachel Page Elliott, long-time historian of the Golden Retriever.

Am. Can. Ch. Beckwith's Malagold Flash, Am. Can. UDT, Am. WC (Ch. Beckwith's Copper Ingot x Ch. Beckwith's Frolic of Yeo CDX). Born 1968. Owned, trained and handled by Carole (Kvamme) Johnson, "Robbie" had the rare distinction of having been Best in Show and Highest Scoring Dog in Trial at the same show. His career started with a bang when he was awarded Best of Breed at the GRCA National Specialty in 1969 from the American-bred class by judge Kitty Drury.

Am. Can. Ch. Jolly Oahu Cougar CD WC, ten years young, winning the Veterans' Class at the 1985 GRCA National Specialty show. The Veterans' classes are particular favorites with exhibitors and spectators alike, and showcase the long-lasting qualities of fine Goldens. Cougar was owned and handled by Laurie Doumaux.

GRCA ACTIVITIES

The most prominent event of the year is the GRCA National Specialty, which includes nearly every activity in which Goldens participate: a conformation show, Obedience Trial, Field Trial and Tracking Test, plus GRCA Working Certificate and WCX Tests. In addition, Sweepstakes, TDX and Hunting Tests are optional and held whenever possible. The National is held in the fall and rotates among the three Regions, where it is hosted by the local GRCA Member Clubs. Entries in recent years often exceed 1,500, and the schedule of events may cover seven days or more.

Other events held with the National are educational seminars, Board meetings, a meeting of the member club delegates, the Honors Parade of title-holders and other special events the host club may have organized. The National is much like a large family reunion for Golden people, and many plan their annual vacations around it.

The GRCA also holds three Regional Specialties yearly, hosted by local clubs, usually including a Specialty Show, Obedience Trial and Working Certificate Test; the WCX, Tracking and Sweepstakes are optional.

THE WORKING CERTIFICATE PROGRAM

The GRCA offers Working Certificate (WC) and Working Certificate Excellent (WCX) titles for Goldens successfully completing the required exercises in basic Field work under judgment. This program, initiated in 1964, was developed to encourage demonstration of Goldens' basic abilities in the field, particularly for dogs whose owners might not participate in Field Trials. Dogs who pass receive a certificate from the GRCA. The WC/WCX titles are not recognized by the AKC but are GRCA titles and are listed in the GRCA Yearbook Supplements.

The WC test consists of the retrieving of two upland game birds on land as a double (two birds shot in succession, then retrieved), and the retrieving of two freshly killed ducks in swimming water as "back-to-back" singles. The dog need not be steady; this is primarily a test of natural ability rather than of training.

The WCX test requires retrieving of three birds (pigeons or other upland game birds) on land as a triple with a shot flyer, and the retrieving of two freshly killed ducks from the water as a double retrieve. The dog is also required to honor (remain in place) while another dog performs the water retrieve.

The GRCA's WC/WCX Committee oversees the program, processes applications for tests by local clubs and periodically reviews the WC/WCX rules. Complete information can be found in a booklet available from the GRCA for a nominal fee. The WC/WCX program has proved very popular and has served to introduce many owners and dogs to Field work, who might well never have thought of doing so.

THE VERSATILITY CERTIFICATE

In 1992 the GRCA established a program to formally recognize dogs who had demonstrated accomplishment in each of the areas of show, Obedience and field work. A point system is used, and the dog must earn at least one point in each area. The system is set up so that a VC is within reach of most Goldens of good overall quality and basic ability. The VCX is to reward dogs who achieve considerably more than a minimum in each area. For instance, a Champion with a CD and a WC will qualify for VC; so will a UD dog with one point in conformation and a WC or a Junior Hunter. To earn a VCX, the dog needs something like a Ch-UD-Senior Hunter, or a UD-Master Hunter with a major win in conformation. The award is not automatic; owners must apply for VC and VCX and submit proof of achievement. VC and VCX are

This trio represents field lines that are dominant in Trial-bred Goldens today. Center, AFC-FC Topbrass Dustbuster, owned by Barbara Howard, bred by Joe and Jackie Mertens. Buster's dam (at left) and sire (at right) are full siblings to other FC-AFCs, and have proven a force in Field Trial and Obedience competition.

GRCA titles only, not recognized by the AKC, but nonetheless are valued by Golden Retriever fanciers as indicating a well-rounded Golden.

THE GRCA YEARBOOK

The Yearbook Supplement is issued biannually and includes the names of all Golden Retrievers earning AKC and GRCA titles, and award winners in all areas of participation. Canadian and British titleholders are also included. Published in loose-leaf format, the large Basic book covers 1932 to 1967. Recent Supplements are nearly 600 pages in length and include more than 500 photographs and individual pedigrees—there is an enormous amount of activity in the Golden world!

Also included in the Yearbook are dogs qualifying for the "Hall of Fame," a system for recognizing achievement at shows, Obedience Trials or Field Trials, and for recording outstanding sires and dams. Outstanding Sire and Outstanding Dam designations are awarded on a system of points earned by the dog's offspring: Sires must have at least five qualifying offspring; dams require three.

The Yearbook is an invaluable reference for any serious Golden fancier and breeder. The full series presents a comprehensive overview of the breed from its first recognition in this country to the present.

THE GRCA CHALLENGE AND PERPETUAL TROPHIES

Through generous donations by members over the years, the GRCA has acquired an extremely impressive array of more than thirty challenge and perpetual trophies. Challenge trophies, if won three times by the same owner, may be awarded outright; perpetual trophies are those that are offered annually but are never to be retired. A number of the trophies are awarded for achievement over the period of a calendar year; others are awarded for wins at the National Specialty. The trophies are on display at each National Specialty and are awarded to the new recipients at the Annual Awards Dinner.

Many of the trophies are unique and irreplaceable works of art. The first trophies donated to the Club are two beautifully hand-engraved sterling bowls first offered by Mr. and Mrs. Samuel S. Magoffin in 1938. The Gilnockie Challenge Cup and the Rockhaven Challenge Cup are for outstanding achievement in Field Trials and bench shows, respectively, over a year's time. Quite unusual is the Ch. Tonkahof Bang Trophy—a heavy sterling silver chain collar from which hang medallions with the GRCA club crest, each engraved with the name of the show champion placing highest in the Specialty Field Trial each year.

THE GOLDEN RETRIEVER NEWS

The GRCA has one of the finest breed club magazines, the *Golden Retriever News*. An average issue may be more than 200 pages. This bimonthly publication is available only to GRCA members and is the Club's major form of communication. It contains reports of Specialties; articles on many matters; a number of regular columns from Conformation, Field, Obedience and Tracking Editors and local club correspondents; "Official Business" and considerable advertising from breeders and exhibitors.

The GRN, as it is often called, is a major component of the GRCA's services to its members. It has evolved over the years from a simple four-page newsletter in the early 1950s into a major publication in the canine world, under the guidance of a series of talented, hard-working editors and contributors.

PUBLIC AWARENESS

Several of the GRCA's major projects began as educational efforts to moderate population growth of the Golden Retriever. The seventy-six-page booklet "An Introduction to the Golden Retriever" is aimed particularly at the person new to Golden Retrievers and heavily stresses responsible dog-ownership and proper care and training. A smaller booklet titled *Acquiring a Golden Retriever* contains succinct information useful to anyone considering taking on the responsibility of a Golden Retriever.

In order to alert new owners of Goldens to the requirements of responsible dog-ownership and the particular character of the Golden, the Public Awareness Letter was created. Called the PAL letter, this simple folded sheet was mailed by the GRCA at their own expense to every single owner of a newly registered Golden Retriever, using labels supplied by the AKC—more than 60,000 pieces a year. It also mentioned the considerable information and educational materials available through the GRCA, and had a mail-in coupon to request further information or order printed material. The AKC later modified its computerized mailing system so that these PAL letters could be mailed in the same envelope as the registration certificate, thus sending information directly to all persons registering dogs.

RESEARCH AND DONATIONS

Attempting to alleviate genetic and health problems for many years, in 1956 the GRCA established the Advisory Council on Hip Dysplasia, which was a panel of radiologists who read X rays submitted by veterinarians for the owners. Making use of cooperative veterinary radiologists, the Advisory Council was very active in disseminating information about hip dysplasia and making Golden fanciers aware of the problem. In 1966 the Advisory Council was expanded into the Orthopedic Foundation for Animals. John Olin, a Labrador Retriever fancier, was largely instrumental in the organization and funding of the OFA, which now serves all breeds and interprets thousands of radiographs yearly, issuing reports and maintaining lists of OFA-registered dogs.

The GRCA also donates substantial sums annually to research projects, through the Morris Animal Foundation and the American Kennel Club, and tries to keep members informed about current developments pertinent to Goldens. Among other organizations that have received funds from the GRCA are several such as Guide Dogs for the Blind and Canine Companions for Independence. In addition to monetary donations, many individual GRCA members contribute time as volunteers with these organizations, and also donate dogs to be used for such training.

The Golden Fund for Rescue is managed by the GRCA's Committee to Assist Rescue. This committee serves as a central advisory and funding source for the many Golden Retriever Rescue organizations throughout the country, local groups that work to rescue Goldens who have been abandoned or are in need, assess them and find them new homes. Some of these groups are not affiliated with any GRCA clubs, but as long as their requests are appropriate, the GRCA will try to assist.

Appendix A

Bibliography

This is not intended to be a complete listing of all available books and videos but to supply opportunities for further reading and viewing that are pertinent. Most are readily available; those indicated as out of print may sometimes be found at secondhand book dealers.

BOOKS AND VIDEOS ON THE BREED

Charlesworth, Mrs. W. M. *The Book of the Golden Retriever.* (Out of print) England: The Field, 1933; 2nd ed., 1947. By a pioneer breeder and exhibitor in Goldens. A shortened version, *Golden Retrievers*, by A. S. Barnes, was printed in New York, 1952.

Elliott, Rachel Page. *The Golden Retriever.* Thirty-one minute video, VHS or Beta (specify), for the GRCA. Available from GRCA, c/o Ann Houston, 8 Kendall Rd., Boxboro, MA 01719. Good overview of the Golden; function, structure, movement, character.

Fischer, Gertrude. *The Complete Golden Retriever.* New York: Howell Book House, 1974.

———. *The New Complete Golden Retriever.* 2nd ed. New York: Howell Book House, 1984. Additional material and photos.

Foss, Valerie. *The Book of Golden Retriever Champions, Show Champions, Field Champions and Obedience Champions: 1946–1985.* England: No pub. given, 1986.

———. *Golden Retrievers Today.* New York: Howell Book House, 1994. Has some of the historical material from the "Book of Champions" plus general care and so on.

————. *The Second Book of Golden Retriever Champions, Show Champions, Field Champions, and Obedience Champions: 1915–1939, 1986–1990*. 1991. The titles tell it all: pedigrees and photos (where possible) of all Golden titleholders in England, plus some other outstanding Goldens and a few from other countries as well.

The Golden Retriever by American Kennel Club and GRCA. Twenty-minute video. New York: American Kennel Club. Brief overview of the breed's show points.

Pepper, Jeffrey. *The Golden Retriever*. Ocean City, NJ: TFH Publications, 1984.

Reflections. Magazines published by Golden Retriever Club of America, 1985 and 1989. Available through GRCA. Articles on history, prominent dogs of the day, and so forth.

Sawtell, Lucille. *All About the Golden Retriever*. London: Pelham Books Ltd., 1971. Also later editions. General breed book by long-time breeder.

Stonex, Elma. *The Golden Retriever Handbook*. (Out of print) London: Nicholson & Watson, 1953. Elma Stonex was not only a longtime breeder of quality Goldens but also the eminent historian of the breed; her research established much of the breed's early history.

Yearbooks. Golden Retriever Club of America: Comprehensive book published 1964–1968 and biannual supplements thereafter, issued in even-numbered years. Published by and available from GRCA. Previous Yearbooks (1939, 1947, 1948, 1950, 1957) are very rare.

BEHAVIOR, BASIC TRAINING AND CARE

Carlson, D. G., DVM, and James M. Giffin, MD. *Dog Owner's Home Veterinary Handbook*. New York: Howell Book House, 1994.

Coren, Stanley. *The Intelligence of Dogs: Canine Conciousness and Capabilities*. New York: The Free Press (Macmillan), 1994. Comprehensive survey of dogs' mental capacities, personality and instincts, by a professor of psychology who is also an experienced dog trainer.

Dunbar, Ian, Ph.D., MRCVS. *How to Teach a New Dog Old Tricks; Sirius Puppy Training Manual*. Oakland, CA: James & Kenneth Publishers, 1991.

Fox, Michael W., MRCVS. *Superdog: Raising the Perfect Canine Companion*. New York: Howell Book House, 1990.

Milani, Myrna, DVM. *The Weekend Dog*. New York: Rawson Associates, 1984. Excellent for those who have to work away from home but still want a dog.

Pfaffenberger, Clarence, Ph.D. *The New Knowledge of Dog Behavior*. New York: Howell Book House, 1964. First popular presentation of research findings on canine behavior, based on Scott and Fuller's work on genetics and social behavior of the dog.

Pryor, Karen. *Don't Shoot the Dog*. New York: Bantam Books, 1985. Softcover. Excellent explanation and application of behavioral concepts utilized by trainers.

Rutherford, Clarice, and David Neil. *How to Raise a Puppy You Can Live With*. Loveland, CO: Alpine Publishing Co., 1981. Also subsequent editions. The book for every new puppy owner.

TRAINING FOR SPECIALIZED AREAS

Alston, George G., with Connie Vanacore. *The Winning Edge: Show Ring Secrets*. New York: Howell Book House, 1992. Excellent guide for the amateur handler in the conformation ring, by an experienced and successful professional.

Bailey, Joan. *How to Help Gun Dogs Train Themselves*. Hillsboro, OR: Swan Valley Press, 1992. Great book on making use of dog's instincts and behaviors in training, from pup's first day onward. Aimed at pointing breeds, but much also applies to retrievers. Softcover.

Bauman, Diane. *Beyond Basic Dog Training*. New York: Howell Book House, 1986. Training for obedience competition.

Burnham, Patricia Gail. *Playtraining Your Dog*. New York: St. Martin's Press, 1980. Also later editions. Mostly obedience-oriented; good understanding of dog character and an approach that works well with Goldens.

Cree, John. *Nosework for Dogs*. London: Pelham Books Ltd., 1980. Covers basic obedience and tracking.

Ganz, Sandy, and Sue Boyd. *Tracking From the Ground Up*. 1991. Authors are experienced TD-TDX trainers and judges. Available from Sandy Ganz, 20 Steeplehill Lane, Ballwin, MO 63011.

Johnson, Glen. *Tracking Dog, Theory and Methods*. Westmoreland, NY: Arner Publications, 1975. Precise and very complete explanation of training dogs for tracking.

Rutherford, Clarice, and Sandy Whicker and Barbara Branstad. *Retriever Working Certificate Training*. Loveland, CO: Alpine

Publications, 1986. Only text specifically covering WC/WCX training; also applicable to Hunting Tests. Softcover.

Spencer, James B. *Hunting Retrievers: Hindsights, Foresight, and Insights.* Loveland, CO: Alpine Publications, 1989. Very good introduction to hunting retrievers and what they do, also the various retriever breeds and Hunting Tests.

———. *Training Retrievers for the Marshes and Meadows.* Fairfax, VA: Denlinger's, 1990. Good coverage of all the basics of retriever training, aimed at the amateur owner.

Volhard, Joachim, and Gail Fisher. *Training Your Dog: A Step by Step Manual.* New York: Howell Book House, 1984. Basic obedience.

Wolters, Richard. *Water Dog.* New York: E. P. Dutton Co., 1964. A book that's been around a long time, but still very good for basic retriever training, especially for the novice.

HEALTH AND BREEDING

Carlson, D. G., DVM, and James M. Giffen, MD. *Dog Owners' Home Veterinary Handbook.* New York: Howell Book House, 1994. *The* dog health book; indexed.

Holst, Phyllis M., MS, DVM. *Canine Reproduction; A Breeder's Guide.* Loveland, CO: Alpine Publications, 1985. Much good solid information not found in other texts on breeding.

Hutt, Frederick B., DVM. *Genetics for Dog Breeders.* San Francisco, CA: W.H. Freeman and Co.1979. Useful, practical, accurate and readable too. A must for serious breeders.

Wilcox, Bonnie, and Chris Walkowicz. *Old Dogs, Old Friends.* New York: Howell Book House, 1991. Living with and caring for the senior dog.

Willis, Malcolm B., BSc, Ph.D. *Practical Genetics for Dog Breeders.* New York: Howell Book House, 1992.

Zink, Christine, DVM, Ph.D. *Peak Performance: Coaching the Canine Athlete.* New York: Howell Book House, 1992. Health care and conditioning for the performance dog.

STRUCTURE AND MOVEMENT

Brown, Curtis. *Dog Locomotion and Gait Analysis.* Wheat Ridge, CO: Hoflin Publishing, 1986. Detailed study of dog gaits and movement. Softcover.

Elliott, Rachel Page. *Dogsteps—A Study of Canine Structure and Movement*. Sixty-nine minute video. New York: American Kennel Club.

————. *The New Dogsteps*. New York: Howell Book House, 1983. Excellent explanation of canine gait and structure; good illustrations and concise text.

Gilbert, Edward M. Jr., and Thelma R. Brown. *K-9 Structure and Terminology*. New York: Howell Book House, 1995. Based on *Dog Locomotion and Gait Analysis* by Curtis Brown; a fully updated and expanded version.

Schlehr, Marcia R. *A Study of the Golden Retriever*. Travis House, Box 414, Flat Rock, MI 48134; 1994 edition. Sixty-four-page softcover with hundreds of line drawings.

Smythe, R. H., MRCVS. *Conformation of the Dog*. London: Popular Dogs Pub. Co., 1962. An interesting discussion of relevance of dog structure and anatomy.

Appendix B

Glossary of Titles and Abbreviations

This section lists the symbols and abbreviations often found in reading pedigrees.

AKC (American Kennel Club) titles:

AFC or AFCh	Amateur Field Champion
FC, FCh, or FTCh	Field Champion, Field Trial Champion
NFC or NFTCh	National Field Trial Champion
NAFC or NAFTCh	National Amateur Field Trial Champion
JH	Junior Hunter (1st Hunting Test title)
SH	Senior Hunter (2nd Hunting Test title)
MH	Master Hunter (3rd Hunting Test title)
CD	Companion Dog (1st Obedience title)
CDX	Companion Dog Excellent (2nd obedience title)
UD	Utility Dog (3rd Obedience title)
UDX	Utility Dog Excellent
OTCh	Obedience Trial Champion
TD	Tracking Dog (1st Tracking title)
TDX	Tracking Dog Excellent (2nd Tracking title)

UDT	Utility Dog Tracker (UD + TD)
UDTX	Utility Dog Tracker Excellent (UD + TDX)
VST	Variable Surface Tracker (Note: AKC has also deemed that a dog with both TDX and VST is to be a "Tracking Champion.")
Ch	Champion (conformation)
D.Ch	Dual Champion (FC + Ch, but not AFC + Ch)

Other abbreviations:

BB or BOB	Best of Breed (show)
BOS	Best of Opposite Sex to Best of Breed (show)
BIS	Best in Show
HSDT	Highest Scoring Dog in Trial (Obedience)
JAM	Judges' Award of Merit (Field Trial, or Specialty show)
OAA	Open All Age stake (Field Trial)
AAA	Amateur All Age stake (Field Trial)
LAA	Limited All Age stake (only Qualified All Age dogs may compete)
OFA	Orthopedic Foundation for Animals
CERF	Canine Eye Registration Foundation
vWD	von Willebrand's Disease
SAS	Subaortic Stenosis

GRCA (Golden Retriever Club of America) titles and designations:

WC	Working Certificate title
WCX	Working Certificate Excellent title
VC	Versatility Certificate

VCX	Versatility Certificate Excellent
OD	Outstanding Dam (based on record of offspring)
OS	Outstanding Sire (based on record of offspring)
SDHF	Show Dogs Hall of Fame (based on show wins)
FDHF	Field Dogs Hall of Fame (based on Field record)
ODHF	Obedience Dogs Hall of Fame (5 or more HSDT)
*	WC, or (before 1964) placement at a sanctioned Field Trial
* *	Any placement or JAM in Derby, or 3rd or 4th or JAM in a Qualifying Stake, at AKC licensed or member Field Trial
* * *	"Qualified All-Age" (1st or 2nd in Qualifying, or any placement or JAM in Open or Amateur All-Age stake at AKC licensed or member Field Trial giving championship points)

Canadian titles generally parallel the American, except in Canada the WC/WCI/WCX titles are officially recognized by the Canadian Kennel Club for all retrievers. The Canadian tests are slightly different than the GRCA's. WCI is Working Certificate Intermediate. In Canada, any UD titlist is also an Obedience Trial Champion; this is not a separate title.

Appendix C

Addresses of Interest

AMERICAN KENNEL CLUB, INC. (AKC)

The AKC registers all litters and individual purebred dogs; it is the largest registry of purebred dogs in the world. AKC also regulates many areas of competition such as dog shows, Obedience Trials, Field Trials, Tracking Tests, Hunting Test, Agility Tests and all titles in these competitions. Many informational items are available, a number of them free. Write or call for information. Registrations and all related matters: American Kennel Club, Inc., 5580 Centerview Drive, Raleigh, NC 27606; (919) 233-9767. All other information: American Kennel Club, Inc., 51 Madison Ave., New York, NY 10010; (212) 696-8200.

THE GOLDEN RETRIEVER CLUB OF AMERICA, INC.

(Parent club for the breed, representing Golden Retrievers with the American Kennel Club). Address of the current secretary of GRCA may be obtained from the AKC (above). GRCA also has many informational materials available, as well as referrals to more than forty-five local-area Golden clubs throughout the country.

CANINE EYE REGISTRATION FOUNDATION (CERF)

CERF, SCC-A, Purdue University, West Lafayette, IN 47907; (317) 494-8179. Registry for all breeds of dogs who have been examined by veterinary ophthalmologists. Newsletter, reports and other information are available.

ORTHOPEDIC FOUNDATION FOR ANIMALS (OFA)

2300 Nifong Blvd., Columbia, MO 65201. Information is available on x-raying for OFA evaluation, and hip dysplasia.

NORTH AMERICAN HUNTING RETRIEVER ASSOCIATION (NAHRA)

P.O. Box 6, Garrisonville, VA 22463; (703) 752-4000. Information on NAHRA-sponsored hunting retriever tests.

UNITED KENNEL CLUB (UKC)

100 East Kilgore Rd., Kalamazoo MI 49001-5598. UKC has registered dogs for many years; they have held limited breed conformation shows, hunting retriever tests and Obedience Trials for some time, and are beginning to hold all-breed conformation shows. Their events are more informal than AKC's, with emphasis on education and enjoyment.

AMERICAN DOG OWNERS ASSOCIATION

1654 Columbia Turnpike, Castleton, NY 12033. The ADOA monitors legislation (federal, state and sometimes local) of concern to dog owners and issues updates and reports to its members. They also have a variety of informative and educational materials concerning dogs and dog ownership; these are available singly or in bulk quantities at minimal cost.